ACCIDENTAL ACTIVISTS

Studies of the Weatherhead East Asian Institute, Columbia University

The Studies of the Weatherhead East Asian Institute of Columbia University were inaugurated in 1962 to bring to a wider public the results of significant new research on modern and contemporary East Asia.

ACCIDENTAL ACTIVISTS

Victim Movements and
Government Accountability in
Japan and South Korea

Celeste L. Arrington

CORNELL UNIVERSITY PRESS   **ITHACA AND LONDON**

The Korea Foundation has provided financial assistance for the undertaking of this publication project.

KOREA KF
FOUNDATION
한국국제교류재단

Cornell University Press gratefully acknowledges receipt of a subvention from the Sigur Center for Asian Studies, Elliott School of International Affairs, The George Washington University, which aided in the publication of this book.

First published 2016 by Cornell University Press
Printed in the United States of America

Library of Congress Cataloging-in-Publication Data

Arrington, Celeste L., 1980– author.
    Accidental activists : victim movements and government accountability in Japan and South Korea / Celeste L. Arrington.
        pages cm — (Studies of the Weatherhead East Asian Institute, Columbia University)
    Includes bibliographical references and index.
    ISBN 978-0-8014-5376-2 (cloth : alk. paper)
  1. Political participation—Japan.   2. Political participation—Korea (South).
3. Government liability—Japan.   4. Government liability—Korea (South).
5. Victims—Japan—Political activity.   6. Victims—Korea (South)—Political activity.   I. Title.   II. Series: Studies of the Weatherhead East Asian Institute, Columbia University.
    JQ1681.A75 2016
    322.4'30952—dc23   2015032414

Cornell University Press strives to use environmentally responsible suppliers and materials to the fullest extent possible in the publishing of its books. Such materials include vegetable-based, low-VOC inks and acid-free papers that are recycled, totally chlorine-free, or partly composed of nonwood fibers. For further information, visit our website at www.cornellpress.cornell.edu.

Cloth printing   10 9 8 7 6 5 4 3 2 1

For Nathan

Contents

Acknowledgments

For first kindling my interest in Japanese politics in its East Asian context, I thank my advisers at Princeton, Gil Rozman and Kent Calder. I broadened my perspective to include the Korean peninsula under the expert tutelage of John Swenson-Wright at the University of Cambridge and benefited from the friendship of J. R. Kim, who would later provide me with invaluable introductions in Seoul.

The seeds of this project germinated at the University of California, Berkeley, and matured at Harvard, the Institute for Advanced Study in Princeton, and the George Washington University thanks to insightful input from many people. Steve Vogel offered especially helpful and extensive feedback and always pushed me to refine my arguments. T. J. Pempel provided perceptive comments throughout the process and opened many opportunities. Ron Hassner's encouragement and penetrating questions improved the manuscript. Kim Voss generously gave thoughtful criticism and advice. Hiwatari Nobuhiro and Kage Rieko in Tokyo and Lee Sook-jong and Park Cheol-hee in Seoul provided academic bases during my fieldwork trips and much sage advice over the years. Oh Seung-youn not only gave me lots of friendly feedback on this project but also shared her family's home with me in Seoul. Many thanks also to Effie, Georgia, Christos, and especially Popi for taking care of Quinn and feeding us so well during two crucial periods of work on this book in Komotiní. I am exceptionally grateful to my friends and colleagues Margaret Boittin, Kim Sunil, Ken Haig, Rachel Stern, Jennifer Dixon, Kenji Kushida, Kristi Govella, Miriam Kingsberg, Amy Catalinac, Reo Matsuzaki, Yukiko Koga, Rachel Stein, Erin Chung, Andrew Yeo, and especially Danielle Lussier and Crystal Chang for reading so many versions of this project and serving as sounding boards along the way. Susan Pharr at Harvard and Danielle Allen at the Institute for Advanced Study generously mentored me, offered wise counsel as fellow female scholars, and spent many hours discussing this project. Ezra Vogel supplied a welcoming place to live in Cambridge and encouragement for my writing. I also thank Kathy Moon and Dave Kang for their support and advice over the years. At the George Washington University, Kimberly Morgan has served as an exemplary mentor and has provided probing comments on numerous parts of this project.

Many individuals generously provided thoughtful feedback on parts of this book. I am deeply indebted to (in alphabetical order) Ariga Kenichi, Wendy Chun, Didier Fassin, Eric Feldman, Shin Fujihira, Danny Hayes, Michelle Jurkovich, Dave Kang, Saori Katada, Steven Lukes, Karuna Mantena, Angel Parham, Michael Reich, Dick Samuels, and Joan Scott. I am also thankful for the opportunities I had to present and receive feedback on portions of this research at UC Berkeley, the University of Tokyo, Sophia University, Tsukuba University, Harvard, Wellesley, the University of Pennsylvania, the Institute for Advanced Study, the Johns Hopkins School of Advanced International Studies, and the George Washington University. Many thanks to Choi Shin-hye, Christine Yong, Byun See-won, Kim Seok-joon, and Moon Yong-il for their superb research assistance. Particular thanks go to Bruce Dickson and the Sigur Center for Asian Studies at the Elliott School for International Affairs for organizing and funding the immensely helpful book workshop. I appreciate the considerable time and thought that Chuck Epp, Melissa Nobles, Dave Leheney, and Adrienne LeBas devoted to the manuscript. My colleagues Susan Sell, Adam Ziegfeld, Henry Hale, and Dot Ohl Smith also took substantial time out to enrich the workshop. My sincere thanks to Cornell's two anonymous reviewers and the Weatherhead East Asian Institute book series' anonymous reviewer for their incisive and detailed feedback.

This book would have been very different without the vital support and timely advice of Roger Haydon and Sara Ferguson at Cornell University Press. Ross Yelsey at the Weatherhead East Asian Institute guided this book into the institute's publications series. I am particularly grateful to Richard Trenner, Jamie Fuller, and especially John Grennan for their expert editing at several stages in the process.

Generous financial support from several institutions helped make this book and the research behind it possible. I thank UC Berkeley's Institute for East Asian Studies, Center for Japanese Studies, and Center for Korean Studies. I benefited greatly from the opportunity to refine this research as an advanced research fellow at Harvard's Program on U.S.-Japan Relations and as the Ginny and Robert Loughlin Founders' Circle Member in the School of Social Science at the Institute for Advanced Study in Princeton, New Jersey. I have also learned much about the broader context of my research by participating in the Mansfield Foundation's U.S.-Japan Network for the Future and the U.S.-Korea Scholar-Policymaker Nexus programs, with support from the Center for Global Partnership and the Korea Foundation. Numerous fellow participants have had helpful suggestions. At the George Washington University, I have been the grateful recipient of several summer research grants from the Sigur Center for Asian Studies and have had the opportunity to participate in the GW Institute for Public Policy research scholar program. The Sigur Center also generously provided funds for this book's production.

Most important, scores of people in Japan and Korea took time out of their busy schedules to answer my questions. They are too numerous to list here, but I offer particular thanks to Kim Yeong-ro, Koo Byeong-sam, Park Chan-un, Oh Ha-na, and Kim Jae-hyeong in Korea and Yamamoto Shimpei, Sakata Kazue, and Kitano Ryūichi, among others, in Japan for kindly giving me multiple interviews and introductions to other people. The insights of all my interlocutors not only enriched my research but also challenged me as a person. I am keenly aware that my book probably fails to fully convey the hardships that so many of them endured and the courage they all have displayed, but I hope it can draw more attention to the ways in which they have contributed to government accountability in Japan and Korea.

I wish to acknowledge my parents, my brothers, my grandfather Powell, and my entire extended family for always asking the difficult questions, about this book and many other things. I am thankful for their love and support. Finally, words cannot adequately convey the gratitude I have for Nathan Arrington, my friend and husband. He has cheerfully tagged along on and vastly improved many adventures, including those that became this book. Quinn's arrival inspired both of us to finish our books and augmented our lives in unimaginable ways. I thank Nathan for his good humor and encouragement, and I lovingly dedicate this book to him.

A Note on Conventions

I have used the Japanese and Korean order for names (family name first and given name last) and the Revised Romanization System for Korean romanization, unless authors have published in English with a particular romanization or westernized name order. For Japanese romanization, I use the modified Hepburn system with macrons for long vowels. I make exceptions to these conventions for common words and proper nouns (e.g., Tokyo, *chaebol*, Park Chung-hee). All conversions from Korean won to U.S. dollars are calculated as 1,100 KRW = $1 and from Japanese yen to U.S. dollars are calculated as 105 JPY = $1.

Introduction

VICTIMHOOD AND GOVERNMENTAL ACCOUNTABILITY

When Lee Se-yong developed leprosy in 1974, his mother told him it would be better if he just died.[1] His disease, she said, was destroying his sister's marriage prospects. That is how dark a shadow leprosy (also called Hansen's disease) continued to cast in Korean society two decades after treatment became readily available. Even though the World Health Organization (WHO) began advocating outpatient treatment for the skin ailment in 1960, Lee Se-yong spent twelve years confined to South Korea's national leprosarium on the island of Sorokdo and lived apart from society until the mid-1990s. He later told me that being sent to Sorokdo "was not just a matter of getting treated and then returning to society; it was a life sentence." People with leprosy suffered not only from the disease but also from stigmatization and governmental policies and neglect. Into the 1980s, some Korean doctors still quarantined or forcibly sterilized leprosy patients. Decades after the disease was confirmed to be only rarely contagious, not hereditary, and fully curable, prejudice toward leprosy survivors persisted. In a 2005 survey, 79 percent of Korean respondents said they would be reluctant or even refuse to use public facilities, like bathhouses and hairdressers, frequented by persons affected by Hansen's disease.[2]

---

1. This paragraph is based on an interview with Lee Se-yong, leprosy survivor, Chungcheong-bukdo (July 23, 2009).

2. NHRCK, *Hansenin Ingwon Siltae Josa [A Study of the Human Rights of Persons Affected by Hansen's Disease]* (National Human Rights Committee Korea, December 2005), 132.

1

Who was to blame for the hardships Lee Se-yong and other leprosy survivors endured? Although Lee Se-yong acknowledges that the South Korean government provided food and shelter for him on Sorokdo, he faults the state for neither correcting public misconceptions about leprosy nor implementing leprosy-related policies that accorded with international medical practice. In 2004, he and other Korean leprosy survivors started calling on the South Korean (Republic of Korea, ROK) government to acknowledge and remedy what they perceived as its past wrongdoing and negligence. Several years earlier, Japanese leprosy survivors had also launched a campaign to hold their government accountable for similar mistreatment. As one leader in the Japanese Hansen's disease community explained, state policies toward leprosy victims "allowed society to treat us inhumanely. Once a person had leprosy, he or she ceased to be a human being."[3] Like many of their Korean counterparts, Japanese victims of the disease had endured institutionalization, forced vasectomies and abortions, and stigmatization. Like their Korean counterparts, they asked their government to redress such mistreatment.

Despite the similarly marginal positions from which Japanese and Korean leprosy survivors sought to redress past suffering, these movements differed in form and outcome. Within months of holding a historic symposium to raise awareness of the plight of Korea's leprosy community in 2004, leaders in the community started drafting special legislation with a lawmaker who had decided to champion their cause. This legislative breakthrough, however, reduced the impetus for mobilizing rank-and-file leprosy survivors and supporters beyond the leprosy community. The movement consequently lacked the leverage to push for comprehensive redress measures like an official apology and compensation, and hundreds of leprosy survivors resorted to suing the state after the special legislation that was passed in 2007 proved insufficient. In contrast, Japanese leprosy survivors took their cause to the courts as a first step in 1998. Their claims initially encountered little receptivity from legislators or the mainstream media. Hence, leprosy survivors and their lawyers combined litigation with grassroots mobilization, following a tried-and-true Japanese model of activism that emphasized empowering plaintiffs and gaining support from ordinary citizens. Leveraging networks of local supporters and a favorable court ruling, they finally achieved national media attention in 2001. The resulting public outrage against the state led some influential politicians, including the prime minister, to engineer sweeping redress. The prime minister's apology in 2001 admitted the state's wrongdoing, and a bill passed unanimously the next month enumerated measures to compensate leprosy survivors, investigate the structural sources of rights abuses, and educate

---

3. Sogano Kazumi, a Japanese leprosy survivor, quoted in IDEA, "Our Struggle and Efforts," *IDEA Newsletter*, December 2004, 6, http://www.idealeprosydignity.org/newsletter/vol9–3/9V3.pdf.

the public about leprosy survivors' rights.[4] One victim welcomed the apology by exclaiming, "I feel like I am finally a human being again!"[5] By comparison, Korea's 2007 special legislation recognized only a few incidents of abuse of leprosy survivors, and financial aid for victims of these incidents was not distributed until 2012. Korea's prime minister apologized on Sorokdo in 2009 for leprosy survivors' "unspeakable suffering amid social discrimination and prejudice" but did not concede any state wrongdoing.[6] An elderly Korean leprosy survivor told me she hopes that "the Korean government will one day apologize and grant compensation to its Hansen's disease population like the Japanese government did."[7] And a plaintiff in one of the Korean leprosy survivors' still-pending lawsuits complained that the ROK government "is just reminding us that we've been living like animals, not like humans, for our whole lives. They are just waiting for us to die."[8]

What accounts for the differences between these parallel movements by citizens to hold their governments accountable for violating their rights? Why did political elites take up leprosy survivors' cause earlier in Korea than in Japan? What impact did Japanese leprosy survivors' lawsuits have on their subsequent efforts to obtain support from lawmakers? How did Japanese survivors of a rare and seemingly antiquated ailment incite such widespread public outrage against the state, while Korean leprosy survivors fought in relative obscurity? And why did Japanese Hansen's disease survivors achieve more redress than their Korean counterparts?

At one level, these examples reaffirm the consensus among observers and activists alike that outsider groups like the Japanese and Korean Hansen's disease survivors depend on support from political elites, civil society groups, the media, experts, or the attentive public if they ever hope to sway government policies. The "problem of the powerless," as Lipsky famously phrased it, is that they must "activate 'third parties' to enter the implicit or explicit bargaining arena in ways favorable to the protesters" in order to extract concessions from the state.[9] For

---

4. Koizumi Jun'ichirō, "Hansenbyō Mondai no Sōkikatsu Zenmenteki Kaiketsu ni Mukete no Naikaku Sōridaijin Danwa [Prime Ministerial Statement Concerning the Swift and Comprehensive Solution of the Hansen's Disease Issue]," May 25, 2001, http://www.kantei.go.jp/jp/koizumispeech/2001/0525danwa.html.

5. "'Ningen Toshite Ikirareru,' Nagasugita Kurayami ni Hikari, Hansenbyō Kōso Dannen ['I Will Be Able to Live as a Human Being,' A Light in the Darkness, Declining to Appeal the Hansen's Disease Lawsuit]," *Asahi Shimbun*, May 24, 2001.

6. Kim Se-jeong, "PM Apologizes to Hansen's Disease Patients for Discrimination," *Korea Times*, May 17, 2009.

7. Interview with Kim Yong-deok, leprosy survivor, Sorokdo (Aug. 14, 2009).

8. Jason Strother, "Korean Leprosy Victims Seek Redress; Time Is Running Out for Many Who Allege Forced Abortions, Sterilizations Decades Ago," *Wall Street Journal*, June 24, 2014.

9. Michael Lipsky, "Protest as a Political Resource," *American Political Science Review* 62, no. 4 (1968): 1145.

example, lawmakers and agency officials are considered especially useful as "elite allies" for outsider groups because they may have insider information about decision making, raise public awareness about issues, insert a group's demands directly into policy discussions, or actually draft and enact legislation.[10] Support from active groups in society can supply organizational resources and access that redress claimants tend to otherwise lack. Lawyers provide the legal expertise outsider groups need to pressure the state through litigation. And sympathy from members of the attentive public can bolster the perceived importance of minorities who are not usually, on their own, numerous enough to constitute a voting bloc. From the state's perspective, issues that political elites, organized groups, and voters care about are harder to ignore or quietly address.

At the same time, the examples of the Hansen's disease movements also draw attention to the complex and dynamic relations among outsider groups and their different third-party supporters, which have received less attention from scholars, as Rucht notes.[11] The processes and interactions that affect when and how third-party supporters give an outsider group leverage over the state actors it targets are insufficiently understood. But the examples above indicate that the degree to which elite allies are helpful to an outsider group depends at least in part on when, relative to other third-party supporters, elite allies take up the group's cause. The Hansen's disease movements also suggest that an initial lack of political opportunities may be surprisingly beneficial for a movement. By comparing the political activism of redress claimants like the Hansen's disease movements, this book unpacks these counterintuitive dynamics and develops a framework for analyzing why some groups achieve more redress than others.

The Argument in Brief

In this book, I show that the *process* of mobilizing third-party supporters and the *interactions* among claimants and their supporters over time have significant implications for redress outcomes. In particular, I argue that gaining an elite ally too early in the claims-making process can be detrimental, even if outsider groups ultimately need elite allies to affect policy. Early elite allies may help by raising

---

10. E.g., Doug McAdam, Sidney Tarrow, and Charles Tilly, eds., *Dynamics of Contention* (New York: Cambridge University Press, 2001); Linda Brewster Stearns and Paul D. Almeida, "The Formation of State Actor-Social Movement Coalitions and Favorable Policy Outcomes," *Social Problems* 51, no. 4 (November 2004): 478–504; Sarah A. Soule and Brayden G. King, "The Stages of the Policy Process and the Equal Rights Amendment, 1972–1982," *American Journal of Sociology* 111, no. 6 (May 2006): 1871–1909.

11. Dieter Rucht, "Movement Allies, Adversaries, and Third Parties," in *The Blackwell Companion to Social Movements*, ed. David A. Snow, Sarah A. Soule, and Hanspeter Kriesi (Malden, MA: Blackwell, 2004), 197.

awareness about an issue or proposing special legislation. But early access to elite allies also reduces incentives to mobilize fellow claimants and sympathetic citizens, leaving these allies with less leverage to persuade other lawmakers to vote for redress legislation and claimants with less leverage to ensure that their elite allies don't compromise away key aspects of redress. Questions of redress thus remain in the realm of "politics as usual," where negotiation and compromise tend to produce lower levels of redress. By contrast, claimants who gain elite allies only after mobilizing broader societal support tend to achieve more redress. An initial lack of political opening encourages grassroots mobilizing, sometimes through litigation or other adversarial tactics. Although such mobilization is difficult, time-consuming, and not without risks, sympathy for redress claimants among active groups in society and the attentive public creates powerful incentives for entrepreneurial politicians (elite allies) to draft more comprehensive redress legislation, persuade fellow lawmakers to vote for it, and thus be seen as having answered constituents' calls for justice. Bottom-up mobilization also increases the chances that key decision makers will perceive themselves as vulnerable, in terms of either votes or approval ratings, if they do not address victims' demands.

Elite allies, much like other types of third-party supporters, choose to champion causes for a variety of reasons. I emphasize that many potential reasons are related to elite allies' interactions with or perceptions of redress claimants and, just as important, their other supporters. Although elite allies can include agency officials or judges, I focus on politicians because they have the power to legislate measures that amount to redress. The way in which politicians support a cause can range from merely cosponsoring a bill to holding hearings on an issue or making public statements about it to actually drafting legislation. Support for a cause may also be at the individual or the collective level, such as when lawmakers form multipartisan leagues to address an issue or when political parties establish task forces on a particular cause. Politicians' precise motives for taking up an issue are often highly contingent, multifaceted, or hidden, but they generally relate to the level of attention the issue has received from other actors. Lawmakers who take up a cause after it has aroused societal interest beyond those directly affected usually do so because they want to be seen as having addressed public dissatisfaction.[12] Collective action by the victims and their supporters helps to signal voters' dissatisfaction to political elites.[13] The main consideration is not whether the public understands the details of an issue or has consistent opinions about it but whether political elites think that the attentive public cares about

---

12. R. Douglas Arnold, *The Logic of Congressional Action* (New Haven: Yale University Press, 1992), 128–30.

13. Susanne Lohmann, "A Signaling Model of Informative and Manipulative Political Action," *American Political Science Review* 87, no. 2 (June 1993): 319–33.

the issue. For other lawmakers, the costs of taking up a victim group's cause early in a conflict tend to be low, but the payoffs for championing redress are also uncertain. Personal values, lawmakers' background, or their desire to enact policies for which they can claim credit usually drives such early elite allies, who are often ardent supporters.[14] This latter scenario, however, tends to look more like "routine politics" and to give other decision makers less incentive to enact sweeping redress.[15] I am not arguing that public opinion drives policy change. Rather, an issue that has public interest gives redress claimants greater leverage and lawmakers different incentives for taking action on that issue.

With this argument, I highlight the importance of examining political activism in dynamic and relational terms, considering not just a movement's confrontation with the state but also the interactions over time among the movement, politicians, public bystanders, and mediating institutions like the news media, activist sector, and legal profession. I suggest the need to rethink our assumptions about third-party supporters, and especially elite allies, by specifying when they are more or less helpful for outsider groups. In his classic work on democratic politics, Schattschneider described the process of mobilizing third-party support as expanding the scope of a political conflict or socializing a conflict.[16] I build on this concept when referring to the process and temporal order in which different third parties take up a victim group's cause as the pattern or sequencing of conflict expansion. My research indicates that the sequencing of conflict expansion affects the incentives and constraints faced by both redress claimants' potential supporters and the decision makers they target. Progress in one of a victim group's interlinked relationships with different target audiences has implications for its other relationships. For example, gaining elite allies early on risks tainting victims and their claims with partisan overtones that could repel other potential supporters. Thus I show that the explanation for varying redress outcomes can be found in the patterns of conflict expansion more than in a movement's tactics or in political structures.

As victim groups try to persuade third parties that they deserve redress for the harm the state allegedly did to them, redress claimants must compete with other groups for public and political attention. They must also overcome counternarratives by more powerful actors, including the state and corporations that they hold accountable. Three key mediating institutions—the news media, the legal profession, and the activist sector—arbitrate among such competing claims in the public sphere. I build off Habermas's influential but controversial concept by

---

14. Patrick J. Sellers, "Strategy and Background in Congressional Campaigns," *American Political Science Review* 92, no. 1 (March 1998): 160.

15. Kent E. Calder, *Crisis and Compensation* (Princeton: Princeton University Press, 1988), 18.

16. E. E. Schattschneider, *The Semisovereign People* (New York: Holt, Rinehart and Winston, 1960).

relying on Hallin's definition of the public sphere as the "nexus of processes and institutions . . . [that] are involved in the construction of political meaning and formation of opinion."[17] Lawyers, activists, and journalists' positions as "public professionals" make them more audible and visible than ordinary citizens in these processes.[18] They play an important role in the processes of conflict expansion because they package and convey information in ways that affect public and political perceptions about issues. They also provide redress claimants with ways of reaching potential supporters. And they may become third-party supporters themselves. Most conceptions of the public sphere focus only on the intermediary functions of the media and civil society organizations,[19] but I include lawyers because of their growing role in efforts to hold democratic governments accountable—what Epp has termed "legalized accountability"—and in the "judicialization" of politics more generally.[20]

As studies of professions or fields have shown, the differentiated spheres of activity that characterize modern societies develop distinctive organizational structures and norms over time that define how each sector's members interact and how they conceive of their work, whether paid or not.[21] As a result, each society's mediating institutions have distinctive relationships with the state and the political sphere, as well as distinctive professional values, internal organizational structures, and types of competition among the subgroups of each sector. Such organizing structures and norms, though rarely static or explicitly acknowledged, set the parameters within which victims' activism occurs. One might expect Korea's influential lawyers' organizations, diverse and accessible news media, and vibrant advocacy sector to create favorable conditions in the public sphere for redress movements. But conditions are actually more favorable in Japan because the apparent political weakness of Japan's activist sector and the homogeneity of

17. Jürgen Habermas, *The Structural Transformation of the Public Sphere*, trans. Thomas Burger and Frederick Lawrence (Cambridge: MIT Press, 1989); Daniel C. Hallin, *We Keep America on Top of the World* (New York: Routledge, 1994), 9.

18. Rachel E. Stern and Jonathan Hassid, "Amplifying Silence," *Comparative Political Studies* 45, no. 10 (October 2012): 1232.

19. E.g., Jürgen Habermas, "Political Communication in Media Society," *Communication Theory* 16, no. 4 (2006): 411–26.

20. Charles R. Epp, *Making Rights Real* (Chicago: University of Chicago Press, 2009); Torbjörn Vallinder, "The Judicialization of Politics," *International Political Science Review* 15, no. 2 (April 1, 1994): 91–99.

21. Pierre Bourdieu, "The Force of Law," *Hastings Law Journal* 38 (1986–87): 805–54; W. Richard Scott and John W. Meyer, "The Organization of Societal Sectors," in *Organizational Environments*, ed. John W. Meyer and W. Richard Scott (Beverly Hills: Sage, 1983), 129–53; Marion Fourcade, *Economists and Societies* (Princeton: Princeton University Press, 2009); Neil Fligstein and Doug McAdam, "Toward a General Theory of Strategic Action Fields," *Sociological Theory* 29, no. 1 (March 2011): 1–26.

its mainstream media make them, along with Japan's tradition of independent activist lawyering, surprisingly conducive to grassroots mobilizing around litigation. Victim groups, enterprising public professionals, and other third parties still have agency within these constraints, though. By describing in chapter 2 the distinctive conditions that the mediating institutions create in Japan's and Korea's public spheres, I show how a country's mediating institutions condition but do not determine patterns of conflict expansion.

Victim Redress Movements as a Subject of Analysis

This book examines the dynamic processes of mobilizing third-party support and their effects through three paired comparative case studies of movements that formed around similar claims in both Japan and South Korea. Like the Japanese and Korean Hansen's disease movements, they are part of the burgeoning global phenomenon of "victim redress movements," which mobilize on the basis of perceived injury. Familiar examples from beyond Japan and Korea include women forced to work in Ireland's Magdalene laundries, families affected by the Bhopal Union Carbide disaster in India, and survivors of the Tuskegee syphilis experiments in the United States. The protagonists of such movements are directly affected parties (*tōjisha* in Japanese, *dangsaja* in Korean) and their families, though they are often supported by concerned citizens, lawyers, and professional activists from advocacy groups or nongovernmental organizations (NGOs).[22] They demand redress from the state. Generally, this includes fact-finding about their suffering, official apologies, compensation, and structural reforms to prevent future victimization. By referring to redress claimants as "victims," I do not intend to validate their claims about the etiology of their suffering, reify their identity, or rob them of agency. Rather, this term reflects the way they self-identify, distinguishes them from their supporters, and underscores the experiences that motivate their activism.

Victimhood is certainly not a new phenomenon, and neither are victim groups. As both a cause and effect of the burgeoning numbers of victim redress movements, however, definitions of rights and conceptions of state responsibilities have expanded worldwide.[23] Concomitantly, making claims on the basis of victimhood has become more legitimate in the past four decades, including in

---

22. Advocacy groups or NGOs sometimes also include the people who are being advocated for. Sex workers, for example, may participate in NGOs that promote the rights of sex workers. In addition, ethnic or religious minorities sometimes use a victimhood framing when their activism includes demands for redress as well as political inclusion.

23. E.g., Charles R. Epp, *The Rights Revolution* (Chicago: University of Chicago Press, 1998).

Japan and Korea, as will be detailed in chapter 2. In the West, although people suffered incredible trauma and suffering prior to the 1970s, victims who demanded compensation before that time encountered more suspicion than sympathy. European victims of railroad disasters were criticized for pursuing mere monetary gain when they sought compensation, and victims of workplace accidents or battlefield trauma faced accusations of laziness or cowardice.[24] As countries in the West gradually recovered from the ravages of the first half of the twentieth century, however, women's movements and victims of racially discriminatory policies in the United States won recognition of new rights through collective action, sometimes through the courts.[25] The traction that Holocaust survivors' personal testimonies gained when they started speaking out in the late 1960s further revealed how Western societies' perceptions of claims made on the basis of victimhood were changing.[26] In the 1970s and 1980s, the combination of diverse victims' political activism and clinical psychology research into trauma rendered victims increasingly credible in the public's eyes.[27] American crime victims, Vietnam War veterans, and hemophiliacs infected with the new disease HIV/AIDS further bolstered the legitimacy of victims' claims about their right to redress and the state's duty to account for its role in their alleged suffering. Then, as many countries—including South Korea—emerged from authoritarian rule, victims of wartime atrocities and repressive regimes used their newfound freedoms to seek justice as part of their countries' transitions to democracy in the early 1990s.

In this milieu, Barkan argues, states seem to have become more willing to recognize victims' moral status and claims.[28] Brooks even referred to the late twentieth century as the "age of apology."[29] Not all redress claimants achieved what they sought, but more and more grievance groups worldwide have leveraged their victimhood domestically and transnationally to hold governments accountable for past misconduct. Sikkink and colleagues referred to this trend in the context of democratic transition as a "justice cascade."[30] Redress movements have learned from one another's missteps and inspired each other. Their activism has also drawn on and resonated with the emergence of human rights discourses internationally.

---

24. Didier Fassin and Richard Rechtman, *The Empire of Trauma* (Princeton: Princeton University Press, 2009), chaps. 1–4.

25. E.g., Michael W. McCann, *Rights at Work* (Chicago: University of Chicago Press, 1994).

26. Andrew Woolford and Stefan Wolejszo, "Collecting on Moral Debts," *Law & Society Review* 40, no. 4 (2006): 872.

27. Fassin and Rechtman, *The Empire of Trauma*, 77.

28. Elazar Barkan, *The Guilt of Nations* (New York: Norton, 2000), xvii.

29. Roy L. Brooks, ed., *When Sorry Isn't Enough* (New York: New York University Press, 1999), chap. 1.

30. Kathryn Sikkink and Carrie B. Walling, "The Justice Cascade and the Impact of Human Rights Trials in Latin America," *Journal of Peace Research* 44, no. 4 (2007): 427–45.

As victim movements have proliferated, scholarly interest in redress and state accountability has grown, especially from the perspectives of transitional justice in third-wave democracies, state apologies, historical or wartime injustice, and human rights.[31] Most prominent in the scholarship on East Asia are the movements surrounding survivors of Japanese atrocities committed in the first half of the twentieth century, including the "comfort women" who were used as sex slaves for soldiers and whose claims have strained Korea-Japan relations in more recent times. But redress claims are not only about history or prior regimes. The cases examined in this book indicate that even today Japan and Korea grapple with similar problems of governmental accountability that every democracy sometimes faces. As East Asia's main democracies and their citizens debate emotionally charged interpretations of history and questions of Japan's responsibility for past wrongs, therefore, they are also tackling questions about redress for more contemporary and common, but certainly not straightforward, episodes of alleged postwar government wrongdoing or negligence. This book's focus is on redress movements related to these less studied and more recent episodes. The atrocities associated with World War II are, one hopes, unlikely to occur again soon, whereas it would be naive to think that examples like those discussed in this book will not recur. This book's findings, therefore, have broad applicability, as they illumine processes related to democracy, political participation, and accountability.

Deciding when to recognize the plight of victims of state policies, to grant them political voice, and to admit responsibility for their victimization is a dilemma that all democracies grapple with. Hence, this book contributes to scholarship in comparative politics and social science in several ways. First, by analyzing political disregard and attentiveness toward the harmful effects of state policies, this book provides a framework for understanding the power dynamics in state-society relations and in relations among societal actors in a given country. It examines how small groups of citizens try to persuade their leaders and other members of the polity that they deserve something more from the state than that which other citizens are afforded—"citizenship plus," if you will—because government actions or inactions harmed them.[32] Second, I pay particular attention to how a victim group's dynamic interactions with other sociopolitical actors shape movement outcomes. I thereby expose some oft-overlooked downsides to gaining elite political backing early in activism. Third, by unpacking how victim movements combine litigation, publicity, and grassroots mobilizing, I challenge

---

31. Inter alia, Brooks, *When Sorry Isn't Enough*; Barkan, *Guilt of Nations*; Priscilla B. Hayner, *Unspeakable Truths* (New York: Routledge, 2001); Jon Elster, *Closing the Books* (Cambridge: Cambridge University Press, 2004); Melissa Nobles, *The Politics of Official Apologies* (Cambridge: Cambridge University Press, 2008).

32. I thank Melissa Nobles for suggesting this concept.

the view that the courts offer a "hollow hope."[33] Litigation alone may have its limits, but when combined with other tactics it can be a powerful tool for mobilizing third-party supporters and using them to gain leverage over decision makers, as studies of legal mobilization have shown.[34] Finally, this book illuminates broader questions about efficacy in the public sphere and democratic political participation. For instance, it analyzes how citizens articulate claims against their government and construct compelling narratives of victimhood as they seek to build coalitions of supporters. It thereby sheds light on why some claimants receive more public and political attention than others, as well as how democratic polities adjudicate questions of governmental responsibility. The dynamic processes and mechanisms that enable some victim groups to achieve greater redress than others reveal much about governmental accountability and the very health of democracy in that country.

Mobilizing Victimhood

While all outsider groups face an uphill battle when trying to affect policy decisions, those who manage to mobilize to hold their own governments accountable for causing them harm face particular difficulties. Yet relatively few scholars have systematically studied victim redress movements as a distinct form of activism by virtue of their membership, goals, and tactics.[35] This section outlines the contested, interactive, and dynamic processes by which people who feel they experienced some collective injury use that injury to gain leverage over the state they hold accountable by mobilizing third parties to their side in the conflict. As Nobles points out, conflicts over governmental accountability and redress are not just about power politics.[36] Moral imperatives, ideas about justice, and emotions also play a role and can be potent levers for persuading third parties to take up a cause or compelling decision makers to meet victims' demands.

Victimhood often connotes powerlessness. Indeed, daunting hurdles to collective action deter potential redress claimants. With the oft-cited terms "naming, blaming, and claiming," Felstiner et al. described the process by which individuals who have experienced some harm identify and seek to remedy their suffering.[37] These stages shed light on the challenges of mobilizing on the basis

---

33. Gerald N. Rosenberg, *The Hollow Hope* (Chicago: University of Chicago Press, 1991).

34. Inter alia, Michael W. McCann, *Rights at Work* (Chicago: University of Chicago Press, 1994).

35. But see Christopher H. Foreman, "Grassroots Victim Organizations," in *Interest Group Politics*, 4th ed., ed. Allan J. Cigler and Burdett A. Loomis (Washington, DC: CQ Press, 1995), 33–53.

36. Melissa Nobles, "The Prosecution of Human Rights Violations," *Annual Review of Political Science* 13 (2010): 167–68.

37. William L. F. Felstiner, Richard L. Abel, and Abel Sarat, "The Emergence and Transformation of Disputes: Naming, Blaming, Claiming," *Law & Society Review* 15, no. 3–4 (1981): 631–54.

of collective victimhood. The cognitive steps of naming an injurious experience and untangling its causes (blaming) are crucial prerequisites to seeking redress. But some people may not know they have suffered because harm can remain imperceptible for years. Many others choose not to admit victimhood because they fear further harm or because of cultural taboos or hegemonic versions of history. Still others may blame themselves, not realizing that government actions contributed to their suffering or that others suffered as they did. Geographically clustered populations of victims tend to recognize their victimhood more readily because their neighbors are similarly affected, but peer pressure against claiming redress can be severe in small communities.[38] In addition, hierarchical relationships of trust, particularly between doctors and patients in the context of lifelong illness, frequently obscure the true causes of suffering and deter claims making.[39] Victims may also feel that pursuing redress from the state is futile or could jeopardize their current situation.[40] Studies indicate that victims often exaggerate the power of the culprit (i.e., the state and/or corporations) to rationalize their inactivity.[41] But dealing with suffering may also sap victims' energies. Many are doubly or triply stigmatized, dispersed throughout society, or suffer from disease, disability, poverty, and trauma.

As a result, many individuals harmed by state policies never even mobilize to seek redress, whether individually or collectively. If they do mobilize, victim groups usually lack the resources normally considered necessary for influencing policymaking processes. Rarely do they have money, large politically active memberships, organizational legitimacy, access to officials, or expertise. Opaque bureaucratic procedures, closed policymaking arenas, and tight-knit relations between government and business interests can limit victims' access to information about the causes of their suffering. And although short or clear causal chains have been found to facilitate collective action and make victims' claims more persuasive, officials' short tenures and "the problem of many hands" in policymaking generally obfuscate questions of responsibility.[42] Claiming restitution may also seem futile in an era of already-strained or predetermined budgets. Especially if the government publicly denies responsibility, the power and resource differentials between victims

---

38. Foreman distinguishes between "condition-directed" and "community-directed" victim organizations. The former lack the connective local ties that would help them mobilize. Foreman, "Grassroots Victim Organizations," 34–35.

39. Marlynn L. May and Daniel B. Stengel, "Who Sues Their Doctors?," *Law & Society Review* 24, no. 1 (1990): 109–10.

40. Albert O. Hirschman, *The Rhetoric of Reaction* (Cambridge, MA: Belknap Press, 1991).

41. Kristin Bumiller, *The Civil Rights Society* (Baltimore: Johns Hopkins University Press, 1988), 73.

42. Debra Javeline, "The Role of Blame in Collective Action," *American Political Science Review* 97, no. 1 (February 2003): 107–8; Dennis F. Thompson, "Moral Responsibility of Public Officials," *American Political Science Review* 74, no. 4 (December 1980): 905–16.

and the state can overwhelm claimants.[43] Moreover, few people, perhaps least of all officials in large organizations like governments, readily admit wrongdoing or negligence. Redress claimants thus begin from positions of weakness.

But victimhood is also less an objective fact than an interpretation of reality. Through collective action, redress claimants aim to activate third-party support by persuading different audiences of the validity of their assertions about how the state contributed to their suffering. Ironically, perceived weakness can be a strength in the process of building coalitions of support. Redress claimants play up their status as "accidental activists" without prior activism experience or political ambitions, even if their activism is far from accidental once they mobilize.[44] Especially if they remain unified and focused on redress, claimants may be seen as innocent sufferers and thus immune to criticism. Furthermore, psychologists have found that the process of speaking out liberates survivors, by helping them understand the causes of their suffering and "find the means of reclaiming authorship over their stories."[45] They tell poignant stories of personal suffering and try to frame their causes in terms that resonate with nonvictims and spark moral outrage or fears of similar victimization. Litigation helps victim groups to articulate particularistic grievances in more general terms, such as rights and justice, that might resonate with bystanders. Redress claimants also appeal to potential supporters by specifying how policy changes—beyond just restitution for themselves—will help prevent similar victimization in the future.

In the processes of building coalitions of support, tactics that normally work for social movements can backfire for redress movements. Whereas aligning with a political party might work for nonvictim groups, it often undermines victim groups' claims because it makes them seem motivated by partisan ideology rather than a desire for justice. Seeking redress through political activism opens claimants up to accusations that they are not "real victims."[46] Money can also tarnish the moral legitimacy and image of innocence that redress claimants cultivate. Instead, victim groups' most effective strategies are those that cultivate clear narratives of victimhood and the state's villainy that draw third parties to their cause. When pooled, victim group members' credibility as affected parties, shared sense of injustice, testimonials of suffering, intense desire to see justice, moral authority, and ability to shame officials can become potent assets.[47] Suing

---

43. William A. Gamson, "Hiroshima, the Holocaust, and the Politics of Exclusion: 1994 Presidential Address," *American Sociological Review* 60, no. 1 (February 1995): 10.

44. Monica McWilliams, "Struggling for Peace and Justice," *Journal of Women's History* 6, no. 4 (1995): 21, citing Susan Hyatt.

45. Shoshana Felman and Dori Laub, *Testimony* (London: Routledge, 1992); Veena Das et al., eds., *Violence and Subjectivity* (Berkeley: University of California Press, 2000), 12.

46. Caroline Joan (Kay) S. Picart, "Rhetorically Reconfiguring Victimhood and Agency," *Rhetoric & Public Affairs* 6 (2003): 118.

47. Joseph A. Amato, *Victims and Values* (New York: Greenwood Press, 1990), 151, 159.

the state, gaining publicity, and lobbying politicians are three of the most common tactics that capitalize on these assets and recruit third parties to gain leverage over the state they hold accountable.

At the same time, previous scholars have noted the potential perils and costs involved in using victimhood as a form of identity politics. For example, victim groups often adopt an all-or-nothing approach that can inhibit reasoned political debate and compromise.[48] Redress claimants may also deny disadvantaged members of the victimized population or other groups a voice in politics. Privileging victimization rhetoric can erase the uniqueness of each victim's experiences and disempower those redress claimants who do not fit the innocent-victim stereotype.[49] The question of who counts as a victim can be as contentious *within* a movement as it is for the government officials adjudicating claims. In his study of the U.S. crime victim movement, for example, Simon traces the emergence of victims as "idealized political subjects" who are supposed to act and speak in certain ways.[50] For governments, meanwhile, victim groups raise tough political questions. There are compelling reasons not to compensate everyone who claims to be a victim of governmental malfeasance. The process of admitting blame and redressing earlier wrongs costs time and resources, sometimes to the detriment of the majority. It could set a precedent that encourages a flood of additional claims too. Besides, how does one equitably calculate the price of human suffering? Redress movements may therefore render policymakers more hesitant and decision making more complicated, especially in the face of litigation. More broadly, by seeking redress through judicial or legislative channels, claimants may inadvertently legitimize the very state apparatus they blame and thus contribute to their own revictimization.[51] Victims' families and supporters also often struggle to retain each victim's individuality as the authorities depersonalize victims in order to process their claims.[52] By analyzing the dynamic processes and the sequences or combinations of mechanisms that enable some victim groups to achieve more redress than others, this book sheds light on both the potential potency and the potential perils of political participation on the basis of victimhood.

Approach and Plan of the Book

My findings are based on three paired case studies of six victim redress movements that emerged in Japan and South Korea around the turn of the millennium,

---

48. Martha Minow, "Surviving Victim Talk," *UCLA Law Review* 40 (1992–93): 1411–45.

49. Ratna Kapur, "The Tragedy of Victimization Rhetoric," *Harvard Human Rights Journal* 15 (2002): 1–37.

50. Jonathan Simon, *Governing through Crime* (London: Oxford University Press, 2007), 106.

51. Wendy Brown, *States of Injury* (Princeton: Princeton University Press, 1995), chap. 3.

52. Jenny Edkins, *Missing* (Ithaca: Cornell University Press, 2011).

when both countries had become consolidated democracies.[53] Japan and Korea present particularly well-matched and interesting contexts for analyzing governmental accountability because policymaking in both countries was historically quite insulated from societal pressure as both "strong states" sought to promote industrial policy and economic development.[54] Authoritarianism in Korea until 1987 and single-party dominance in Japan until 1993 further limited governmental accountability. Yet institutional and cultural changes, as well as models of effective activism, have enabled more and more victims in Japan and Korea to collectively leverage narratives of victimhood to make claims for redress. Some have elicited remarkable concessions, while others still struggle in vain.

My aim is to examine why some movements obtain greater redress than others. I capitalize on the fact that parallel mobilization around analogous forms of suffering occurred in Japan and Korea to minimize perceived differences among the types of issues, characteristics of claimants, and their grievances. While a growing number of excellent studies have examined redress issues related to World War II-era suffering in Northeast Asia,[55] this book focuses on collective action by more recent victims and the particular dynamics of holding one's own government accountable. In so doing, it elucidates the ways in which the tools and landscapes of power are changing in two of East Asia's erstwhile strong states. It also reveals surprising confluences in Japanese and Korean societies over coming to terms with similarly harmful government actions and inactions since World War II, even amid the headline-grabbing tensions between these two democracies over Japan's perceived lack of contrition for wartime atrocities.

Partly because of the wide range of governmental actions that could be construed as redress, measuring redress outcomes for comparative analysis is complicated. Also, factors other than a victim group's activism may spur policy decisions that benefit that group. I therefore eschew simplistic notions of success or failure and measure variations in redress outcomes according to four dimensions of redress: an inquiry, official apologies, compensation, and preventative reforms. These dimensions incorporate material and symbolic objectives shared by victim groups worldwide. As the analytical framework in chapter 1 shows, decision makers may respond fully, partially, or not at all to victim groups' demands

---

53. Sidney Tarrow, "The Strategy of Paired Comparison," *Comparative Political Studies* 43, no. 2 (February 2010): 230–59.

54. Chalmers A. Johnson, *MITI and the Japanese Miracle, 1925–1975* (Stanford: Stanford University Press, 1982); Alice H. Amsden, *Asia's Next Giant* (New York: Oxford University Press, 1989).

55. Inter alia, Jennifer Lind, *Sorry States* (Ithaca: Cornell University Press, 2008); Thomas U. Berger, *War, Guilt, and World Politics after World War II* (Cambridge: Cambridge University Press, 2012); Gi-Wook Shin, Soon-Won Park, and Daqing Yang, eds., *Rethinking Historical Injustice and Reconciliation in Northeast Asia* (New York: Routledge, 2007); Jun-Hyeok Kwak and Melissa Nobles, eds., *Inherited Responsibility and Historical Reconciliation in East Asia* (New York: Routledge, 2013).

related to each dimension. Government officials might, for instance, redesign policymaking procedures to prevent future harm but never acknowledge any wrongdoing or provide compensation. Alternatively, they might investigate the alleged victimization but grant no-fault payments rather than compensation. I am less interested in the independent impact of a victim group on redress outcomes than in the processes and mechanisms that tend to produce greater levels of redress. In the three issue areas examined in this book, victim redress movements already exist. Examining only successful cases of victims' mobilization runs the risk of overstating or falsely identifying the key explanatory factors. This is why I analyze the levels of redress that victim groups achieve once they form, rather than just success or failure. Identifying factors that make victim groups more or less effective helps clarify why governments ever accept responsibility for detrimental decisions. In the six cases this book examines, victims' conflicts with the state expanded in different ways, and redress outcomes ranged from no redress to full redress. Redress movements without parallels in the other country, such as those concerning Korean victims of authoritarian-era abuses, have also achieved varying results.

Overall, the Japanese movements in this book obtained greater redress than the Korean ones, though there is also variation within each country. These outcomes may seem surprising, considering the vibrant and politically influential reputation of Korean activism. Yet, as will be elaborated in chapter 2, I find that the organizational structures and norms of the mediating professions are more conducive to bottom-up patterns of conflict expansion in Japan than in Korea for path-dependent reasons. Beginning with the pollution lawsuits of the 1960s, Japanese lawyers, journalists, and nonvictim activists have developed extensive networks and practices that facilitate grassroots, multipartisan, and victim-centered activism. The mainstream national media also encourage grassroots mobilization by being relatively homogeneous and difficult to break into. In Korea, on the other hand, the pro-democracy struggle of the 1980s and the subsequent professionalization of the activist sector catalyzed a different process of social learning that has rendered politicized activism more common. It also created a diverse and more accessible media environment. Thus, outsider groups in Korea tend to seek and gain access to elite allies more readily, partly as a result of conditions created in the public sphere by the country's mediating institutions.

In addition to the Japanese and Korean leprosy survivors described at the start of this chapter, my paired case studies include the Japanese and Korean movements of victims of hepatitis C-tainted blood products and victims of North Korean abductions. Thousands of Japanese and Koreans contracted hepatitis C from tainted blood products prescribed in the 1970s and 1980s to treat hemophilia or to stop bleeding during labor or surgery. These victims blame their infections on government regulators and the pharmaceutical companies that made the tainted blood products. Also in the 1970s and early 1980s, North Korea kidnapped hundreds of Japanese and ROK nationals, ostensibly for propaganda purposes, spy training, or covert operations. The families of these abductees blame North Korea, and they are usually considered in the context of foreign policy and the threat North Korea poses to the region. But these families have also campaigned to hold their own governments accountable for first failing to protect their loved ones or acknowledge that North Korea had abducted them and later failing to rescue them. Comparing the abductee families' activism with wholly domestic redress movements reveals similar patterns in activism related to this seemingly idiosyncratic issue. The abductee movements illustrate the downsides to gaining elite allies early in a conflict, even if claimants subsequently mobilize broad societal concern, as happened in Japan. More broadly, these six cases give us a chance to investigate parallels in the processes of holding governments accountable across a range of issues, from systemic discrimination to medical drug safety to national security and counterespionage. Chapters 3 to 5 analyze why these three pairs of movements achieved varying levels of redress.

To elucidate the contested processes of constructing victimhood and claiming redress, I conducted 225 interviews with victims, lawyers, journalists, nonvictim activists, scholars, politicians, and government officials in Japan and Korea in 2007–9, 2012, 2013, and 2015.[56] I also analyzed media coverage, legal briefs and rulings, governmental reports, movement documents, and scholarly accounts of the redress conflicts in Japanese and Korean. I use Felstiner et al.'s three stages of naming, blaming, and claiming—plus an added stage of "shaming"—to structure my analysis of the six paired case studies in chapters 3 to 5. Each chapter analyzes how a group of individuals acknowledged their suffering, how the state's liability was first framed, how different stakeholders cooperated and competed to identify a means of righting the wrong done, and how the political momentum for redress developed. In recognition of the many victims of state policy who have yet to acknowledge their plight, let alone organize to collectively demand redress, I investigated the periods both before and after any of these six

---

56. As much as possible, I tried to interview leaders of all the relevant organizations and used referrals or cold-contacting to reach an array of rank-and-file members of these groups. Scholars and journalists also helped me access some of the officials involved in these conflicts, but actors on the plaintiffs' side of the disputes were generally more willing to be interviewed than actors on the defendants' side (i.e., from the state and/or corporations). To make up for this disparity in response rates, I interviewed relatively neutral observers, such as scholars. Interviews lasted two hours on average, were usually in Japanese or Korean, and were loosely structured around a predetermined set of questions. Whenever my subjects agreed, interviews were recorded. Recordings and interview notes, compiled during and immediately after each interview, are on file with the author.

populations mobilized. Interviews and memoirs elucidated victims' motivations for and experiences in mobilizing and the substantial hurdles to collective action that they overcame. Most victims initially made their claims individually through normal grievance articulation channels, such as by contacting an elected representative or meeting with a relevant government official. Once they began collectively claiming redress, however, they sought to gain third-party supporters through shaming tactics that exposed the state's failure to admit wrongdoing and redress their suffering. With supporting casts of lawyers, journalists, and civil society groups, redress claimants used diverse combinations of litigation, publicity-oriented activities, and conventional lobbying in the iterative stages of claiming and shaming. While this multistaged process of turning a private injurious experience into a public issue is sequential, it is rarely predictable. Felstiner et al. emphasize how high the attrition rates are at each stage. Indeed, many grievances are never even articulated, and countless others fall on deaf ears.

As will be detailed in the empirical chapters, the six movements I compare are not independent. In fact, even as tensions flared between Japan and Korea over interpretations of history and Japan's accountability for past atrocities, these six movements looked to each other as reference points and sometimes actively collaborated. Such interactions may complicate the analysis, but we would miss an opportunity if we examined only Japanese or only Korean redress movements. Factors that we might take for granted in one country—such as Japanese courts' procedural rules to protect plaintiffs' privacy or the conditions created by each country's mediating institutions—come into sharper relief through comparative analysis. By comparing movements across time, I also expose variations in efficacy *within* each movement and evidence of learning or diffusion *between* movements. And these cases reveal how social learning affects not just subsequent redress movements but also third parties' receptivity to redress claims. These comparisons advance our understanding of when and how claims to victimhood work to hold a government accountable.

EXPLAINING REDRESS OUTCOMES

Victim redress movements may be increasingly common worldwide, but they achieve varying levels and forms of redress. For example, the families of more than four hundred South Korean nationals abducted and ostensibly still detained by North Korea have received an average of 31 million won (about $28,200) each from the ROK government since they first became able to apply for recognition from the ROK government in 2007. The nine South Korean abductees who have escaped North Korea since 2000 also received stipends of 191 million won (roughly $173,600) each and other forms of resettlement assistance. Meanwhile, the five Japanese abductees, whose return to Japan in 2002 received far more media coverage, get monthly allowances from the Japanese government of 170,000 yen (about $1,600) each plus pensions. But the families of Japanese abductees who have not returned to Japan receive no stipends from the Japanese government, and, unlike in South Korea, there is no official process for applying to have a missing relative recognized as a North Korean abductee. Redress outcomes vary not only in monetary terms, though. Redress comes quickly for some victim groups but slowly for others. Japanese Americans interned during World War II had to wait until 1988 to receive an apology and restitution from the U.S. government. Yet some people affected by the BP oil spill in the Gulf of Mexico in 2010 and the earthquake-tsunami-nuclear disaster in northeast Japan in March 2011 started receiving government payouts within a year. For some redress claimants, governments may try to minimize concessions, as the U.S. government has done for civilian victims of the Agent Orange used in Vietnam. Other victim groups, such as the survivors of the families of victims of the ROK's lethal suppression of leftists on Jeju Island in 1948, eventually obtain multipronged redress that includes official apologies, memorials, truth commissions, and state subsidies.

Ideally, a healthy and well-functioning democracy has leaders and institutions that are responsive to both social problems and citizens' specific grievances. Although this may not always be true, victims act upon this expectation when holding their governments accountable for their suffering. Redress claimants tap into the array of mechanisms that democratic systems have for encouraging governmental agencies and officials to give a public account when they fail to fulfill the obligations of their office. The classic accountability mechanism is the ballot box, open to all voting-age citizens. Between elections, a narrower set of actors and institutions helps hold the state accountable. Where a free press exists, the media play a watchdog role. Organized interests and NGOs also monitor state actions. Citizen groups may alert such mediating institutions to some problem or lodge complaints with the agencies tasked with overseeing other parts of the government. Such accountability processes involve both the formal authority to check state actors through electoral, political, administrative, professional, financial, legal, or constitutional means and the informal power to sway or shame government officials.[1] As the discussion above indicates, not all victim groups are equally effective at activating these mechanisms. And members of democratic polities struggle to respond to all redress claimants, let alone the diverse grievances that arise when modern social, economic, and political processes go awry.

Analyzing when and why mobilizing on the basis of victimhood works is an admittedly complicated task. Yet this chapter identifies several consistent patterns in the politics of holding the state accountable in Japan and Korea, as well as other advanced industrial democracies. In its explanation for varying redress outcomes, this book concurs with the consensus view that third-party support is important for redress claimants, but it also reveals oft-overlooked dynamics by scrutinizing the interactions over time among grievance groups, their adversaries, and their advocates. Specifically, I find that redress outcomes tend to be less extensive if a victim group has gained early access to an elite ally because it makes the question of redress seem more like politics as usual. On the other hand, mobilizing support from the attentive public and active groups in society *before* gaining elite political allies gives lawmakers a range of incentives to answer victims' demands for redress. Redress claimants do not fully control who takes up their cause when, and democratic governments do not always respond to claimants backed by societal outrage, but conflicts that expand from the bottom up tend to produce more redress.

---

1. Andreas Schedler, "Conceptualizing Accountability," in *The Self-Restraining State*, ed. Andreas Schedler, Larry J. Diamond, and Marc F. Plattner (Boulder: Lynne Rienner, 1999), 1, 22.

Conceptualizing Redress Outcomes

Before examining these dynamics of conflict expansion, let me clarify what I am measuring and comparing. Rather than focusing on a movement's success or failure, I measure variations across four categories of outcomes that correspond to redress claimants' typical goals: (1) information about the etiology of claimants' suffering, (2) official apologies, (3) government assistance and compensation, and (4) structural reforms to prevent future victimization.[2] By considering outcomes according to these four generic dimensions of redress, I acknowledge that victims' specific demands may change, be hidden for strategic reasons, or be contested.[3] These four components are also not an exhaustive list of possible outcomes, which can include victims' empowerment or revictimization, more cautious policymaking, or the exclusion of other groups. Yet measuring outcomes rather than success enables me to consider both the intended and the unintended consequences of redress movements because, as Andrews and others note, factors besides a victim group's activism may spur redress-related decisions.[4] This generic scale of outcomes also avoids judgments about what the proper form of redress should be. Instead, I assess the extent to which a state's specific actions fulfill each of these components of redress: fully (a score of 2), partially (a score of 1), or not at all (a score of 0). Even the most comprehensive redress on this scale is unlikely to satisfy every claimant, and I do not pretend that it can restore the status quo ante. Figure 1.1 depicts how three of the six movements examined in this book score on a scale of redress, ranging from low to high.

This scale serves two key functions: it accounts for different permutations of actions that states may take to redress alleged victimization, and it facilitates cross-issue and cross-national comparisons of redress outcomes. Not only can redress take many different forms, but state officials also make decisions related to these four dimensions of redress across various stages of the policy process, both before and after passing actual legislation.[5] A government might place redress on the political agenda and even pass special legislation but then delay

---

2. Brooks categorizes redress differently, depending on whether policies are (1) remorseful or not, (2) monetary or not, and (3) compensatory or rehabilitative. Roy L. Brooks, ed., *When Sorry Isn't Enough* (New York: New York University Press, 1999), 8–9.

3. Joel F. Handler, *Social Movements and the Legal System* (New York: Academic Press, 1978), 35–41.

4. Kenneth T. Andrews, "Social Movements and Policy Implementation," *American Sociological Review* 66, no. 1 (2001): 72; Marco G. Giugni, "Was It Worth the Effort?," *Annual Review of Sociology* 24, no. 1 (1998): 371–93; Edwin Amenta et al., "The Political Consequences of Social Movements," *Annual Review of Sociology* 36 (April 2010): 287–307.

5. Paul D. Schumaker, "Policy Responsiveness to Protest-Group Demands," *Journal of Politics* 37, no. 2 (1975): 494–95.

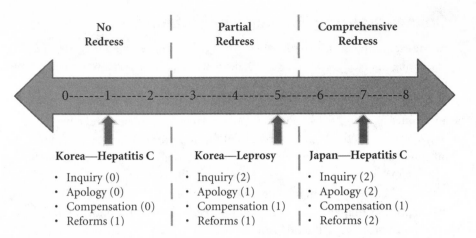

FIGURE 1.1 Levels of redress outcomes

before implementing it. Other researchers can, however, categorize outcomes in cases from around the world according to these four dimensions of redress, as elaborated below. It is possible, but by no means guaranteed, that a victim group scoring low today might achieve more comprehensive redress at a later date. Yet by disaggregating redress, this typology avoids the trap of assuming that, for instance, commissioning an inquiry into some collective suffering necessarily entails the state's acknowledging past wrongdoing and providing restitution.

The first dimension of redress concerns the degree to which the state acknowledges victims' suffering, which is usually signaled by the decision to launch an official inquiry. The mandate, composition, autonomy, budget, visibility, and decisions of these fact-finding commissions vary and are often the subject of fierce political battles. In the wake of the Sewol ferry's sinking in Korea in 2014, for example, the opposition and ruling parties disagreed over whether the commission investigating the accident's causes should have prosecutorial powers. Generally, a partial response to victims' demands for truth might involve investigating only particular episodes of alleged victimization or limiting the independence of the inquiry commission.

The second dimension relates to the amount of liability the state accepts for causing harm. Does the state accept full blame, does it restrict the number of cases for which it admits liability, or does it refuse to accept responsibility at all? State admissions of responsibility are most meaningful when heads of state or high-level officials apologize publicly and spur changes in societal perceptions, often through commemoration ceremonies, museums, monuments, public education campaigns, or even punishment for key figures. But officials frequently try to limit the time period for which the state can be held responsible or offer condolences rather than an apology when providing a partial response to claimants' demands.

The third dimension of redress concerns the benefits that a government awards to victims. These range from a no-fault settlement or condolence money (*mimaikin* in Japanese, *wirogeum* in Korean) to medical subsidies and pensions to compensation that acknowledges liability. In determining such outlays, decision makers debate budgetary issues but also questions of fairness and the implications of admitting fault. Providing financial relief but not compensation or compensating only a subset of the population of victims would constitute a partial response to victims' demands.

The fourth dimension of redress relates to policymaking processes. The key question is, To what extent do the principles, actors, and power relations of policymaking that enabled the alleged victimization change in order to prevent future suffering? We see one example of partial reform when the state creates a new forum to ostensibly incorporate victims' opinions but then restricts the forum's agenda. The state may mix and match components of redress by, for example, launching an official inquiry and reforming decision-making processes but not apologizing or granting compensation. The cumulative score based on these four dimensions points to three levels of redress outcomes.

At the low end of the scale, victim groups achieve *no redress* when a government refuses to conduct an inquiry, apologize, grant compensation, or enact structural reforms. Claimants may also receive no redress if a state conducts an inquiry but finds no merit in their claims. Officials, however, often refuse to conduct such inquiries, let alone grant other forms of redress, because they want to avoid expending scarce resources on victims or having to publicly admit blame. If pushed, officials may make some concessions, specifying that these do not constitute redress. From the state's perspective, nonredress concessions can undermine a movement by sowing dissent within it. Korean activist groups involved in the comfort women's movement, for example, ostracized victims who accepted no-fault payments from the Asian Women's Fund, a private foundation the Japanese government established in 1995. Offering no-fault condolence payments, often without an inquiry, is a common government tactic worldwide. In order to accept such payments, victims typically relinquish the right to make restitution claims in the future. For example, the U.S. government's Victim Compensation Fund for families of victims of the 9/11 terrorist attacks prohibits recipients of payouts from filing lawsuits. For many victims, such settlements may seem sufficient and easier than fighting for full redress. Indeed, the majority of families affected by the 9/11 attacks accepted payouts from the fund. But as one study showed, many who accepted such payouts later regretted or had misgivings about not suing, which they believed would have provided more information and accountability.[6]

---

6. Gillian K. Hadfield, "Framing the Choice between Cash and the Courthouse," *Law & Society Review* 42, no. 3 (September 2008): 663.

In cases of *partial redress*, the state accepts responsibility for the suffering of only a subset of claimants or only part of the period of alleged victimization. Governments control a powerful lever in the politics of redress: the definition of who counts as a "victim." They may restrict official parameters of victimhood for several reasons. First, a line needs to be drawn somewhere to contain the material and nonmaterial costs of redress. For example, the Japanese government provided medical subsidies only to atomic bomb survivors (*hibakusha*) who resided in Japan until lawsuits by representatives of the tens of thousands of Korean survivors forced the Japanese government to loosen the requirements for gaining *hibakusha* status in 2002. Second, a dearth of scientific information or other knowledge at the time of the alleged victimization may genuinely exempt the state from liability. Although victims enjoy greater credibility than they did forty years ago, they still must convincingly show exactly how the state is to blame. In the absence of proof that the harm was preventable, the state can plausibly deny liability. Third, officials may overlook disadvantaged subgroups of victims who either cannot or do not speak up. After the AZF chemical factory explosion in France in 2001, for instance, inpatients at the neighboring mental institution suffered injury but were ignored by officials.[7] Fourth, officials may seek to undermine the cohesion of a victim group by giving redress to only some claimants. To avoid such a fate and achieve the broadest definition of who counted as a victim of the violence on Jeju Island in 1948, the Korean movement compromised on the question of monetary reparations when campaigning for special redress legislation in 1999.[8] Movements that achieve partial redress sometimes fizzle, but the injustice of partial redress can also reinvigorate victims' activism.

Comprehensive redress involves an official investigation into the alleged victimization, apologies, compensation for all victims, and reforms of relevant policymaking processes. It usually takes a long time and several tries to elicit such redress. Victims of the ROK military's violent suppression of protests in Gwangju in 1980, for instance, achieved comprehensive redress only after receiving partial redress at earlier junctures. The ROK government initiated an inquiry in 1988, provided compensation and medical subsidies to some victims in 1990, and expanded compensation eligibility requirements several years later.[9] The state then acknowledged wrongdoing in a special law passed in 1995, which enabled the prosecution of two former presidents the following year.[10] The ROK went on to create a national cemetery in Gwangju in 1997 and restore the honor (*myeongye*

---

7. Didier Fassin and Richard Rechtman, *The Empire of Trauma* (Princeton: Princeton University Press, 2009), 145–48.

8. Hun Joon Kim, *The Massacres at Mount Halla* (Ithaca: Cornell University Press, 2014), 121.

9. Linda S. Lewis, "Commemorating Kwangju," in *Korean Society*, ed. Charles K. Armstrong (New York: Routledge, 2002), 183n36.

10. Kuk Cho, "Transitional Justice in Korea," *Pacific Rim Law & Policy Journal* 16 (2007): 579–612.

hoebok) of a broader swath of pro-democracy activists through new legislation in 2000. Only rarely do states simultaneously commission wide-ranging official inquiries, show public contrition, compensate victims, establish welfare and re-habilitation programs, construct memorials, and include victims in policy im-plementation and future decision-making processes. Such full redress, though desired by most victim groups worldwide, is costly. For example, 3.5 million people, or 7 percent of the Ukrainian population, qualify as victims of the 1986 Chernobyl nuclear disaster and are thus eligible for free medical care and educa-tion and pensions.[11] This costs 5 percent of Ukraine's annual budget. To deflect attention from such cost concerns, many claimants emphasize moral questions of justice and fairness when demanding comprehensive redress. The rest of this chapter elaborates a framework for explaining such differing outcomes.

Explaining Variations in Redress Outcomes

As accidental activists, redress claimants on their own generally lack the leverage to hold their government accountable and elicit redress policies. They are rarely numerous enough to give lawmakers electoral incentives to answer their demands. And interest groups with greater legitimacy, organizational resources, political connections, or expertise stand a better chance of capturing public and political attention. As a result, victim groups—much like other challenger groups—depend on support from lawmakers, agency officials, the media, lawyers, scholars, civil society organizations, or the attentive public to affect policy decisions. Support from such third parties increases the chances that a victim group will be heard, gain a spot on the agenda, have redress legislation considered and passed, ensure the implementation of such legislation, and effect lasting change. Lipsky argued that challenger groups are "successful [only] to the extent that the reference pub-lics of [their] targets can be activated to enter the conflict in ways favorable to [their] goals."[12] Under the logic of democratic theory, the assumption is that back-ing from other societal or political actors renders a relatively powerless victim group more threatening or persuasive to the decision makers with the power to ultimately fulfill redress claimants' demands. Victim groups share this assumption because their activism targets not only the state they seek to hold accountable but also lawmakers, civil society groups, the media, and the attentive public.

Yet the interactive processes that shape when and how such third parties take up a cause and give an outsider group leverage over the decision makers it targets are

11. Adriana Petryna, "Biological Citizenship," *Osiris*, 2nd ser., 19 (2004): 255.

12. Michael Lipsky, "Protest as a Political Resource," *American Political Science Review* 62, no. 4 (1968): 1157.

insufficiently understood. As discussed in the introduction, for example, close association with a lawmaker can be useful for getting an issue on the agenda or sparking initiatives to propose redress legislation. But it can also saddle a set of redress claims with partisan baggage and repel potential supporters in the opposite ideological camp. Furthermore, it may lower incentives for a movement to do the hard and sometimes risky work of cultivating a broader consensus that the state did wrong and should redress the victims. This section explores how existing studies of policy outcomes concur about the importance of third-party support for outsider groups but overlook the dynamic interactions among a group's third-party supporters. In doing so, it traces the theoretical roots of my interest in patterns of conflict expansion, or the temporal order in which third parties take up a group's cause.

For years, a common instinct when analyzing variations in the strategies and effectiveness of grievance groups was to focus on the characteristics and resources of the claimants. This impulse undergirded the resource mobilization approach in the social movements literature and echoes through studies that examine how different actors bargain and compromise when crafting policies. Implicitly or explicitly, proponents of this approach either highlight resources that help attract third-party supporters or conceive of those supporters as a resource. In their classic article, for example, McCarthy and Zald contend that effective challenger groups require not just organizational resources but also support from people familiar with legal and political processes and allies in the political system.[13] Aldrich focuses on support from active groups and the public by arguing that Japanese officials tend to site "public bads" like nuclear power plants in areas where local civil society is perceived to be less cohesive and thus to have less capacity to mobilize opposition to siting decisions through social networks.[14] Similarly, some studies of what makes rights litigation effective argue that staff, funding, and internal organization are crucial because they help claimants coordinate lawsuits with extrajudicial activism, which is designed to attract publicity and thus public sympathy and lawmakers' attention.[15] Global human rights norms, meanwhile, are also often considered potential resources for local activists because they help raise third parties' awareness of a state's nonconformity to international standards and frame causes in terms that resonate with different audiences.[16] Bob,

13. John D. McCarthy and Meyer N. Zald, "Resource Mobilization and Social Movements," *American Journal of Sociology* 82, no. 6 (1977): 1212–41.

14. Daniel P. Aldrich, *Site Fights* (Ithaca: Cornell University Press, 2008).

15. For a review of this literature, see Ellen Ann Andersen, *Out of the Closets and into the Courts* (Ann Arbor: University of Michigan Press, 2006), 4–5; see also Handler, *Social Movements and the Legal System*; Susan M. Olson, *Clients and Lawyers* (Westport, CT: Greenwood Press, 1984).

16. Kiyoteru Tsutsui and Hwa Ji Shin, "Global Norms, Local Activism, and Social Movement Outcomes," *Social Problems* 55, no. 3 (2008): 391–418.

for example, argues that challenger groups must pitch and match their causes to the priorities of transnational advocacy groups in order to access their financial resources, connections, and organizational capacities.[17] Scholars who focus on movement-controlled variables may diverge over whether elite political allies or broader societal support is more important, but they agree that third parties' support constitutes a resource for claimants.

A victim group's characteristics and resources alone are, however, insufficient for explaining varying redress outcomes. As will be shown in this book's case studies, resources become valuable only relative to the needs and perceptions of others. For example, the bureaucratization that Gamson found enhanced other social movements' capacity to court allies and affect policymaking can undermine redress claimants' moral legitimacy as *accidental* activists.[18] And victims' sheer numbers lead to ambiguous predictions about redress outcomes. On the one hand, numerical strength might help claimants attract publicity and officials' attention. Alternatively, one could argue that governments will tend to grant more redress to smaller victim groups because it is less costly than paying redress to a large number of claimants. Hence, as Burstein and Linton point out, scholars increasingly agree that characteristics of the state and third parties affect the availability and utility of a movement's resources.[19]

Such approaches place more explanatory weight on state institutions and aspects of the political context that are beyond challenger groups' control but still affect their expectations of success. The logic behind such explanations, however, still often pertains to societal or political support for the challenger group. Although numerous factors have been incorporated under the umbrella of "political opportunity structure" and the concept has arguably been stretched,[20] many proponents of this approach give explanatory prominence to the structures that affect political support for challengers. For example, Tarrow specifies political realignments, the presence of influential allies, and divisions among elites as key dimensions of opportunity for challenger groups.[21] The collapse of long-standing conservative political alignments in Japan and Korea and the increasing openness of policymaking in the 1990s undeniably enabled all six redress movements

17. Clifford Bob, *The Marketing of Rebellion* (Cambridge: Cambridge University Press, 2005).

18. William A. Gamson, *The Strategy of Social Protest*, 2nd ed. (Belmont, CA: Wadsworth, 1990), 91–93.

19. Paul Burstein and April Linton, "The Impact of Political Parties, Interest Groups, and Social Movement Organizations on Public Policy," *Social Forces* 81, no. 2 (December 2002): 386–87.

20. Jeff Goodwin and James M. Jasper, "Caught in a Winding, Snarling Vine," *Sociological Forum* 14, no. 1 (1999): 27–53; David S. Meyer and Debra C. Minkoff, "Conceptualizing Political Opportunity," *Social Forces* 82, no. 4 (June 2004): 1457–92.

21. Sidney Tarrow, *Power in Movement*, 3rd ed. (Cambridge: Cambridge University Press, 2011), 165–66.

studied here to challenge the state, but these factors do not explain why the movements achieved different levels of redress. Shorter-term political realignments or political opportunities—due to looming elections, interparty and intraparty competition, and unexpected crises—provide better analytical leverage, as will be elaborated in the next section.

Although this is not always explicitly acknowledged, arguments about political opportunities rest on the effects of *relationships* among claimants, state actors, and third parties. For example, in periods of electoral flux, lawmakers, especially in the opposition, are more likely to take up a victim group's cause to illustrate the ruling coalition's failings or prove themselves more responsive than another faction.[22] Perceived vulnerability due to political or economic crises can also give the ruling coalition incentives to pass legislation to address challengers' grievances in order to retain power, as Calder argues in his study of Japanese policymaking.[23] When the ruling party's hold on power is tenuous, challenger groups may have an easier time persuading political leaders to take bold initiatives related to redress, such as those Prime Minister Koizumi took for Japanese leprosy survivors.[24] Institutionalist approaches emphasize structural factors that affect not only elite allies' availability but also officials' vulnerability to pressure from victims and their supporters. For this reason they are more relational than is often recognized. For instance, Maclachlan illustrates how rifts in the iron triangle of the Liberal Democratic Party (LDP), bureaucrats, and big business and the structure of center-local relations in policymaking enabled Japanese consumer groups to leverage local citizens' support to influence national policy decisions.[25] The analytical framework I lay out below draws on such studies but emphasizes the interactive and dynamic dimensions of such relationships among claimants, their allies, and the state. I also show that these institutionalist studies have overlooked how an initial absence of political opportunities can be surprisingly beneficial to movements in the longer run.

A useful offshoot of this institutional approach draws attention to the "legal opportunity structure," which includes the perceived accessibility and unity of the judicial system, the stock of laws and precedents on which victims could draw, and the presence of allies in court.[26] Epp contributes a more relational

---

22. Hanspeter Kriesi et al., *New Social Movements in Western Europe* (Minneapolis: University of Minnesota Press, 1995), chap. 9.

23. Kent E. Calder, *Crisis and Compensation* (Princeton: Princeton University Press, 1988).

24. Herbert Kitschelt, "Linkages between Citizens and Politicians in Democratic Polities," *Comparative Political Studies* 33, no. 6–7 (2000): 845–79.

25. Patricia L. Maclachlan, *Consumer Politics in Postwar Japan* (New York: Columbia University Press, 2002).

26. Andersen, *Out of the Closets and into the Courts.*

perspective by arguing that more legalized structures of government account-ability that have emerged in the past few decades in the United States stem from collaborations among activists and reformist officials in the context of threats of litigation. Since many victim groups claim redress through the courts, the concept of legal opportunity structure is useful. Its proponents also give promi-nence to third-party support for claimants. For example, favorable rulings turn the courts into elite allies, akin to sympathetic lawmakers or agency officials, who give claimants legitimacy, attract media attention, and embolden other redress claimants. The loosening of rules on standing, or the right to bring suit, and reinterpretations of the statute of limitations in Japan and Korea have signaled courts' increased receptiveness to claims against the state.[27] And growing judicial activism, especially by Korea's Constitutional Court, has turned the courts into potent allies for some grievance groups. Although not necessary for challengers to affect policy, favorable rulings can spawn or signal rifts among state actors that provide opportunities for claimants to then persuade political elites to take up their cause.

Explanations that focus on state-related factors or the broader political and judicial context shed important light on the institutions that structure third par-ties' incentives for taking up a victim group's cause. This book's main argument does not deny the importance of these factors, especially as they affect political elites' sensitivity to appeals or pressure from redress movements. Yet although institutionalist explanations are a useful corrective for explanations that focus only on claimants' actions and resources, they often downplay claimants' agency and the contingency of political conflicts over redress.

A third approach to explaining movement outcomes therefore looks to more ephemeral factors, such as dramatic events or the particularities of an issue. Such explanations, though, also hinge on third parties and their interactions, under the assumption that changes in elite or public opinion lead democratic officials to alter policies. Accidents, "focusing events," or "internal shocks" are seen as creat-ing opportunities to inject new options and participants into policymaking pro-cesses.[28] For example, although he is discussing a massive natural disaster, Samu-els notes that crises can become tools for change because their emotional impact creates political openings.[29] Such events may be beyond a victim group's control, but they can be strategically used, along with revelations of new information, to

---

27. On Japan, see Lawrence Repeta, "Limiting Fundamental Rights Protection in Japan," in *Criti-cal Issues in Contemporary Japan*, ed. Jeff Kingston (New York: Routledge, 2013), 41–42.

28. John W. Kingdon, *Agendas, Alternatives, and Public Policies* (Boston: Little, Brown, 1984), 99; Paul A. Sabatier and Christopher M. Weible, "The Advocacy Coalition Framework," in *Theories of the Policy Process*, ed. Paul A. Sabatier (Boulder: Westview Press, 2007), 204.

29. Richard J. Samuels, *3.11* (Ithaca: Cornell University Press, 2013).

raise public and political awareness of an issue. Sometimes, redress movements also create dramatic events by augmenting institutional tactics (i.e., lobbying or litigation) with disruptive tactics like marches or sit-ins. But studies of protests warn that excessive disruption, like perceptions of political ambition, can alienate other civil society groups or the attentive public.[30]

In addition, certain types of claims may resonate with audiences more than others. For instance, human rights scholars suggest that ordinary people and by extension the news media relate to issues of injustice and bodily harm and thus pay attention to causes framed in these terms.[31] The specifics of victims' claims—such as whether children suffered or whether harm was clearly preventable—represent potential confounding factors that this book's paired case study research design controls for. Divergent outcomes between analogous movements indicate that factors endogenous to the type of alleged victimization cannot explain variations in redress outcomes. But support from third parties, such as active groups in society, can also alter perceptions of an issue. For example, Barkan argues that restitution for the wartime internment of Japanese Americans became an *American* issue rather than just a Japanese American issue after the American Bar Association and other civil rights groups took up the cause.[32] Yet dramatic events and issue characteristics matter for explaining redress outcomes only to the extent that they affect the order in which bystanders take up a victim group's cause. And, as Soule and Olzak point out, such explanations are not incompatible with perspectives that emphasize political structures or movement characteristics.[33]

Indeed, a growing number of scholars argue that some combination of movement-controlled variables, the broader political and institutional context, and contingent factors explains movement outcomes.[34] To varying degrees, such explanations also showcase how grievance groups' impact on policy processes is indirect and depends on the level of support they receive from societal and political actors. In their "political mediation" model, for example, Amenta and colleagues contend that both collective action that mobilizes bystanders and favorable political conditions facilitated the Townsend movement in the United States.[35]

30. Andrews, "Social Movements and Policy Implementation," 76; Doug McAdam, *Political Process and the Development of Black Insurgency, 1930–1970* (Chicago: University of Chicago Press, 1982).

31. Margaret E. Keck and Kathryn Sikkink, *Activists beyond Borders: Advocacy Networks in International Politics* (Ithaca: Cornell University Press, 1998), 205.

32. Elazar Barkan, *The Guilt of Nations* (New York: Norton, 2000), 42.

33. Sarah A. Soule and Susan Olzak, "When Do Movements Matter?," *American Sociological Review* 69, no. 4 (2004): 478.

34. For a meta-analysis, see Burstein and Linton, "The Impact of Political Parties."

35. Edwin Amenta, Bruce G. Carruthers, and Yvonne Zylan, "A Hero for the Aged?," *American Journal of Sociology* 98, no. 2 (1992): 308–39.

Giugni, meanwhile, argues that movement outcomes are best explained by the "joint effects" of support from elite political allies, social movement activity, and favorable public opinion.[36] And Burstein's sustained study of public opinion and activism reveals that movements affect policy only indirectly, by altering public opinion on an issue, heightening public concern, or changing lawmakers' perceptions of voters' preferences.[37] The analytical framework I elaborate in the next section builds off these insights, drawing particular attention to the overlooked effects of the sequencing or temporal order of interactions among such factors.

An Analytical Framework: Conflict Expansion Processes

To explain variations in redress outcomes, I focus on when and how support from third parties enables victim groups to influence, albeit indirectly, officials' decisions related to redress. My research indicates that it is not sufficient to examine this process as having just two camps: on one side, the decision makers that victim groups target and, on the other side, victim groups and their supporters. Rather, we need to pay more attention to the multiplicity of interactions and relationships among victim groups, their supporters, and their adversaries. In particular, I argue that the extent to which elite allies are helpful in redressing claimants depends at least in part on when, relative to other third parties, these political elites take up a victim group's cause. Support from political elites is crucial for ultimately achieving policy changes, but gaining elite allies early in a conflict has disadvantages. On the other hand, the initial absence of political opportunities can be surprisingly felicitous in the longer term for victim redress movements.

This argument is based on an analysis of the processes of mobilizing and leveraging third-party support and of the interactions among claimants and their supporters over time. Even though early elite allies may raise awareness about a neglected issue or draft legislation, they can also adversely affect a victim group's other relationships and thus also redress outcomes. First, early access to political elites can undercut or discourage efforts to mobilize other members of the allegedly victimized population or to appeal for support from public bystanders. As a result, redress claimants' elite allies will have less leverage with which

---

36. Marco G. Giugni, *Social Protest and Policy Change* (Lanham, MD: Rowman & Littlefield, 2004).

37. Paul Burstein, "Social Movements and Public Policy," in *How Social Movements Matter*, ed. Marco G. Giugni, Doug McAdam, and Charles Tilly (Minneapolis: University of Minnesota Press, 1999), 3–21.

to push through legislation, and the victim group will have less leverage with which to hold its elite allies to their promises. Even if victims' political allies do subsequently help mobilize broader societal support, they tend to exert more influence than redress claimants over issue framing and thus societal perceptions of the movement.[38] Debates over what steps should be taken to redress victims will therefore tend to look more like routine politics and be hammered out through compromises, which usually produce lower outcomes. If claimants gain elite allies only after they have mobilized some support from active groups in society or the attentive public, then they tend to achieve greater redress, even if it takes longer. Political elites who take up a cause after it has aroused societal interest have different incentives and constraints than do early elite allies. This latter scenario tends to entail "de-routinized" policymaking related to redress and policy debates that are more open to new voices and ideas.[39] Decision makers are also more likely to perceive inaction on redress demands as dangerous, whether for their electoral prospects or for their approval ratings, and thus to grant more redress. With this argument, I show the importance of taking a dynamic and relational approach to analysis because progress with one set of third-party supporters, such as elite allies, affects other relationships that redress claimants have with third-party supporters.

Mobilizing on the basis of victimhood to claim redress involves a variety of relational processes. My core argument highlights elite allies, which usually means legislators and political leaders (or sometimes agency officials or judges) who take concrete steps to support a particular cause, because victim groups ultimately depend on them to enact measures related to redress.[40] Yet, as the case studies demonstrate, victim groups are also in conversation with and interact with fellow victims, lawyers, reporters, civil society groups, the attentive public, the courts, and government officials. These sociopolitical actors range from actively supporting redress claimants to ignoring or actively opposing them. They choose to champion causes for many different reasons. But I show that these actors' interactions with and perceptions of other third parties—not just redress claimants—affect their decisions about when and how to support a victim group's cause. Progress in one relationship, therefore, can have consequences for a victim group's other relationships. Carpenter makes a similar point about how interactions among advocacy organizations and causes shape issue

---

38. For a similar point, see Michael R. Reich, *Toxic Politics* (Ithaca: Cornell University Press, 1991), 214–15.

39. Calder, *Crisis and Compensation*, 18.

40. Christopher H. Foreman, "Grassroots Victim Organizations," in *Interest Group Politics*, 4th ed., ed. Allan J. Cigler and Burdett A. Loomis (Washington, DC: CQ Press, 1995), 43; Brooks, *When Sorry Isn't Enough*, 6.

entrepreneurs' decisions about when and how to promote issues in global politics.[41] In more domestic contexts, interrelated interactions among redress claimants and their third-party supporters have similarly important implications for
redress outcomes because victim groups affect policy processes only to the extent
that they have support from third parties.

Relational processes, rather than a victim group's strategic choices or political structures, determine when political elites take up the group's cause. My goal
is to draw attention to the potential downsides of early access to elite allies, not
develop a theory of elite action. But I will outline how choices figure into the relational processes at the core of my argument. Political elites' specific reasons for
championing particular causes are personal, multifaceted, and often hidden, but
they generally include reelection, career advancement, or adhering to personal
convictions.[42] Effective lobbying to persuade politicians to take up a cause makes
use of their potential objectives and incentive structures, which are conditioned
by their perceptions of redress claimants' other third-party supporters, as well as
by party politics, electoral institutions, social cleavages, the nature of elite alignments, and events.

When a victim redress movement gains elite allies is thus the result of multiple interactions. For redress claimants, working directly with a lawmaker to
draft legislation can seem less time-consuming and risky than suing the state
or courting publicity to mobilize broader societal support. The appeal of potentially quicker results explains why some claimants lobby politicians as a first
step, especially when they have ready access to them. From politicians' perspective, the rewards for taking up a victims' cause are uncertain early in a conflict.
For politicians who support an incipient redress movement, personal values and
career considerations seem to matter more than calculations of potential votes
to be had, as the public remains largely unaware of victims' claims. Claimants
I interviewed described using specific kinds of information or particular victims to cue politicians and connect with relevant aspects of a lawmaker's background. Poignant personal stories of suffering from a member of the same party,
constituency, profession, or faith are more likely to resonate with a legislator.
Redress claimants who have sued the government report that gaining elite allies
in the opposition party is even easier than getting meetings with ruling-party
politicians because victims give opposition lawmakers personally identifiable examples of government failure. Victims may also provide information and especially compelling testimony for legislative hearings or serve on a policy advisory

---

41. R. Charli Carpenter, *"Lost" Causes* (Ithaca: Cornell University Press, 2014).
42. R. Douglas Arnold, *The Logic of Congressional Action* (New Haven: Yale University Press,
1992), 5.

committee to help advance a cause that the lawmaker believes in. Or the elite ally might see a way of advancing his or her career by demonstrating issue expertise with a particular issue. Although the benefits of taking up a cause early on are uncertain, the costs are also low. Politicians who take up a victim group's cause before it gains widespread attention are often committed allies, and they often help raise support from other third parties. And policy change is more likely if an issue gets on the agenda.[43] But the presence of elite allies can also undermine or repel potential third-party supporters because it makes it seem as if the issue is already being addressed or because it associates the issue with a partisan agenda. Ultimately, early elite allies can help get an issue on the agenda or a bill drafted, but actually getting legislation passed requires support from more lawmakers.

Political elites who take up a cause that has already aroused societal interest do so more for electoral reasons or to address perceived public dissatisfaction. Latecomers may also be responding to signals from active groups in society about what issues deserve attention. Shorter-term political realignments due to looming elections, interparty and intraparty competition, and unexpected crises render political elites more receptive to such signals or public dissatisfaction. Lobbying politicians who are considering a bill or implementing a new law therefore centers on demonstrating the level of broader societal concern for a victim group's cause and the costs of ignoring the cause. The act of delivering hundreds of thousands of signed petitions to government offices, for instance, creates a media event and physically shows politicians the public's concern. Whether or not the public is actually outraged matters less than convincing lawmakers that it is. In addition, backing from active groups in society also signals to politicians an issue's salience and can help relatively powerless victim groups create and enforce "contracts" with lawmakers who became their allies.[44] Not only does societal concern for an issue motivate politicians to become elite allies, but it also gives these allies fodder for trying to persuade other lawmakers to vote for redress legislation. Redress claimants can help in this process. For example, they might conduct surveys of legislators to shame certain parties for their lack of sympathy for the victims' cause. The process of trying to convince other lawmakers to support redress legislation can also spur key decisions related to redress by increasing the ruling party or coalition's perceived vulnerability, in terms of either electoral outcomes or approval ratings.

---

43. Frank R. Baumgartner and Bryan D. Jones, *Agendas and Instability in American Politics* (Chicago: University of Chicago Press, 1993).

44. Megumi Naoi and Ellis S. Krauss, "Who Lobbies Whom?," *American Journal of Political Science* 53, no. 4 (2009): 874–92.

Schattschneider's concept of expanding the scope of a conflict offers a useful way of characterizing the processes whereby different societal and political actors take up a victim group's cause, even though he did not spell out the multiplicity of relationships just discussed. Burstein and colleagues extend this logic to point out that if third parties enter a political conflict on redress claimants' side, then the claimants gain bargaining resources relative to the state they seek to hold accountable.[45] Raising awareness of an issue among civil society groups and citizens not involved in the movement gives claimants leverage because, as democratic theory indicates, elected representatives are more likely—but certainly not guaranteed—to respond to a victim group's demands if their constituents care about the group's cause or they think their constituents care. Elite allies, meanwhile, can pressure policymakers from positions of institutional authority and draft redress legislation. To describe the processes of gaining such third-party backing, I use the terms "conflict expansion" and "socialization" instead of "politicization" because avoiding the partisanship implied in the term "politicization" is a crucial part of victims' efforts to portray themselves as accidental activists.

By arguing that early access to elite allies can be detrimental, I am making a broader point about the link between different patterns of conflict expansion and redress outcomes. In particular, I draw inspiration from Pierson's insights about the effects of the temporal ordering of events or processes on institutions.[46] My analytical framework also responds to calls for more relational approaches to analyzing social movements.[47] I find that different patterns of conflict expansion affect redress outcomes by shaping the incentives and constraints faced by both redress claimants' potential supporters and the decision makers they target. Elite allies who take up a cause because they perceive that their constituents care about a victim group's cause, for example, tend to be driven by electoral calculations and also constrained by their constituents' concern. I use the term "bottom-up" as shorthand for causes that gain societal support before gaining political elites' support. Top-down conflict expansion signals the reverse pattern. The terms "bottom-up" and "top-down" call to mind the gap in political power between government officials at the top and challenger groups at the bottom, as well as the dynamic and relational nature of building awareness of and support for a cause.

---

45. Paul Burstein, Rachel Einwohner, and Jocelyn Hollander, "The Success of Political Movements," in *The Politics of Social Protest*, ed. Bert Klandermans and J. Craig Jenkins (Minneapolis: University of Minnesota Press, 1995), 275–95.

46. Paul Pierson, *Politics in Time* (Princeton: Princeton University Press, 2004), chap. 2.

47. Doug McAdam, Sidney Tarrow, and Charles Tilly, eds., *Dynamics of Contention* (New York: Cambridge University Press, 2001); Dieter Rucht, "Movement Allies, Adversaries, and Third Parties," in *The Blackwell Companion to Social Movements*, ed. David A. Snow, Sarah A. Soule, and Hanspeter Kriesi (Malden, MA: Blackwell, 2004), 197–216.

Schattschneider himself acknowledged that conflict expansion is not just about the number of people involved but also about participants' relative power.[48] Yet what my analytical framework highlights is that the relational processes of conflict expansion are about power relations, as well as about perceptions and emotions. Nobles similarly pointed out that moral imperatives, conceptions of justice, and affect also play an important role in activating third-party support and leveraging it to shape policy outcomes.[49] Interactions among such diverse actors create different dynamics in conflicts that expand from the bottom up or from the top down.

TABLE 1.1   Patterns of conflict expansion and associated redress outcomes

	CONFLICT EXPANSION PROCESS	OUTCOME
Bottom-up	Victim group → public → politicians	Comprehensive redress
Top-down	Victim group → politicians → public (?)	Partial redress
Limited	Victim group ← → bureaucrats and ministers	No redress

Table 1.1 summarizes the redress outcomes associated with each pattern of conflict expansion. I include limited conflict expansion, in which collective bargaining between officials and victims occurs far from public scrutiny or politicians' interest. Each pattern of conflict expansion involves different relational processes, which exert a distinctive form of pressure on decision makers and thus tend to produce to different redress outcomes. Although the specifics of any given political context create slightly different dynamics, I expect each pattern of conflict expansion to produce similar outcomes in any democracy.

Each of these sequencing patterns is an ideal type, as reality is much messier. Efforts to mobilize political and societal support are often interrelated and temporally overlapping as victim groups explore where their claims first gain traction. For example, claimants might try to capture citizens' attention through local public events and media appearances but receive coverage in only a few specialized news outlets. Though such tactics might have failed to capture societal interest, the news stories might grab a lawmaker's attention and spawn an elite ally. Identifying the sequencing of conflict expansion in a particular case therefore requires analysis of the dynamic interaction of victim groups' tactics and their target audiences' receptivity.

I conceptualize support from the attentive public, active groups in society, and political elites in the following way. Public support is notoriously hard to

48. E. E. Schattschneider, *The Semisovereign People* (New York: Holt, Rinehart and Winston, 1960).

49. Melissa Nobles, "The Prosecution of Human Rights Violations," *Annual Review of Political Science* 13 (2010): 167–68.

gauge because, as Page pointed out, opinion polls ask only about issues that are already salient.[50] I thus triangulate among the following indicators of public sympathy: signatures on victim groups' petitions, supportive survey results, and more subjective measures such as participants' or reporters' recollections of bystanders' receptiveness to claimants' public events and demonstrations. Existing civic groups signal support for redress claimants through statements or participation in events. Citizens may also form new organizations specifically to back redress claimants, especially in Japan, where supporter groups (*shien dantai*) are common.[51] Politicians signal support for redress claimants by attending victims' events, organizing public hearings and task forces, speaking on the record about victims' claims, or sponsoring legislation. Although I acknowledge that all these categories of actors are less discrete in reality, for analytical purposes I try to distinguish elite allies from politicians who merely vote for redress legislation.

A focus on the interactive and dynamic processes of conflict expansion reaffirms that redress claimants do not ultimately control the order in which different third parties take up their cause. And conflict expansion is an inherently risky process because it may also broaden the definition of the key problem, which can dilute a victim group's objectives. Although Reich also argued that conflict expansion is important for achieving policy change, he titled his study of victims of chemical disasters *Toxic Politics* because "for the victims, paradoxically, the politics of contamination can become as poisonous as the chemicals themselves."[52] Internally, victims may disagree with each other about strategy and tactics. Externally, members of the public may criticize victims' activism as being motivated by greed or partisan agendas; this means that victims must choose their political allies with care. Although the families of victims of the Newtown mass shooting in 2012 were not explicitly seeking redress, they encountered this problem when a U.S. congressman denounced the families' allies as using them as "political props" while lobbying for stricter gun regulations. Constructing narratives of victimhood and using them to gain leverage through third-party supporters are inherently contested processes. The next chapter analyzes the historical and social contingencies of victim redress movements in the context of how democracy developed in Japan and Korea. I pay particular attention to each society's mediating institutions. The media, lawyers, and civic groups are key nodes in the

---

50. Benjamin I. Page, "The Semi-Sovereign Public," in *Navigating Public Opinion*, ed. Jeff Manza, Fay Lomax Cook, and Benjamin I. Page (Oxford: Oxford University Press, 2002), 332–35.

51. Patricia G. Steinhoff, "Doing the Defendant's Laundry," *Japanstudien: Jahrbuch des Deutschen Instituts für Japanstudien* 11 (1999): 55–78.

52. Reich, *Toxic Politics*, 1–2.

relational processes just described because they can be both potential third-party allies and channels through which to reach potential supporters in society and the political class. Ultimately, though, this book locates the explanation for varying redress outcomes in patterns of conflict expansion, which are the interactive and dynamic processes through which redress claimants gain and leverage third-party support to extract concessions from the state.

2

CONSTRUCTING VICTIMHOOD AND VILLAINY IN JAPAN AND KOREA

Redress claimants' efforts to gain third-party supporters entail constructing narratives of victimhood and villainy that convince others that certain inferences about the causes of an injurious experience are correct and deserve attention. As Stone notes, such "causal stories" are crucial for turning a grievance into an issue because they explain why something happened, assign blame, and frame a difficult situation as "amenable to human intervention."[1] In trying to persuade others that the state should redress the harm it allegedly did to them, however, redress claimants compete with other voices for attention. They must also grapple with the implications that claims to victimhood have historically acquired in their society. This chapter outlines the parameters within which victim groups campaign to gain third parties' support in Japan and Korea. In doing so, it illuminates the contingent and interactive mechanics of conflict expansion.

Third parties respond to victimhood claims for a variety of reasons. Studies of framing processes indicate that groups with salience and credibility are most likely to gain and sustain attention.[2] Salience denotes the degree to which people relate to claimants and care about their grievance. Claims with emotional appeal or historical resonance, for example, may gain salience more readily. Credibility

1. Deborah A. Stone, "Causal Stories and the Formation of Policy Agendas," *Political Science Quarterly* 104, no. 2 (1989): 282–83.
2. For an overview, see Robert D. Benford and David A. Snow, "Framing Processes and Social Movements," *Annual Review of Sociology* 26, no. 1 (2000): 619–22.

refers to both the empirical verifiability of victims' claims and the perceived organizational legitimacy of the victim group. Yet redress claimants generally lack the technical expertise or documentation to prove that state actions caused their suffering. Indeed, the issues examined in this book—infectious disease control, medical drug regulations, the safety of the blood supply, and national security and counterespionage—all involve expert or classified knowledge that ordinary citizens rarely have. Through tactics such as seeking publicity and conventional lobbying, claimants instead use personal accounts of suffering to empirically verify their claims and dramatize an issue for different audiences. They may also link their claims to historical narratives to tap reservoirs of potential supporters. Additionally, the tactic of suing the state bolsters claimants' legitimacy when a court agrees to hear their case or certifies evidence. But more powerful groups, including the state or the corporate actors that claimants fault, often contest victims' claims about the etiology of their suffering.

The news media, the legal profession, and the activist sector—society's mediating institutions—play an important role in shaping third parties' perceptions of such competing claims in the public sphere. They filter and package information, contextualize issues in broader historical terms, signal issue salience, and supply redress claimants with the means of reaching target audiences. As outlined in the introduction, a country's mediating institutions develop characteristics over time that may be more or less helpful for victim groups seeking to mobilize societal support before gaining politicians' support and vice versa. Some societies' mediating professions behave in ways that encourage grievance groups to adopt tactics that try to mobilize grassroots support first, as is the case in Japan. Mediating institutions in other nations, such as Korea, may be more attuned to issues that begin from society's elite or to activism aimed at the political class. But individuals, whether members of victim groups or other sociopolitical actors, still have agency within these constraints. Indeed, varying redress outcomes *within* Japan and Korea attest to the fact that conflict expansion entails dynamic and interactive processes. Third parties take up victim groups' causes for their own particular reasons. Tactical decisions are also pragmatic and flexible, in that victim groups pursue whatever seems to be working. Rather than determining the exact sequencing of conflict expansion, therefore, a country's mediating sectors shape the range and expected utility of redress claimants' tactical options. Recognizing that the movements discussed in the next three chapters are embedded in the contingencies of politics in each country, this chapter analyzes the distinctive relationships that victimhood claims have to democracy in Japan and Korea and the characteristics that mediating institutions have developed over time in both countries.

Victimhood as a Basis for Political Participation in Japan and Korea

As victimhood claims proliferated in the postwar era in Japan and Korea, as elsewhere around the world, they became deeply intertwined with the development of democracy, albeit in different ways. Each society's historically acquired and distinctive connotations of victimhood set the parameters within which the victim groups in this book sought redress. Shared understandings of what political participation based on victimhood meant also colored different third parties' receptivity to the groups' claims. Here, I include both societal processes of collective memory formation and official narratives, which Berger usefully distinguishes in greater detail.[3] This section merely sketches this historical context, and the following section focuses on how this political evolution both shaped and was shaped by each society's mediating institutions.

Much as Western societies formerly treated redress claimants with suspicion, ordinary Japanese initially shunned the millions of physically and mentally scarred veterans, war widows, orphaned and homeless children, and *hibakusha* left after Japan's defeat in World War II.[4] Once U.S. occupying authorities lifted censorship restrictions, however, victims' accounts, especially from *hibakusha*, gradually spurred public discussions of war memories. As a result, viewing the entire Japanese populace as a victim of militarism and more generally of modern war—victim consciousness (*higaisha ishiki*)—gained currency on both sides of the political spectrum in the 1950s and 1960s.[5] Aligned with the left, *hibakusha* activists and the concomitant antinuclear movement popularized a pacifist discourse that emphasized Japan's special moral status as the sole country to have endured atomic bomb attacks. On the other side of the political spectrum, conservative political forces cemented their dominance in the late 1950s by propounding a different narrative of national victimhood that celebrated Japan's rapid economic recovery after devastating victimization and defeat but downplayed questions of Japan's wartime aggression. As a result, veterans' widows, *hibakusha*, and other groups could gain benefits by registering their victimhood with the state. Only during the anti-Vietnam War protests did some progressive groups, which were the perennial opposition in Japanese politics, begin to

---

3. Thomas U. Berger, *War, Guilt, and World Politics after World War II* (Cambridge: Cambridge University Press, 2012).

4. John W. Dower, *Embracing Defeat* (New York: Norton, 1999), 61–64, 119–20.

5. James Joseph Orr, *The Victim as Hero* (Honolulu: University of Hawai'i Press, 2001), chap. 3.

counterbalance these discourses of national victimhood with conscious efforts to understand Japan's history of victimizing others in the context of war.[6]

A separate discourse of victimhood emerged in Japan in the late 1960s to challenge the LDP's dominance in Japanese democracy and the devastating pollution caused by the country's rapid industrial development. Pollution victims blamed first industry and then government—the engines of Japan's economic growth—for their diseases. The concerned citizens and progressive lawyers who supported these redress claimants articulated new conceptions of environmental rights and became the backbone of Japan's nascent environmental movement.[7] Pioneering the use of lawsuits to achieve redress and social change, these movements also constituted a "victim-centered" model of political activism that has been widely used since then.[8] As Japan's middle class grew and the opposition scored electoral victories at the subnational level, people also came to expect their government to safeguard a broader range of rights. Women, consumers, victims of faulty medical drugs and tainted food products, and Japan's outcasts (*Burakumin*) mobilized from the 1970s on, usually facing bureaucratic resistance but sometimes transforming regulatory practices and policy.[9] They leveraged political opportunities at the subnational level to pressure the national government to alter policy.[10] The victim or affected party (*tōjisha*) gained even more credibility in Japan in the early 1990s as hemophilia patients who had contracted HIV from tainted blood products sought redress.[11] One observer of Japan described such activism as "seeking and realizing social justice for those who have been shortchanged for too long."[12]

Neighboring Korea emerged from thirty-five years of Japanese colonial occupation in 1945 with an even more profound sense of victimhood. National division—imposed from outside—and the ensuing Korean War (1950–53) further wounded the entire ethnic nation (*minjok*). But the trauma of this

---

6. Inter alia, Jennifer Lind, *Sorry States* (Ithaca: Cornell University Press, 2008), 52–53; Vera Mackie, "In Search of Innocence," *Australian Feminist Studies* 20, no. 47 (July 2005): 212.

7. Frank K. Upham, "Litigation and Moral Consciousness in Japan," *Law & Society Review* 10, no. 4 (Summer 1976): 579–619; Margaret A. McKean, *Environmental Protest and Citizen Politics in Japan* (Berkeley: University of California Press, 1981).

8. Simon Avenell, "From Fearsome Pollution to Fukushima," *Environmental History* 17, no. 2 (April 2012): 268.

9. Michael R. Reich, *Toxic Politics* (Ithaca: Cornell University Press, 1991); Susan J. Pharr, *Losing Face* (Berkeley: University of California Press, 1990).

10. Patricia L. Maclachlan, *Consumer Politics in Postwar Japan* (New York: Columbia University Press, 2002).

11. Eric A. Feldman, *The Ritual of Rights in Japan* (Cambridge: Cambridge University Press, 2000).

12. Jeff Kingston, *Japan's Quiet Transformation* (London: Routledge, 2004), 33.

"fratricidal conflict" blurred the lines between victim and victimizer.[13] After the armistice in 1953, ordinary Koreans were also too preoccupied with putting food on the table to sympathize with anyone making claims on the basis of victimhood. Everyone had suffered. South Korea's increasingly authoritarian leaders, meanwhile, focused on rebuilding, jumpstarting the economy, and competing with the North. Economic development involved setting aside questions of colonial victimization in order to normalize relations with Japan in 1965 and open the door to Japanese economic aid and investment. Competition with North Korea also provided a justification for the ROK government to curtail its citizens' rights in the name of national security and to suppress opposition voices. During a brief window of democratic rule from 1960 to 1961, associations of bereaved families and students tried in vain to pursue redress for the ROK military's massacres of civilians suspected of being communists before and during the Korean War.[14] But after a coup in 1961, anyone who openly criticized the regime's abuses of power was tarred as a communist sympathizer and subjected to surveillance, interrogation, imprisonment, or worse. Residents of localities affected by the pollution that accompanied Korea's rapid industrialization also tried to seek redress in the 1970s, to little avail.[15] At the same time, increasingly repressive military rule and rising income inequality during the Park Chung-hee (1961–79) and Chun Doo-hwan (1979–87) regimes engendered a *minjung* (people's) discourse, which was articulated and propagated by intellectuals and students who sought to transform Korea's historical trajectory from one of passive victimization into one of agency.[16]

The bereaved families and survivors of the May 1980 pro-democracy uprising in Gwangju came to embody this narrative of mobilized victimhood. ROK military and special forces—whose movements were allegedly approved by U.S. military officials—had killed hundreds and injured scores in their nine-day suppression of civilian protests in that city.[17] The dead and wounded became symbols of the dictatorship's oppression of all ROK citizens' basic rights and fueled the spread of pro-democracy protests. *Minjung* activists partnered with Korea's mistreated workers, religious groups, and even middle-class professionals to

13. Bruce Cumings, *The Origins of the Korean War*, vol. 2 (Princeton: Princeton University Press, 1990), 619.

14. E.g., Hun Joon Kim, *The Massacres at Mount Halla* (Ithaca: Cornell University Press, 2014), 45–50.

15. Jaehyun Joo, "Dynamics of Social Policy Change," *Governance* 12, no. 1 (January 1999): 57–80.

16. Namhee Lee, *The Making of Minjung* (Ithaca: Cornell University Press, 2009).

17. Linda S. Lewis and Ju-na Byun, "From Heroic Victims to Disabled Survivors," in *Contentious Kwangju*, ed. Gi-Wook Shin and Kyung Moon Hwang (Lanham, MD: Rowman & Littlefield, 2003), 54.

assemble a broad coalition that demanded political liberalization. The resulting transition to democracy in 1987 and political reforms enabled the formation of a variety of victim movements, fed by a "pent-up resentment of victimhood" created by Japanese occupation, national division, and authoritarian oppression.[18] And, as the ROK's first civilian president in decades, Kim Young-sam made "settling the past" (*gwageo cheongsan*)—both with Japan and inside the ROK—a way of deepening democracy after he was elected in 1992.

Through protest and later the courts, Korea's flourishing civil society organizations pressed the government to recognize and safeguard long-neglected civil and political rights, and then economic and social rights. Like other third-wave democracies, Korea gradually tackled transitional justice issues from the Korean War and authoritarian era through numerous truth commissions in the first decade of the twenty-first century.[19] In the 1990s, activists also started exposing the experiences of Japanese colonial rule to cultivate a collective identity of national victimhood. World War II victims—Korean women forced into sexual slavery, Koreans mobilized to work in Japanese factories and mines, Korean atomic bomb survivors, and Korean laborers abandoned on Sakhalin Island at the end of the war—sought restitution from the Japanese government.[20] Additionally, Korea's growing confidence in East Asia and improving relations with North Korea encouraged reinterpretations of the Korean War that depicted the peninsula as a victim of foreign aggression.[21] In this milieu, people whose families were separated during the war sought information and reunions, while those branded as leftists by the ROK's authoritarian regimes campaigned to clear their records and receive restitution. Narratives of national victimization, which painted foreign powers and the ROK's past dictators as the main culprits, resonated especially well with Korea's newly enfranchised political left. Yet, as in Japan, the growth of Korea's middle class also spurred victims of pollution, collapsed buildings, defective consumer products, flooding, and accidents to demand that their democratic government safeguard a broader range of rights and enforce stricter regulations.

While not unproblematic, the increasing legitimacy of victims' activism in Japan and South Korea has both contributed to and benefited from changing sociopolitical and legal conditions since the early 1990s. These changes have strengthened democracy and governmental accountability in both countries, making them well-matched contexts in which to examine the politics of redress.

---

18. Gi-Wook Shin, Soon-Won Park, and Daqing Yang, eds., *Rethinking Historical Injustice and Reconciliation in Northeast Asia* (New York: Routledge, 2007), 20.

19. See the Truth and Reconciliation Commission of the ROK, www.jinsil.go.kr/english.

20. E.g., Chunghee Sarah Soh, *The Comfort Women* (Chicago: University of Chicago Press, 2008); William Underwood, "Redress Crossroads in Japan," *Asia-Pacific Journal* 30–1–10 (July 26, 2010).

21. Sheila Miyoshi Jager and Jiyul Kim, "The Korean War after the Cold War," in *Ruptured Histories*, ed. Sheila Miyoshi Jager and Rana Mitter (Cambridge, MA: Harvard University Press, 2007), 234.

Historically, policymaking in both Japan and Korea was relatively insulated from public scrutiny and judicial oversight. During thirty-eight years (1955–93) of uninterrupted rule by the LDP, Japanese officials used "bureaucratic informalism" to grant preemptive but partial concessions to potential challengers to avoid "resolutions that might have broad application to other situations."[22] In Korea, anticommunist and conservative rulers used draconian laws, the mobilization of prostate organizations, coercion, and media censorship to stymie challenges to authoritarian rule (1961–87).[23]

Conditions in both countries became more conducive for outsider groups, including victim redress movements, in the 1990s. Korea's democratizing reforms began in 1987 but accelerated under Kim Young-sam (1993–98) and his successor, Kim Dae-jung (1998–2003). Meanwhile, the bursting of Japan's economic bubble, political scandals, and declining electoral support for the ruling LDP and especially for left-leaning opposition parties from the late 1980s on catalyzed major realignments in party politics and opened the door to institutional reforms.[24] In both countries, growing governmental transparency, new legal instruments, more competitive electoral politics, increasingly accessible and activist judicial systems, new definitions of rights, rising civic activism, and greater media scrutiny of politics have provided victim groups with better means of holding their governments accountable. New product liability laws, information disclosure laws, and administrative procedure acts have given citizens somewhat better leverage and information with which to monitor and challenge governmental actions.[25] Additionally, institutional and cultural disincentives to litigation have diminished with judicial and legal education reforms, as well as social changes in both countries.[26] The growing number of successful redress movements also created a lexicon and tactical tool kit for subsequent victim activists to emulate. Networks of lawyers and other supporters facilitated each new set of redress claimants. And yet the Japanese and Korean governments have not been equally responsive to all redress movements. This book seeks to understand why not.

---

22. Pharr, *Losing Face*, 168–69; see also Frank K. Upham, *Law and Social Change in Postwar Japan* (Cambridge, MA: Harvard University Press, 1987), chap. 1.

23. Paul Y. Chang, "Unintended Consequences of Repression," *Social Forces* 87, no. 2 (December 2008): 653–57.

24. T. J. Pempel, *Regime Shift* (Ithaca: Cornell University Press, 1998).

25. Patricia L. Maclachlan, "Information Disclosure and the Center-Local Relationship in Japan," in *Local Voices, National Issues*, ed. Sheila A. Smith (Ann Arbor: University of Michigan, 2000), 9–30; Tom Ginsburg, "Dismantling the Developmental State-Administrative Procedure Reform in Japan and Korea," *American Journal of Comparative Law* 49 (2001): 585–626; Jeeyang Rhee Baum, *Responsive Democracy* (Ann Arbor: University of Michigan Press, 2011).

26. Inter alia, Tom Ginsburg, ed., *Legal Reform in Korea* (New York: Routledge, 2004); Dai-Kwon Choi and Kahei Rokumoto, eds., *Korea and Japan* (Seoul: Seoul National University Press, 2007); Setsuo Miyazawa, "Symposium: Successes, Failures, and Remaining Issues of the Justice System Reform in Japan," *Hastings International and Comparative Law Review* 36, no. 2 (Summer 2013): 313–48.

Mediating among Victims, Their Allies, and Their Adversaries

As the sociopolitical changes described in the previous section were occurring, each country's mediating institutions developed particular characteristics. In fact, the distinctive relationships that these institutions developed with the state and the political sphere both contributed to and benefited from the trends discussed above. Social learning processes also ingrained certain patterns of organizing and behaving within each mediating sector, which affected the menu, or "repertoire" of tactics and "organizing templates" that victim groups could choose from.[27] Although victim groups might combine tactics in innovative ways, I found that they frequently work with lawyers, other civil society groups, and journalists within these parameters as they claim redress and shame the state. Lawyers can provide legal expertise, access to political elites, and rights-based issue framing. Nonvictim activists can boost the impact of victims' activities by showing solidarity or providing logistical assistance. Journalists influence both the form and the level of public awareness about an issue and uncover information relating to victims' claims of state wrongdoing. At the same time, redress claimants can help lawyers and activists promote broader goals and can provide news media with content that sells copy or attracts audiences. Thus the legal profession, the activist sector, and the news media have central positions in the web of interactions that constitute conflict expansion, and the distinctive characteristics they have developed in Japan and Korea deserve further attention.

For redress movements, I find that the most salient dimensions on which the Japanese and Korean mediating institutions differ are lawyers' autonomy, the media environment's diversity, and the activist sector's level of professionalization and organization. These characterizations risk oversimplifying multifaceted and evolving sectors of society, but they facilitate comparisons with other countries' mediating institutions.[28] Autonomy for lawyers means freedom from state interference, as well as low levels of integration with political parties, law firms, and other organizations that might have interests of their own. With autonomy, lawyers are more likely to challenge the state or other powerful actors in society. In the activist sector, meanwhile, professionalized and centrally organized

27. Charles Tilly, "Repertoires of Contention in America and Britain, 1750–1830," in *The Dynamics of Social Movements*, ed. Meyer N. Zald and John D. McCarthy (Cambridge, MA: Winthrop, 1979); Elisabeth S. Clemens, "Organizational Repertoires and Institutional Change," *American Journal of Sociology* 98, no. 4 (January 1993): 755–98; Paul D. Almeida, "The Sequencing of Success," *Mobilization* 13, no. 2 (2008): 165–87.

28. For a related analysis, see Celeste L. Arrington, "Leprosy, Legal Mobilization, and the Public Sphere in Japan and South Korea," *Law & Society Review* 48, no. 3 (September 2014): 563–93.

groups tend to have elite connections and wield political influence but to suffer from weak links to ordinary citizens. Citizen-centered activist organizations may have stronger grassroots linkages but lack the means to influence policymaking. Finally, when a country's news media include diverse outlets that cover topics from a range of perspectives, they create low barriers to entry for groups seeking publicity. But the segmentation that develops among such diverse outlets catering to niche audiences also limits the number of people groups can reach. Though a more homogeneous media environment poses higher barriers to entry, it increases the likelihood that a group's message will reach more people.

This section details how the Japanese and Korean mediating sectors compare on these three dimensions, which are generalizations about admittedly heterogeneous sectors. One might expect that victim redress movements would benefit from Korea's politically connected legal profession, diverse and accessible media environment, and contentious and effective activist tradition. Yet I find that the organizational structures and norms of Korea's mediating institutions are more conducive to political activism that targets political elites and politics at the center. By contrast, Japan's seemingly weaker civil society sector, relatively homogeneous mainstream media, and independent "cause lawyering" tradition facilitate grassroots mobilizing, which tends to ultimately produce greater levels of redress. As mentioned earlier, within-country variations in redress outcomes indicate that these features of each country's mediating institutions do not determine outcomes, but rather constrain conflict expansion processes. Victim groups and other sociopolitical actors still interact with agency in the public sphere.

Lawyers' Autonomy

The Japanese and Korean private bars have followed divergent trajectories since 1945, even though the countries' judicial systems and state-run structures of legal education share institutional similarities as a result of Japanese colonial rule. For space reasons, I focus here on the organizational structures and norms of cause lawyers within the private bar because they are most likely to become involved in redress conflicts. As the work led by Sarat and Scheingold posits, "cause lawyering" denotes the range of activities in which lawyers leverage their professional skills to advance a particular cause, whether related to specific rights violations or the broader public interest.[29] Although Japanese and Korean lawyers who

---

29. Austin Sarat and Stuart A. Scheingold, eds., *Cause Lawyering* (New York: Oxford University Press, 1998); Austin Sarat and Stuart A. Scheingold, eds., *Cause Lawyering and the State in a Global Era* (Oxford: Oxford University Press, 2001); Stuart A. Scheingold and Austin Sarat, *Something to Believe In* (Stanford: Stanford Law and Politics, 2004).

represent victims of state wrongdoing or negligence do not necessarily call themselves cause lawyers, they and their work fit this concept.[30] Lawyering refers to the
"organizational forms and practice that embody an ideology about law and legal
work."[31] After the 1950s, Japan developed a relatively flexible, issue-specific, and
decentralized cause lawyering tradition, whereas Korean cause lawyering, which
did not emerge until democratization in the 1980s, is more centrally organized
and politicized. Korea resembles what Hilbink calls the "elite/vanguard" model of
cause lawyering, while Japan fits his "grassroots" model better.[32] Compared with
Korea's cause lawyering tradition, Japan's is more independent from political and
organizational ties and thus facilitates tactics that aim to mobilize societal support before attracting elite allies.

In part, Japanese cause lawyers operate more autonomously because Korean
lawyers did not gain democratic freedoms until after 1987. Historically, quotas
on the number of people allowed to pass the bar exam kept the population of
lawyers per capita low in both countries and established lawyers as members of
each country's elite.[33] But because of authoritarian Korean government controls,
the country still had only half as many private attorneys per capita as Japan in
1995. The few Korean lawyers who challenged regime decisions faced arrest or
harassment as procommunist agitators and had their licenses revoked.[34] Driven
by Christian ideals of social justice and/or leftist ideology, some lawyers persevered to defend the workers, students, and other dissidents whom the authorities increasingly arrested for antistate activities as protests against the regime
mounted in the 1980s. But the state curtailed the Korean Bar Association's (KBA)
autonomous activities until the late 1980s.

By contrast, Japan's 1949 Lawyers' Law, which included human rights and social
justice in its first article, had already enshrined the notion of attorneys as a *zaiya*
(out-of-power) force to balance state power and the emerging LDP-dominated
political establishment by the 1950s. Although formally under the Japan Federation of Bar Associations (JFBA), regional bar associations became more active than

---

30. For a discussion of terminology in the Korean context, see Patricia Goedde, "From Dissidents
to Institution-Builders," *East Asia Law Review* 4 (2009): 66–69.

31. Christine B. Harrington, "Outlining a Theory of Legal Practice," in *Lawyers in a Postmodern World*, ed. Maureen Cain and Christine B. Harrington (New York: New York University Press,
1995), 55.

32. Thomas M. Hilbink, "You Know the Type," *Law & Social Inquiry* 29, no. 3 (Summer 2004):
673–90.

33. Shozo Ota and Kahei Rokumoto, "Issues of the Lawyer Population: Japan," *Case Western
Reserve Journal of International Law* 25 (1993): 316.

34. Based on the excellent history in Patricia Goedde, "How Activist Lawyers Mobilized the Law
for Social and Political Change in South Korea, 1988–2007" (PhD diss., University of Washington,
2008), 91–102.

their politically restrained Korean counterparts and developed an ethos of being more sensitive to aggrieved groups than were other segments of Japanese society. Japan's private bar also became an attractive alternative but still elite profession for individuals whose protest activities as students were frowned upon by potential government or industry employers. Japanese lawyers enjoyed democratic freedoms and earned high salaries because of their scarcity, enabling a subset of them to pursue cause lawyering in addition to their normal work from the 1960s on.

As is the case worldwide, many cause lawyers in Japan and Korea have progressive political beliefs, but cause lawyers in Japan evolved to be more independent from political and organizational constraints than Korea's are. In the 1960s, four pathbreaking lawsuits by Japanese victims of industrial pollution (*kōgai*) established a model for subsequent campaigns to hold the state and powerful firms accountable through the courts.[35] It combined litigation with publicity and local consciousness-raising and then leveraged grassroots support to pressure political elites for policy change, as elaborated below. Although many of the lawyers involved in such early legal mobilization campaigns were at least indirectly associated with the Socialist or Communist Parties, the pro bono legal teams (*bengodan*) formed for such lawsuits operated relatively independently from political organizations.[36] Personal contacts through the JFBA and other bar associations (especially through their human rights committees) facilitated lawyers' initial mobilization for such cases. Lawyers also mobilized friends through Japan's several left-leaning cause lawyering organizations—the largest of which is Jiyū Hōsōdan (Lawyers' Association for Freedom), which included about 10 percent of all attorneys at its peak in the 1970s and still has more than two thousand members—but the legal teams had separate organizational structures.[37] Moreover, cause lawyers' political affinities have pragmatically shifted to the center along with the demise of the political left in Japan and the rise of electoral competition between two moderate parties. Rather than focusing on mobilizing political connections, the Japanese cause lawyering tradition that emerged emphasizes grassroots mobilizing around victims or plaintiffs.

Korean cause lawyering began with a more progressive and politicized bent, as it centered on defending political dissidents and challenging the regime. Many of the earliest cause lawyers had ties to Jeongbeophoe (Association of Lawyers for the Realization of Justice), which thirty lawyers secretly formed behind the façade of the KBA's Human Rights Committee in 1986. After democratization, this group

---

35. Robert L. Kidder and Setsuo Miyazawa, "Long-Term Strategies in Japanese Environmental Litigation," *Law & Social Inquiry* 18 (1993): 623.
36. Interview with Kawabata Yoshiharu, lawyer, Tokyo (July 23, 2012).
37. Interview with Izumisawa Akira, lawyer, Tokyo (June 29, 2013).

was renamed Minbyeon (Lawyers for a Democratic Society) and included more than nine hundred lawyers by 2014. Cause lawyers also developed a reputation for fighting powerful interests, starting with the collective lawsuit that they helped residents of the flooded Mangwon-dong area of Seoul launch against Hyundai and the Seoul government in the late 1980s. By working with and through NGOs to abolish laws left over from the authoritarian era, promote civil and political rights, and combat *chaebol* (business conglomerates) impunity, Korean cause lawyers helped make litigation a common and potent political tactic by the first decade of this century.[38] Minbyeon retained close ties to progressive political parties throughout the 1990s but also encouraged professionalization and issue diversification among its members' activities.[39] Especially during the progressive presidency of Roh Moo-hyun (2004–9), who was himself a Minbyeon member, Korean cause lawyers developed close ties to or served in government and were thus "domesticated" into the political establishment.[40] Although Korea's cause lawyers have grown more heterogeneous in the quarter century since democratization, their modus operandi involves closer cooperation with political parties and lawyers' associations than is the case in Japan. As a result, the lawyers who help redress movements in Korea are, on balance, more likely to turn to political elites early in their activism to mobilize elite support for their cause.

The Degree of Organization and Centralization in Civil Society

With their experience and expertise, civil society organizations can help victims identify and pry open windows of opportunity for political activism. They can also reduce the challenges of collective action by signaling their solidarity, providing logistical assistance, mobilizing experts, and pressuring state actors. Moreover, since activist groups are relatively more "attuned to how societal problems resonate in the private life spheres," they can help victims identify mobilizing frames that previously captured public and political attention.[41] By civil society organizations, I mean the formal and informal citizens' and advocacy groups that do not aim to turn a profit, win elections, or advance specific economic or professional interests.[42] Korea's civil society sphere is dominated by centrally organized,

---

38. Joon Seok Hong, "From the Streets to the Courts," in *South Korean Social Movements*, ed. Gi-Wook Shin and Paul Y. Chang (London: Routledge, 2011), 105–13.

39. Interview with Yang Hyunah, law professor, Seoul (July 25, 2013).

40. Tom Ginsburg, "Law and the Liberal Transformation of the Northeast Asian Legal Complex," in *Fighting for Freedom*, ed. Terrence Halliday, Lucien Karpik, and Malcolm Feeley (Oxford: Hart, 2007), 55.

41. Jürgen Habermas, *Between Facts and Norms* (Cambridge: MIT Press, 1996), 366.

42. See, among others, Marc Morjé Howard, *The Weakness of Civil Society in Post-Communist Europe* (Cambridge: Cambridge University Press, 2003), 32–42.

professionalized, and politically connected groups that have arguably become more effectively institutionalized than the country's political parties since democratization. By comparison, Japanese civil society groups are predominantly small volunteer organizations that lack the resources and access normally needed for effective political advocacy at the national level. While one might call Korea's activist sector "advocates without members," Pekkanen characterizes Japan's civil society as "members without advocates."[43] For victim groups, these distinctions mean that Japan offers more fertile soil for mobilizing ordinary citizens who sympathize with and support victims' particularistic demands for redress at the grassroots level. In contrast, Korea's activist sector, though vibrant and politically effective, encourages victim groups to frame their claims in broader and often political terms that will attract a coalition of other advocacy groups and appeal to politicians at the national level, making top-down patterns of conflict expansion more likely in the Korean context.

In Japan and Korea, the number of groups intermediating between the state and society grew rapidly in the 1990s. The expansion of Korea's civil society was particularly rapid, as it grew from a position of comparative organizational scarcity to a position of parity with Japan in terms of organizational density by 1996.[44] Decades of authoritarian controls had limited Korean citizens' freedom of association and made the state the primary target for those who dared to organize and protest.[45] Compared with Japan, therefore, a greater proportion of Korean activist groups are based in the capital, where they focus on national policy questions.[46] Korean civil society groups have also adopted more professionalized organizational forms than their Japanese counterparts. Activist groups have an average of 8.5 employees, and over 20 percent have more than 10 employees.[47] One of Korea's largest and most influential activist groups is the Citizens' Coalition for Economic Justice (CCEJ, Gyeongsilyeon), which was founded by five hundred professionals in 1989. With more than thirty thousand members and numerous staff, CCEJ runs a publishing house, an in-house magazine, and several research institutes. Initially, former dissidents, who became moderate professionals and sought to distance themselves from the more radical *minjung*

---

43. Robert Pekkanen, *Japan's Dual Civil Society: Members without Advocates* (Stanford: Stanford University Press, 2006); Theda Skocpol et al., eds., *Civic Engagement in American Democracy* (Washington, DC: Brookings Institution Press, 1999), chap. 13.

44. Hagen Koo, "Civil Society and Democracy in South Korea," *Good Society* 11, no. 2 (2002): 42.

45. Chang, "Unintended Consequences of Repression."

46. Yutaka Tsujinaka, "From Developmentalism to Maturity," in *The State of Civil Society in Japan*, ed. Frank J. Schwartz and Susan J. Pharr (Cambridge: Cambridge University Press, 2003), 90.

47. Third Sector Institute, *The Explosion of CSOs and Citizen Participation* (CIVICUS Civil Society Index Report for South Korea, Hanyang University, 2006), 39, http://www.civicus.org/media/CSI_South_Korea_Country_Report.pdf.

movements of the 1980s, formed the core of Korea's burgeoning civil society sector in the 1990s.[48] Retaining the previous era's contentiousness and focus on democratization, these professional activists helped achieve many political reforms, but, along with the numerous lawyers involved in the activist sphere, they may have discouraged ordinary citizens from participating. Citizens may have felt they lacked the expertise, status, or eloquence to debate issues of public concern. Rather than being "movements *of* the grassroots masses," Korea's activist sector, one critic noted, comprises organizations made up of professionals and activists "*for* the grassroots masses."[49]

Japanese activist groups, on the other hand, tend to be smaller and more local operations that depend more on ordinary citizens than on paid staff. They also tend to focus on a narrower range of issues than their Korean counterparts, which have wide-ranging agendas touching on many spheres of social life.[50] Since relatively few civil society groups in Japan have legal status as nonprofit organizations (NPOs), statistics characterizing the entire activist sphere—both registered and not—are rare. Nonetheless, a 2007 survey of registered NPOs in Japan revealed that the majority had fewer than fifty members and fewer than five paid staff.[51] The prevailing model of activism in Japan looks more like a local study group, even if such groups sometimes form informal national networks. This tendency traces back to the localized networks of citizens who formed self-help and service-oriented associations that often cooperated with the state after World War II.[52] In the 1960s, single-issue and formally nonpartisan citizen groups with relatively pragmatic and even parochial goals also formed the backbone of the environmental, peace, women's, and antinuclear movements.[53] Japan's strong and development-minded central government reinforced this tendency by maintaining a regulatory environment that discouraged the formation of adversarial civic groups with professional staff or a national scope—attributes that scholars consider essential for sustained

48. Sunhyuk Kim, "South Korea," in *Civil Society and Political Change in Asia*, ed. Muthiah Alagappa (Stanford: Stanford University Press, 2004), 148–49.

49. Jeong Jonggwon, "Simin Undong e daehan Bipanjeok Pyongga [Critical Assessment of the Citizens' Movement]," *Gyeongje wa Sahoe [Economy and Society]*, no. 45 (2000): 132–48.

50. Sook Jong Lee and Celeste Arrington, "The Politics of NGOs and Democratic Governance in South Korea and Japan," *Pacific Focus* 23, no. 1 (2008): 75–96.

51. Prime Minister's Office, *Heisei 18nendo Shimin Katsudō Dantai Kihon Chōsa Hōkokusho [2006 Report on Citizen Activities' Associations]* (April 2007), 21–22.

52. Rieko Kage, "Making Reconstruction Work," *Comparative Political Studies* 43, no. 2 (2010): 163–87; Mary Alice Haddad, "Transformation of Japan's Civil Society Landscape," *Journal of East Asian Studies* 7, no. 3 (2007): 413–37.

53. Ellis S. Krauss and Bradford L. Simcock, "Citizens' Movements," in *Political Opposition in Local Politics in Japan*, ed. Scott C. Flanagan, Kurt Steiner, and Ellis S. Krauss (Princeton: Princeton University Press, 1981), 187–227; Margaret A. McKean, "Political Socialization through Citizens' Movements," in Flanagan, Steiner, and Krauss, *Political Opposition*, 228–75.

and informed activism.[54] Avenell contends that even the 1998 NPO Law, which was hailed as improving the regulatory environment, still privileges more cooperative "citizen participation-style" activist groups.[55] Observers rightly bemoan the political impotence of Japanese civil society groups, but these weaknesses actually aid victim redress movements because they can gain societal supporters by tapping into the grassroots infrastructure of Japanese civil society.

In comparison, Korean activism tends to have a more politicized flavor and utilize large national coalitions to achieve social and political change. Initially legitimized by their moral authority as former dissidents, Korean activists sustained their importance in the context of democratic consolidation in the 1990s through high-visibility tactics at the national level and attention to partisan issues. As part of these efforts, coalitions of Korean activist groups launched highly effective campaigns to monitor public officials, promote women's rights and environmental reforms, scrutinize the national budget, improve consumer safety, advance shareholder rights and corporate transparency, call for *chaebol* reform, expose political corruption, and blacklist unsuitable candidates running for election.[56] These coalitions attracted much media coverage and sparked bursts of temporary mass participation in demonstrations or boycotts.[57] Such coalitional activism, however, tends to be ad hoc and organized in a top-down fashion, which can be politically effective but can also crowd out marginal voices. Indeed, civic groups in Korea have been criticized for "labelling some issues as trivial and instead imposing 'greater' goals" like democratic deepening.[58] Moon similarly argues that "rather than being an open marketplace for political interests and ideas, . . . the Korean activist sector has great power to decide who belongs and who does not, whose grievances and pains are worthy of collective attention."[59] And observers increasingly fault Korean activist groups for failing to adequately connect with citizens and marginalized populations and instead cultivating dense interpersonal ties with the political elite.[60] During President

54. Pekkanen, *Japan's Dual Civil Society*, 177.

55. Simon Avenell, "Civil Society and the New Civic Movements in Contemporary Japan," *Journal of Japanese Studies* 35, no. 2 (2009): 282.

56. Charles K. Armstrong, ed., *Korean Society* (London: Routledge, 2007), 4.

57. Third Sector Institute, *Explosion of CSOs*, 10.

58. Sunhyuk Kim, "Civil Society in South Korea," *Journal of Northeast Asian Studies* 15, no. 2 (Summer 1996): 95.

59. Katharine H. S. Moon, "Resurrecting Prostitutes and Overturning Treaties," *Journal of Asian Studies* 66, no. 1 (2007): 153.

60. Jennifer S. Oh, "Strong State and Strong Civil Society in Contemporary South Korea," *Asian Survey* 52, no. 3 (June 2012): 533; Patricia Goedde, "The Making of Public Interest Law in South Korea via the Institutional Discourses of Minbyeon, PSPD, and Gonggam," in *Law and Society in Korea*, ed. Hyunah Yang (Cheltenham, UK: Edward Elgar, 2013), 140–41.

Roh Moo-hyun's "participatory government," when activist groups gained un-precedented access to policymaking processes, observers joked that the abbrevia-tion "NGO" referred to "next government official."[61] Although Korea's vibrant and diversifying civil society sector has achieved remarkable gains in terms of removing the vestiges of authoritarianism and advancing citizens' well-being, it tends to encourage tactics that focus on mobilizing political elites in Seoul more than ordinary citizens.

By contrast, Japanese activism focuses more on consciousness-raising, sin-gle issues, service provision, and local politics. For instance, Japanese advocacy groups concerned with foreign residents' welfare and rights provide support for foreigners' daily lives and campaign for their inclusion in political processes at the local rather than the national level.[62] Civil society groups also usually eschew formal affiliation with political parties, even if their members or their cause may overlap with a political party. Supporter groups (*shien dantai*) are a common Japanese organizational form that is particularly helpful for victim groups.[63] They usually consist of about a dozen ordinary citizens who coalesce around an individual victim, accused person, or lawyer and volunteer to provide moral support inside and outside the courthouse, organize public rallies or protests, and distribute informational fliers. Frequently such supporters may also supply organizational resources, such as ties to local unions or other civic groups. Most important, supporters tell their friends about victims' causes, which spreads awareness. The high hurdles to entry into Japan's national media (discussed next) push victim groups to seek local media attention as a first step, which actually works well with the predominantly grassroots character of Japan's activist and cause lawyering traditions. Japan's preponderance of single-issue, local activist groups is thus conducive to bottom-up patterns of conflict expansion.

The Media Environment's Diversity

Previous scholars have pointed out that the media shape the version of victims' claims that ultimately enters the public discourse through their selection and placement of stories, inclusion or exclusion of facts and sources, emphasis within a story, and duration of coverage.[64] Such choices are influenced by reporters'

---

61. Interview with Patricia Goedde, law professor, Seoul (June 10, 2008)

62. Erin Aeran Chung, "Korea and Japan's Multicultural Models for Immigrant Incorporation," *Korea Observer* 41, no. 4 (Winter 2010): 649–76.

63. Patricia G. Steinhoff, "Doing the Defendant's Laundry," *Japanstudien: Jahrbuch des Deutschen Instituts für Japanstudien* 11 (1999): 55–78.

64. E.g., William A. Gamson and Gadi Wolfsfeld, "Movements and Media as Interacting Systems," *Annals of the American Academy of Political and Social Science* 528 (July 1993): 119.

desires to convey information, write scoops, gain promotions, or uphold personal convictions, as well as by professional standards, news cycles, editors' priorities, and competitive pressures. As a result, some countries' news media develop greater diversity in terms of their content and political stances across news outlets and, concomitantly, higher levels of audience fragmentation. Such is the case in Korea, where an increasingly wide range of news outlets vie for readers and viewers since democratization. Japan's comparatively homogeneous mainstream national media pose high barriers to entry for outsider groups such as redress claimants, pushing them to seek coverage from the country's local and nonmainstream media.[65] Together with Japan's victim-centered cause lawyering tradition and decentralized civil society sphere, the national media's homogeneity encourages tactics targeted at local groups and ordinary citizens. Moreover, for those groups that capture the mainstream media's attention in Japan, news outlets' tendency to match competitors' content and the populace's relatively uniform news consumption habits make it likely that claimants' narratives of victimhood will reach wide audiences, making bottom-up conflict expansion more likely. By comparison, outsider groups in Korea face lower initial entry barriers but struggle to gain broad coverage and sustain a coherent narrative, as news outlets compete by being different and catering to niche audiences.

Decades of authoritarian rule in Korea and single-party democracy in Japan, as well as journalistic practices, have contributed to the distinctive character of each country's media environment. Japan's news media have enjoyed freedom of the press and a reputation for objectivity and thoroughness for over sixty years. But its reporters' (*kisha*) club system also engendered relatively uniform content across outlets and close relations between the mainstream media and the state that reinforced the LDP-dominated political establishment. The reporters' clubs attached to most government agencies and major corporations became journalists' primary reporting venues, and journalistic norms privileged officials as sources of information. Officials would offer exclusive briefings or documents to club members, under the premise of granting equal access to information, until the Democratic Party of Japan (DPJ) instituted briefings for nonmainstream reporters, who had been excluded from the clubs, while it was in power from 2009 to 2012.[66] Generally, Japanese reporters pride themselves for conveying unbiased, officially validated, and detailed facts, or "standard news," as one reporter put it to me. But critics have called their

65. For more, see Celeste L. Arrington, "Media Environment Diversity and Activism" (unpublished manuscript).

66. Maggie Farley, "Japan's Press and the Politics of Scandal," in *Media and Politics in Japan*, ed. Susan J. Pharr and Ellis S. Krauss (Honolulu: University of Hawai'i Press, 1996), 135–38.

reporting "pack journalism" and "saturation coverage" that promotes unifor-mity and unanalyzed minutiae in news stories.[67] Such practices create high bar-riers to entry for marginal groups. Freeman criticized the Japanese media for working "together with, or on behalf of, the political core—capturing, subvert-ing, misleading, or alternatively ignoring the political periphery."[68] The media became more critical of the state after political scandals in the late 1980s and the LDP's temporary fall from power in 1993. Some of Japan's main papers also created positions for roving reporters (*henshūiin*) who track down stories and report different perspectives.[69] Yet, although half of Japanese citizens sur-veyed in 2009 trusted the national newspapers and broadcasters' content, fewer than 20 percent thought they paid attention to "society's weak."[70] And since the March 11, 2011, earthquake-tsunami-nuclear disaster, criticism of "the main-stream media's relatively unquestioning reporting of the state's point of view in the disaster's wake" has escalated, particularly online.[71]

Korea's shorter history of press freedom has engendered reporting practices that create lower barriers to entry for outsiders. Before democratization, succes-sive authoritarian governments in Seoul discouraged businesses from running ads in dissenting papers, pressured media companies to fire dissident journal-ists, and rewarded loyal media outlets with subsidies and tax breaks.[72] After a movement for press freedom emerged in the 1970s, the state instituted even more media controls and overt censorship in the 1980s.[73] Such government interference and many journalists' experiences as dissidents in the 1980s engendered a "skepti-cism of the government line" among Korean reporters (even at establishment news outlets) that has made them more "open to new voices" than their Japanese coun-terparts.[74] The reporters' rooms (*gijashil*), which were established under Japanese colonial auspices, have also become a minor part of reporting practices because

67. E.g., Ofer Feldman, *Talking Politics in Japan Today* (Brighton, UK: Sussex Academic Press, 2005), 18–20.

68. Laurie Freeman, "Mobilizing and Demobilizing the Japanese Public Sphere," in Schwartz and Pharr, *The State of Civil Society*, 236.

69. Interview with Nakayama Shōzo, *Yomiuri Shimbun* journalist, Washington, DC (April 12, 2013).

70. Japanese Newspaper Federation (NSK), *Beesu Media to Seikatsusha [Main Media and Ordi-nary People]* (Tokyo: Annual Report, 2009), 49.

71. Quote from an interview with Ideishi Tadashi, NHK reporter, Tokyo (June 24, 2013). See also James Hadfield, "Takashi Uesugi: The Interview," *TimeOut Tokyo*, April 1, 2011, http://www.timeout.jp/en/tokyo/feature/2776/Takashi-Uesugi-The-Interview.

72. Kyu Ho Youm, "South Korea's Experiment with a Free Press," *International Communication Gazette* 53, no. 1–2 (January 1994): 112–14.

73. Thomas Kern and Sang-hui Nam, "Citizen Journalism," in Shin and Chang, *South Korean Social Movements*, 174–75.

74. Interview with a *Hankyoreh Sinmun* journalist, Seoul (May 22, 2015).

they were tainted by their association with governmental controls over the media. In addition, Korean reporters tend to provide more analysis, and their reporting is less fact-driven than Japanese reporting. In a 2008 survey, two-thirds of Koreans agreed that newspapers and broadcasters supplied "politically partial" news.[75] In this environment, victim groups can often find a national news outlet eager to run a story that embarrasses the ruling establishment—for example, *Chosun Ilbo* under Roh Moo-hyun and *Hankyoreh Sinmun* under Lee Myung-bak. But the continued existence of the vaguely worded National Security Law (NSL) and the government's increasing use of criminal defamation charges in the first decade of this century arguably constrain what news outlets will report.[76]

Partly stemming from these distinctive historical trajectories, Japan's media environment is characterized by ownership concentration and fewer ideological differences among outlets. Despite regulations that prohibit cross-media ownership, the main national newspapers (listed in order from liberal to conservative)—*Asahi Shimbun, Mainichi Shimbun, Nikkei Shimbun, Yomiuri Shimbun*, and *Sankei Shimbun*—are part of large business groups that also own commercial TV and radio stations, weekly magazines, publishing houses, sports teams, and other businesses. These five newspapers boast some of the largest circulations in the world.[77] Japan's main newspapers and broadcasters have discernibly different editorial stances on issues such as war guilt or revision of the Constitution's pacifist Article 9. But they have long practiced "competitive matching" in format, content, and sources for news stories.[78] From 2008 to 2012, the *Asahi, Yomiuri*, and *Nikkei* even ran a joint website that displayed the three papers' top stories side by side. Until the 1990s, Japan's large and respected public broadcaster NHK dominated the five commercial broadcasters, which were each affiliated with a national newspaper, under regulations that restricted new entrants to the broadcasting market.[79] After the deregulation of cable and satellite TV in the 1990s, Japanese audiences gained access to more channels.[80] Soft news or infotainment talk shows have also drawn some viewers

75. Rhee June-woong, "Tendentiousness of Korean Journalism and the Problem of the 'Distinction between Facts and Opinions,'" *Korea Journalism Review* 4, no. 2 (Summer 2010): 53.

76. Stephan Haggard and Jong-Sung You, "Freedom of Expression in South Korea," *Journal of Contemporary Asia* 45, no. 1 (January 2015): 167–79.

77. Japanese Audit Bureau of Circulations, *Shimbun Hakkōsha Repōto Hanki Fukyūritsu [Newspaper Publishers' Half-Year Report on Diffusion Rates]* (December 2014), http://adv.yomiuri.co.jp/yomiuri/busu/busu01.html.

78. D. Eleanor Westney, "Mass Media as Business Organizations," in Pharr and Krauss, *Media and Politics in Japan*, 69.

79. Ellis S. Krauss, *Broadcasting Politics in Japan* (Ithaca: Cornell University Press, 2000), chap. 7.

80. Gregory W. Noble, "Let a Hundred Channels Contend," *Journal of Japanese Studies* 26, no. 1 (January 2000): 79–109.

away from NHK's famously fact-driven, proestablishment, and nonanalytical news broadcasts.[81] Yet the range of issues these shows cover still tends to be relatively congruent. As a result, challenger groups depend on the more accessible nonmainstream media—including local news outlets, weekly magazines, and foreign media—to break stories about government misconduct. Although many such magazines are affiliated with the main newspapers and face financial difficulties, they have strong traditions of investigative journalism.[82] Moreover, relatively autonomous local and regional news outlets, some of which rival the national dailies in reach and impact (unlike the situation in Korea), combine with Japan's decentralized cause lawyering and activist traditions to facilitate victims' efforts to mobilize grassroots support.

Despite its downsides, the relative homogeneity of Japan's mainstream media helps groups that do make it into the mainstream news to spread a more consistent message and reach broader audiences, which are less fragmented in Japan than in Korea. Although the role of online news is changing Japan's media environment, Japanese citizens still seem to favor the traditional media for news. The percentage of Japanese who read a newspaper daily fell only from 70 to 56 between 2001 and 2013.[83] And, according to a 2006 survey, 77 percent of Japanese still watched NHK news regularly.[84] During the 2011 triple disaster, 81 percent of Internet users said they relied on NHK broadcasts most for information, whereas just 43 percent turned to portal sites such as Yahoo or Google.[85] Twitter gained popularity because it enabled families and friends to find each other when cell phone service was down after the earthquake. But it and, to a lesser extent, social media platforms such as 2channel, Mixi, and Niko Niko Dōga (like YouTube), still cater to niche audiences as they transition from being forums for relatively mundane, nonpolitical discussions to facilitating more political and social commentary.[86] Moreover, in 2011, only 34 percent of Japanese named the Internet as an "essential source of information," compared with 56 percent for newspapers

81. Masaki Taniguchi, "Changing Media, Changing Politics in Japan," *Japanese Journal of Political Science* 8, no. 1 (2007): 147–66.

82. David McNeill, "Japan's Contemporary Media," in *Critical Issues in Contemporary Japan*, ed. Jeff Kingston (New York: Routledge, 2014), 69.

83. Japanese Newspaper Federation (NSK), "2013nen Zenkoku Media Sesshoku Hyōka Chōsa [2013 National Survey of Media Users and Evaluation]" (Tokyo: NSK, 2013), 34–35.

84. Keio University, "Research Survey of Political Society in a Multi-Cultural and Pluri-Generational World," July 2007, http://www.coe-ccc.keio.ac.jp/data_archive_en/data_archive_en_csw_download.html.

85. Ministry of Internal Affairs and Communications, *Jōhō Tsūshin Hakusho [Information and Communications White Paper]* (2011), 15, http://www.soumu.go.jp/johotsusintokei/whitepaper/ja/h23/pdf/index.html.

86. Interview with Yoshioka Jumpei, NHK reporter, Tokyo (June 24, 2013).

and 50 percent for TV.[87] Thus, compared with Koreans, Japanese people tend to consume more congruent news in more congruent ways, which enables those movements that capture national publicity to ignite broad public outrage that threatens decision makers.

Korea's media market is more diverse and segmented. Compared with Japan's main papers, Korea's eleven national newspapers present a wider range of ideological perspectives and topics. The three largest Korean papers—*Chosun Ilbo*, *JoongAng Ilbo*, and *DongA Ilbo* (collectively nicknamed *Cho-Joong-Dong*)—remain relatively homogeneous and conservative and control two-thirds of the market, partly as a result of having toed the authoritarian government's line in the 1980s. But at the other end of the political spectrum are the influential *Hankyoreh* and *Kyunghyang* newspapers, which benefit from and contribute to progressive Koreans' abiding distrust toward *Cho-Joong-Dong*. Founded in 1988, *Hankyoreh* prides itself on its democratic ownership structure, which insulates reporters from the external political and the internal editorial interference associated with *Cho-Joong-Dong*. Until the Asian financial crisis of 1997–98, *chaebol* or individual families owned most other newspapers, but financial challenges diversified ownership structures and regional newspapers became even more minor players, unlike those in Japan.[88] Meanwhile, the dominant public broadcasters (KBS and MBC) and a commercial broadcaster (SBS) have faced competition from a wider range of channels since deregulation in 2002. Cross-media ownership was prohibited until 2011, at which point the *Cho-Joong-Dong* and *Maeil Kyeongjae* newspapers launched four new general programming cable channels to take advantage of controversial relaxed rules. Progressive outlets and the media workers' unions decried newspapers' foray into TV as "the end of a healthy media structure in our society."[89] But, since the 1990s, all Korean presidents have at times favored media outlets that match their political leanings and cited democratic objectives to justify indirect attacks on opposing media, indicating stronger "political parallelism" in the media than in Japan.[90]

Ideological polarization among Korean news outlets and citizens' evolving consumption patterns have spurred greater audience fragmentation than in Japan, which hampers redress claimants' efforts to reach wide audiences with a coherent narrative of victimhood. Although observers still criticize *Cho-Joong-Dong* for

---

87. "Shimbun 'Kakasenai' 56% . . . Media Yoron Chōsa [Newspapers Named Indispensable by 56% in Poll]," *Yomiuri Shimbun*, January 22, 2011.

88. Ki-Sung Kwak, *Media and Democratic Transition in South Korea* (London: Routledge, 2012), 72.

89. Lee Kyung-mi and Jung Hwang-bong, "Media Workers' Union Protests Launch of ChoJoong-Dong Networks," *Hankyeoreh Sinmun*, December 2, 2011.

90. Daniel C. Hallin and Paolo Mancini, *Comparing Media Systems* (Cambridge: Cambridge University Press, 2004).

having undue influence over political agendas, just 9 percent of Koreans reported reading a newspaper daily in 2013.[91] When asked in 2010 where they went for news, 62 percent of Koreans said television, 25 percent said Internet portal sites, and just 7 percent said newspapers.[92] But these patterns diverged by age. More than half of those younger than thirty relied on the Internet for news, while three-quarters of those over fifty turned to television for their news. With declining ad revenues and audience sizes, Korean news outlets are also increasingly tailoring content to the demographics advertisers most want to reach. One journalist noted that Korean news outlets compete by offering "distinctive content, often along progressive and conservative lines."[93] Additionally, Internet-based news providers have flourished more in Korea than in Japan. Often run by professional journalists, Korea's online news outlets combine traditional journalism with popular innovative practices such as citizen journalism (e.g., OhMyNews), blogging, readers' comments, and podcasts like the irreverent *Naneun Ggomsu Da*.[94] While the Japanese version of OhMyNews launched in 2004 lasted only four years after 2004 because of a lack of visitors, live streams of police violence during the 2008 beef protests in Korea attracted millions of viewers to Korea's OhMyNews site.[95] Korea's traditional news outlets—and the organizational structures and norms they propagate—still play an important role, despite citizens' distrust of them, because portals and online news providers rely on them for content and political elites look to them for information. But with the rise of TV, cable, and the Internet worldwide, scholars have worried that people will no longer encounter different points of view.[96] This concern is particularly applicable to Korea.[97] The fragmentation of Korean audiences has also contributed to and been caused by the ideological, regional, and generational divisions in Korean society.[98] In sum, although Korea's media encourage a greater diversity of voices in the public sphere and have loyal audiences, they facilitate consensus mobilization less than Japan's media environment does.

---

91. Korea Press Foundation, "Suyongja Uisik Josa [Survey of Media Users]" (Media Statistics Information System, 2013), http://mediasis.kpf.or.kr/surveyStatistics/KPF_mediaSurvey.aspx?MASTER_CODE=99928&menu_Index=0.

92. Gallup Korea, *Mirae Hanguk Report Josa Gyeolgwa [Survey Results from the Future Korea Report]* (October 2010), http://panel.gallup.co.kr.

93. Interview with An Jun-ho, *Chosun Ilbo* journalist, Seoul (Feb. 11, 2009).

94. Kern and Nam, "Citizen Journalism," 182.

95. Seung-Ook Lee, Sook-Jin Kim, and Joel Wainwright, "Mad Cow Militancy," *Political Geography* 29 (2010): 364.

96. Todd Gitlin, "Public Sphere or Public Sphericules?," in *Media, Ritual, and Identity*, ed. Tamar Liebes, James Curran, and Elihu Katz (London: Routledge, 1998), 168–74.

97. Kim Su Jung, "Emerging Patterns of News Media Use across Multiple Platforms and Their Political Implications in South Korea" (PhD diss., Northwestern University, 2011), chap. 5.

98. Sook-Jong Lee, "Democratization and Polarization in Korean Society," *Asian Perspective* 29, no. 3 (2005): 118–21.

Claiming and Shaming Tactics

These features of the mediating institutions in Japan and Korea help account for the particular mixture of tactics that redress movements tend to adopt in each country, but the most common tactics are litigation, publicity-oriented tactics, and lobbying. When faced with government intransigence, victim groups usually continue to claim redress through accepted channels, but they supplement these efforts with shaming tactics that aim to mobilize third parties' support to help pressure decision makers to grant concessions. Shaming a government entails exposing its failure to perform its duties. Shaming works not only in East Asian contexts, where saving face is socially important. The potency of shaming the state in any democratic context (and sometimes even in nondemocratic ones) stems from the fact that it can enable victim groups to ignite public outrage and thereby spark a political crisis. Ideally, the scandal of government wrongdoing or negligence will attract media coverage and be addressed in the legislature. Litigation, publicity-oriented tactics, and conventional lobbying leverage narratives of victimhood to claim redress directly and pressure the state indirectly by attracting sympathy from societal and political actors through shaming.

Litigation

Not all victim groups claim redress by suing their government, and those that do usually turn to litigation only after exhausting other channels. Bringing legal claims remains a daunting process in any country because of high costs, evidentiary requirements, and the likelihood of a protracted court battle. Governments represent particularly formidable defendants because they have better access to experienced counsel, compelling evidence, and expert witnesses. A government may also cite legal technicalities, such as the statute of limitations or sovereignty to deflate plaintiffs' arguments. Yet my research confirms studies that have found that litigation, even in the absence of rulings favorable for plaintiffs, has potential benefits as a tactic for groups seeking redress.[99] First, preparing a case with lawyers and formally articulating grievances in legal terms helps establish consistency among plaintiffs' stories. It can also augment a redress campaign's salience by framing victims' grievances in terms of universal legal rights and principles with which the public can identify. Both Japanese and Korean cause lawyers facilitate such processes, as they are an inherent part of filing a legal complaint. Second, when a court grants standing to victims and agrees to hear their case, it publicly legitimates the

---

99. Inter alia, Upham, *Law and Social Change in Postwar Japan*, 27; Michael W. McCann, *Rights at Work* (Chicago: University of Chicago Press, 1994), 57; Robert A. Kagan, *Adversarial Legalism* (Cambridge, MA: Harvard University Press, 2003).

victim group and its claims. Third, evidence produced during a trial, a court's recommendations for a settlement, or actual rulings can put direct pressure on state
officials to achieve a political resolution. Japanese lawyers who represent redress
claimants, for example, often prepare short memos detailing particular legal arguments to deliver to the politicians they lobby; these counterbalance the Ministry
of Justice's briefings to politicians. Court rulings or statements in plaintiffs' favor
can also indicate or spawn rifts in the political establishment.

Beyond such direct effects, litigation often has indirect or "radiating" effects
that help build a movement, generate publicity, and boost the impact of other tactics.[100] For example, news of a lawsuit alerts similarly harmed individuals to their
victimhood, raises their rights consciousness, and sometimes inspires naming,
blaming, and claiming. Moreover, since Korean and Japanese trials are discon-
tinuous, meeting just once every few months, and based more on documentary
evidence than on oral argument, redress movements must work harder to remain
salient between court dates. Especially in Japan, important witnesses' testimonies,
transitions between phases of the court process, and interim rulings tend to offer
plaintiffs' attorneys a pretense for organizing press conferences, rallies, or other
events to gain publicity and energize supporters. Besides building momentum for
the movement, mobilizing fellow victims and supporters is important for transforming legal decisions into policy change. This is especially critical with collective lawsuits (*shūdan soshō/jipdan sosong*), which are the closest equivalent in
Japan's and Korea's civil law traditions to class action lawsuits in the United States.
In collective lawsuits, victims cannot rely on a few representative victims to attach
their names to the lawsuit on behalf of a larger class because court decisions apply
only to the plaintiffs actually listed on the lawsuit. Legislation is thus necessary to
ensure that victims who did not join a lawsuit also receive redress benefits.

Since judiciaries tend to support the existing political order and lack the power
to realize some components of redress, even if courts rule in the plaintiffs' favor,
the most effective redress claimants coordinate litigation with publicity oriented
activities and conventional lobbying (as discussed below).[101] Litigation is not
necessary for redress movements to reach the public or mobilize political allies,
and Upham argued that the Japanese government intended to prevent litigation
from becoming "an institutional channel for resolving disputes [and] setting national policy."[102] But since the environmental lawsuits of the late 1960s, Japanese

---

100. Marc Galanter, "The Radiating Effects of Courts," in *Empirical Theories about Courts*, ed.
Keith O. Boyum and Lynn Mather (New York: Longman, 1983), 117–42.

101. Michael W. McCann, "Law and Social Movements," *Annual Review of Law and Social Science*
2 (2006): 23.

102. Upham, *Law and Social Change in Postwar Japan*, 21–22.

cause lawyers have honed a potent model for activism that is victim-centered and strives to mobilize local resources, such as groups of citizen activists and local media coverage, to achieve political change. Japanese cause lawyers mobilize issue-specific teams for each new legal campaign via personal contacts or ad hoc task forces in local bar associations. Although scores of lawyers may sign on just as moral supporters, the active core usually includes an experienced and politically moderate lead counsel (to avoid partisan taint), several midcareer and more politicized secretary-generals, and a number of younger lawyers for the grunt work.[103] Through successive campaigns, such legal teams have developed institutionalized practices of divvying up activities related to legal technicalities, media strategy, plaintiff relations, and lobbying.[104] Lawyers' involvement extends well beyond the courtroom but strives for nonpartisanship in order to uphold victims' status as accidental activists. In addition to providing legal expertise, lawyers in such teams act as facilitators (rather than leaders) when making tactical decisions with claimants. One prominent lawyer explained it this way: "If the lawyers stand in front and the victims hide behind them, then we can't assign true blame and we can't make any sort of appeal to society."[105] This inclination to be coactivists alongside plaintiffs helps foster relationships of trust and empowers redress claimants to play important roles in activism beyond the courtroom.

To further Korea's democratic consolidation in the 1990s, a different model of combining litigation with broader activism developed. Whereas Japanese cause lawyering "puts victims at the forefront" to attract media attention and spark public outrage,[106] Korean cause lawyering places more importance on using lawyers' connections to mobilize supporters. Minbyeon members collaborated closely with the prominent progressive NGO People's Solidarity for Participatory Democracy (PSPD, Chamyeoyeondae) and progressive opposition parties to use litigation and lobbying to overturn authoritarian-era statutes, improve minorities' political rights, curb corruption, and address past wrongdoing by authoritarian regimes.[107] Through these highly effective campaigns, Korean cause lawyers developed a tendency to focus their energies upward—toward political elites rather than toward the grassroots—and take more prominent positions in activism. Many of them also gained excellent access to legal, political, and organizational resources through their membership in activist lawyering organizations and work

---

103. Personal communication with Ota Shozo, law professor (June 15, 2011).
104. Interview with Yahiro Mitsuhide, lawyer, Fukuoka (May 12, 2009).
105. "Interview with Human Rights Lawyer Yasuhara Yukihiko," *Heso Magazine*, October 2008.
106. Interview with Itai Masaru, lawyer, Kumamoto (May 15, 2009).
107. Ginsburg, "Dismantling the Developmental State-Administrative Procedure Reform"; Kuk Cho, "Transitional Justice in Korea," *Pacific Rim Law & Policy Journal* 16 (2007): 579–612; Hong, "From the Streets to the Courts."

they did for large NGOs as volunteers or paid in-house counsels, which are rare in Japan. For example, PSPD, which was founded in 1994 by a prominent Minbyeon lawyer, still often "mobilizes and provides logistical support for lawyers fighting for various progressive causes."[108] While support from such organizations can boost victims' leverage over state actors, these groups also have their own priorities, which sometimes clash with redress claimants' objectives. Only since the end of the first decade of this century has cause lawyering in Korea started becoming "more of a professional ethic of legal service . . . [than] a political tool," as cause lawyers have moved away from Minbyeon's sphere of influence and taken up other causes.[109] But they generally place less importance on empowering redress claimants. Indeed, one Korean cause lawyer commented that the close coordination between lawyers and plaintiffs he had observed in Japan contrasted with the norm in Korea, where "lawyers do most of the work and rarely communicate with plaintiffs about legal tactics."[110] Thus, even though using litigation to change policy has become more effective in both Japan and Korea, it entails different patterns of interaction among claimants, lawyers, and other third parties, partly because of the distinctive characteristics of each country's mediating institutions.

Publicity

Shaming the state through publicity is perhaps redress claimants' most potent tool for propagating narratives of victimhood that mobilize societal and then political supporters. Victim groups often host open or closed online discussions and use e-mail and cell phone mailing lists to distribute newsletters or updates to fellow victims or supporters. But redress claimants depend on the news media to broadcast their stories because such minimedia cannot reach as many people as the mass media can with their wide distributions and status.[111] Claimants therefore frame their claims in terms that appeal to news outlets and their audiences. In their seminal article, Gamson and Wolfsfeld noted that challenger groups seek standing or respect as a source of information, particular issue framing, and sympathy when they pursue media coverage.[112] Issue framing refers to the process of creating and sustaining meaning for the public, other victim group members, and opponents by situating a specific grievance within broader discourses.[113]

---

108. Interview with Park Geun-yong, PSPD, Seoul (May 28, 2015).
109. Goedde, "From Dissidents to Institution-Builders," 88.
110. Interview with Lee Jeong-il, lawyer, Seoul (July 13, 2012).
111. Myra Marx Ferree, "Resonance and Radicalism," *American Journal of Sociology* 109 (2003): 11.
112. Gamson and Wolfsfeld, "Movements and Media as Interacting Systems," 121.
113. Benford and Snow, "Framing Processes and Social Movements," 613–14.

Generally, redress claimants strive for resonance with audiences by instilling a sense of empathy or fear. Particularly persuasive causal stories lead ordinary citizens to believe that they could just as easily have been the ones injured by state policy or to view the situation as one wherein the state failed or abused its powers and violated victims' rights.

Victims' subjective and often emotional "testimonials of suffering" are potent tools for attracting attention and pity, even if proof of the state's liability remains elusive.[114] Specific stories of suffering are also less likely than statistics about a broader pattern of victimization to overwhelm the public and inhibit compassionate responses to real human suffering.[115] Dramatizing claims with personal details from personally identifiable claimants brings an issue to life,[116] though it also requires sacrificing privacy and risking potentially critical public scrutiny. Redress movements, therefore, often have some public faces, such as the "real-name plaintiffs" (jitsumei genkoku) in the Japanese hepatitis C case discussed in chapter 4. In the 1980s, Japanese lawyers for HIV-infected hemophiliacs pioneered a system (which does not exist in Korea) of using only numerical identifiers for plaintiffs who wanted to remain anonymous (tokumei genkoku) in court proceedings and documents to protect them from discrimination.[117] Media interviews and photos of real-name plaintiffs in Japan bolster the human interest appeal of a movement, especially since court hearings are less dramatic and adversarial in Japan (and Korea) than in, for example, the United States. Both personal testimonies and the scandal of government misconduct have the potential to appeal to news outlets competing for market share. As directly affected parties or court-certified plaintiffs, claimants may also be able to surmount reporters' common preference—especially in Japan—for accredited sources such as government officials.

But narratives of victimhood are impermanent and contested. The state and industry actors that victims blame constitute influential potential "counterframers." Keeping embarrassing instances of failure out of the public eye saves face, limits financial outlays, and helps officials retain control over the terms of debate. Japanese journalists' especially strong preference for official sources also gives the state levers of control. The Korean government has recently turned more and

114. Salmaan Keshavjee, Sheri Weiser, and Arthur Kleinman, "Medicine Betrayed," Social Science & Medicine 53, no. 8 (October 2001): 1081–94.

115. Jenny Edkins, Missing (Ithaca: Cornell University Press, 2011); Joseph A. Amato, Victims and Values (New York: Greenwood Press, 1990), 209–212.

116. Todd Gitlin, The Whole World Is Watching (Berkeley: University of California Press, 1980), 146–47.

117. Koga Katsuhige, Shūdan Soshō, Jitsumu Manual [A Practical Manual for Collective Litigation] (Tokyo: Nihon Hyōronsha, 2009), 34–36.

more to libel charges, which carry criminal weight in Korea, to control media and public discourse on sensitive issues. Additionally, as Schattschneider acknowledged, the original contestants may lose control over the terms of their conflict even to their supporters, as they expand the scope of the conflict to include civil society groups or politicians with their own objectives.[118] The public may over time come to see the victims as undeserving of compensation if they appear divided, overly partisan, ideological, or dishonest. Partisan taint is particularly difficult to avoid in Korea's politicized public sphere.

Temporarily adopting more disruptive or contentious shaming tactics can help victims sustain publicity, remain united, and put the government on the defensive. Social movements in Japan and Korea have historically used violence and faced state repression. Yet disruptive but nonviolent tactics such as rallies, demonstrations, sit-ins, vigils, die-ins, and marches are more common. Marching with photos of deceased relatives, as the Korean parents of high schoolers who perished in the Sewol ferry sinking in 2014 did, demonstrates the poignancy and performative nature of shaming tactics. Such nonviolent tactics work especially well in later stages of the policy process when efforts to pass or implement redress legislation stall. Claimants shame politicians for reneging on their promises, which Keck and Sikkink called "accountability politics" in another context.[119] Events that give passersby pause and demonstrate levels of public indignation against the state are especially good publicity. The Japanese HIV victims' sit-in outside the health ministry in snowy conditions in February 1996, with some plaintiffs wearing hospital pajamas and carrying their own IV bags, remains a powerful example of how redress movements can "turn the public against the government," which denied responsibility even as claimants were dying.[120] The impact of such public events is especially amplified in the Japanese media because of outlets' tendency to compete by matching. In sum, publicity can enable redress claimants to both attract the attentive public's support and signal to politicians how important their cause is, giving politicians reason to support victims and pressure the government.

Lobbying

While litigation and publicity-oriented tactics are indirect in that they seek to mobilize judicial and societal pressure on decision makers, conventional lobbying is

---

118. E. E. Schattschneider, *The Semisovereign People* (New York: Holt, Rinehart and Winston, 1960), 4.

119. Margaret E. Keck and Kathryn Sikkink, *Activists beyond Borders* (Ithaca: Cornell University Press, 1998), chap. 1.

120. Interview with Ayukyo Machiko, lawyer, Tokyo (May 30, 2008).

both direct and indirect. Redress claimants appeal directly to elected and agency officials because they ultimately depend on them to enact measures related to redress. But lobbying also gives the claimants credibility and visibility in the eyes of other potential third-party supporters. As a result, they usually lobby at all stages of seeking redress. Lobbying includes both the process of mobilizing and monitoring politicians who are elite allies and the process of contacting politicians who are not elite allies. Of course, whether and when political elites decide to back redress claimants depends on elites' calculations and their interactions with the claimants and their other supporters. And as-yet-uninterested politicians may become elite allies. Yet, as this book's analytical framework emphasizes, lobbying and its outcomes are interconnected with redress claimants' efforts to mobilize other forms of third-party support to pressure the state.

Since victim groups usually lack the connections or electoral clout to stand out amid the plethora of voices clamoring for a politician's finite time and energy, when and how lobbying occurs depends at least partly on redress claimants' ties with members of their society's mediating institutions. For instance, victims' lawyers may have personal ties to an elected official or a member of his or her staff and can help victims to frame their claims in ways that resonate with the lawmaker's interests. This is especially true with Korea's politically connected lawyers. But, as the case studies will show, many Japanese lawyers have also developed political contacts, albeit with all parties, over successive victim redress movements. Redress claimants I interviewed described using specific kinds of information or particular victims to cue politicians and connect with relevant aspects of a lawmaker's background, such as his or her party, professional background, university, or faith, in order to obtain meetings. Furthermore, although Japanese reporters' relatively cozy ties to political elites through the press clubs make them less attuned to outsiders, these ties also make reporters good channels through which to seek meetings with elected or agency officials. Nonvictim activists may similarly provide introductions, especially in Korea, where many activists run for office. If speaking with the lawmaker directly is impossible, then claimants often explain their cause to his or her secretaries. Although such meetings do not offer claimants visibility, they can be highly effective in raising awareness of particularistic issues like victims' redress.

Lobbying politicians who are not already allies in the narrow sense takes on very different implications depending on when it occurs in the course of a political conflict over redress and what relationship it bears to a movement's other tactics. Early lobbying can help raise basic awareness of an issue or a bill that an elite ally is preparing. Later, if a movement has gained media attention, lawmakers may be more willing to meet with redress claimants to gain a photo op, even if they do little to advance the movement's cause. The Japanese media facilitate such coverage and even help the movement, as journalists pay greater attention to events that involve political elites. Lobbying in a conflict's latter stages is also an important way of signaling broader societal concern and enables claimants to leverage such concern to persuade lawmakers to vote for redress legislation. As Soule and King find, public support for a cause is more important when lawmakers are considering and passing legislation than at the agenda-setting stage.[121] While one legislator can propose a bill, more legislators must be persuaded of its merits for it to pass. Delivering hundreds of thousands of signed petitions to a government agency or lawmaker's office, for instance, can attract media attention and physically show politicians the level of public concern. Backing from active groups in society also signals to politicians an issue's salience. Redress movements sometimes conduct surveys of legislators to shame political parties for their lack of support for the victims' cause. Thus conventional lobbying serves various objectives over the course of a campaign for redress and, when combined with litigation and publicity, can help draw third parties to redress claimants' side in their conflict with the state while also directly pressuring officials to make concessions.

Mobilizing Victimhood as an Interactive and Historically Contingent Process

If a population of injured persons overcomes the substantial hurdles involved in grievance articulation and initial mobilization, the resulting victim organization has the potential to transform its weakness—its victimhood—into strength by taking its complaints to court, attracting publicity, and lobbying politicians. My research indicates that these tactics work best in combination and in the order discussed above. But not all victim groups pursue these three claiming and shaming tactics in that order. And the specific form and connotation each tactic takes differ cross-nationally, depending on how they interact with that society's mediating sectors. These sectors have the capacity to open or close windows of opportunity, supply or deny resources, and validate or invalidate victims' issue framings. Sympathetic members of the mediating professions can enhance the efficacy of redress claimants' activism when they transmit victims' grievances with fidelity, "furnish them with possible solutions, and dramatize them in such a way that they are taken up and dealt with by parliamentary complexes."[122] A society's cause lawyers, civil society sector, and news media, therefore, affect the range

---

121. Sarah A. Soule and Brayden G. King, "The Stages of the Policy Process and the Equal Rights Amendment, 1972–1982," *American Journal of Sociology* 111, no. 6 (May 2006): 1871–1909.

122. Habermas, *Between Facts and Norms*, 359.

and efficacy of victim groups' tactical options. As this chapter demonstrates, Japan's relatively more autonomous legal profession, homogeneous mainstream media, and volunteer-based activist tradition facilitate tactics aimed at mobilizing societal supporters *before* gaining elite allies. In comparison, Korea's politically connected legal profession, diverse media environment, and professionalized and centrally organized activist sector encourage challenger groups to seek support from politicians earlier. Each country's mediating institutions developed these characteristics over time through social learning processes, much as victimhood claims developed particular connotations in each country. Such historically contingent constraints are not impossible to overcome, but crafting coherent narratives of victimhood and using them to attract third-party supporters is fundamentally a contested process. Patterns of conflict expansion are thus not entirely within redress claimants' control. Rather, as the case studies in the next three chapters will show, they are the result of victim groups' dynamic interactions with other actors and their sociopolitical environment.

3

HANSEN'S DISEASE SURVIVORS' RIGHTS

Leprosy may seem like an antiquated ailment, but thousands of survivors of the disease are still living in Japan and South Korea today. Stigmatized and misunderstood through much of world history, leprosy (also called Hansen's disease) is rarely infectious and not heritable.[1] It has been treatable since the 1940s, and the World Health Organization has recommended outpatient treatment since 1960. If detected early, it no longer causes the disfiguration that visibly marred leprosy sufferers in previous generations. Yet for most of the twentieth century, Japanese and Korean people affected by Hansen's disease were ostracized in specialized sanatoria (leprosaria) and subjected to various human rights abuses, including forced abortions and vasectomies, as a result of their governments' policies and societal discrimination.[2]

Around the turn of the millennium, leprosy survivors in both countries mobilized to hold their governments accountable for contributing to their suffering. But they have achieved differing levels of redress. Japanese leprosy survivors

---

1. The Norwegian physician Gerhard Armauer Hansen discovered the bacillus that causes leprosy, *Mycobacterium leprae*, in 1873. The stigma against people with leprosy dates at least as far back as biblical references to various skin diseases commonly translated as leprosy (*tzara'at* in Hebrew or *lepra* in Greek).

2. Hansen's disease survivors succeeded in persuading their governments to replace the term "leprosy" (*raibyō/nabyeong*) with "Hansen's disease" in all official documents in 1995 in Japan and in 1999 in Korea. But since "leprosy" is more common in English, I use the two names of the disease interchangeably.

leveraged publicity, a landmark court ruling, and public outrage to elicit an official inquiry, an apology from the prime minister, compensation, and structural reforms within three years of first suing the state in 1998. The passage of the Hansen's Disease Basic Law in 2008 rendered redress even more comprehensive by formalizing agreements that the state and the Hansen's disease community had reached in negotiations after 2001. Korean leprosy survivors, meanwhile, sought redress from two states: first Japan and then Korea. After suing for the right to compensation under Japan's 2001 law, elderly Korean leprosy sufferers who had survived harsh treatment under Japanese colonial rule over the Korean peninsula (1910–45) won compensation in 2006. Their transnational activism inspired younger members of the community to lobby for special legislation to redress the ROK government's post-1948 mistreatment and neglect of Korean leprosy survivors. To date, though, they have achieved only partial redress. Legislation passed in 2007 established a fact-finding commission to review victims' claims related to particular incidents of mistreatment but avoided statements about the state's liability. No-fault stipends from the state for those certified as victims were also delayed until 2012. In 2014 and 2015, however, favorable rulings in the lawsuits that approximately 650 leprosy survivors have filed against the Korean government since 2011 bolstered victims' claims. But the state has appealed all the rulings and comprehensive redress remains elusive.

Several factors contributed to the divergent outcomes in these parallel and interlinked movements. Most important, Japanese redress claimants gained support from ordinary citizens and civic groups before attracting elite political allies. Litigation in three locales, a legal team of more than a hundred lawyers, a network of citizen-run "supporter groups" (*shien dantai*), and plaintiffs' novel organizational identity apart from the country's existing leprosy patient association helped claimants build broad support for their movement and, by 2001, turn redress into an issue that politicians could no longer ignore. In Korea, by contrast, a lawmaker's interest in the issue of redress preceded broader societal concern. In fact, early access to an elite ally, who started drafting special legislation in 2005, reduced the impetus to mobilize leprosy survivors and cultivate broader societal sympathy. Unlike the Japanese claimants, Korea's leprosy community initially eschewed a new organization focused on redress, litigation against the state, and publicity-grabbing tactics. Consequently, Korean Hansen's disease survivors lacked the leverage that broad public outrage against the state provided for Japan's leprosy movement. Through a comparison of leprosy-related activism in Japan and Korea, this chapter explores how early access to political elites can be detrimental for outsider groups. Some degree of initial political closure drives movements to invest more in grassroots mobilization, which tends to produce greater redress outcomes in the long run.

Naming and Blaming:
Sequelae, Society, and the State

People afflicted with Hansen's disease in Japan and Korea experienced hardship during the past century due to varying combinations of the effects (sequelae) of the disease, social stigma, and government policies. Leprosy is a chronic disease caused by a bacillus that affects the skin, peripheral nerves, and mucous membranes. If untreated, people with leprosy can lose sensation in their extremities or develop physical handicaps and blindness. Although the exact mode of transmission is still unknown, the vast majority of people are not susceptible to the bacterium. In the early 1940s, researchers at a U.S. leprosarium in Louisiana discovered that sulfone drugs provided effective treatment. Multidrug therapy (MDT) rendered the disease curable in the early 1980s, and the WHO has provided MDT free of charge to leprosy patients worldwide since 1995. Poorer countries still struggle with high rates of leprosy because inadequate sanitation and underdeveloped public health infrastructures that seem to facilitate the spread of leprosy-causing bacteria and delay diagnosis. Korea's leprosy population peaked at 37,571 in 1970 but declined by 2014 to 11,904 (of whom fewer than 300 are bacterially active), thanks to economic development and improved medical care.[3] The number of leprosy sufferers in Japan, a more advanced nation, peaked in 1900 at 30,359, stood at 4,404 in 2001, and fell to below 2,000 in 2012.[4] Physical disabilities plague three-quarters of Korean leprosy survivors because of the inadequate medical care they received in the recent past.[5] If detected early, new cases of leprosy need not result in such sequelae because the disease has become easy to cure.

Still, societal revulsion toward leprosy survivors and misperceptions about the disease have persisted. Long endemic to both Japan and Korea, leprosy was feared for the visible deformities it caused before treatment was available. Japanese society historically classed people with leprosy as "nonpersons" (*hinin*). Buddhist tradition conceived of leprosy as punishment for sins in a past life, and Chinese medicine traced the etiology of leprosy to bad family lineage.[6] Consequently,

---

3. NHRCK, *Hansenin Ingwon Siltae Josa [A Study of the Human Rights of Persons Affected by Hansen's Disease]* (National Human Rights Committee Korea, December 2005), 166 (hereafter cited as *Hansen's Disease Human Rights Report*). And Korean Centers for Disease Control, *2014 Hansen Saeop Jichim [2014 Hansen's Disease Guidelines]*, 51.

4. NCLR, *Zenkankyō Undōshi [The History of Activism by the National Council of Leprosarium Patients]* (Tokyo: Ikkōsha, 1977), 191. Recent data: "Collection of Hansen's Disease Links," http://www.geocities.jp/libell8/14data.htm.

5. A survey of 6,328 leprosy sufferers by Hanvit Welfare Association in 2008. Hanvit, *Hansenin Pihaesgeon Pihaeja Myeongyehoebok mit Bosang deung e Gwanhan Beopryul Ipbeop Gongcheonghoe [Public Hearing for the Revised Hansen's Disease Victim Assistance Law]* (National Assembly, 2009), 134 (hereafter cited as *Public Hearing on the Revised Law*).

6. Susan L. Burns, "Making Illness Identity," *Japan Review* 16 (2004): 194–95.

victims of the disease and their families occupied precarious positions in society. Before the twentieth century, sufferers whose families would not or could not care for them roamed the land as beggars, often congregating near temples or in "leper villages." Older Koreans recall seeing villagers throw stones at them or scatter salt on the ground to prevent infection. Tales about vagrants with leprosy kidnapping children, allegedly to use their organs as a form of treatment, had existed for centuries.[7] Even in the 1960s, Korean parents warned children to stop crying "or else lepers [*mundungi*] will come get you."[8] Most Korean and Japanese people who entered leprosaria in the twentieth century severed ties with their families to protect them from such prejudice.

Prewar Leprosy Control Policies

For some people affected by Hansen's disease, the compulsory segregation promoted by the Japanese authorities and Western missionaries in the early twentieth century provided relief from social prejudice. For many others, state policies reinforced prejudice, tore apart families, and caused untold trauma. Japan's first Leprosy Prevention Law (law no. 11) was enacted in 1907 and mandated institutionalization for leprosy sufferers who could not receive care at home. After annexing Korea in 1910, Japanese colonial authorities built a leprosarium on the Korean island of Sorokdo for similar purposes. As in Japan, Western missionaries had already established several leprosaria in Korea. But in the 1920s, officials throughout Japan's empire launched "leprosy-free prefecture campaigns," rounding up leprosy sufferers to rid the home islands and colonies of the embarrassing "unmodern" scourge.

In the name of modernization and public health, revisions to the Leprosy Prevention Law in 1931 gave the Japanese government power to quarantine any leprosy sufferer in one of the newly established national leprosaria. Prior to the discovery of a treatment for the disease, public health authorities in other countries—including the United States—also institutionalized leprosy patients. Once confined to a leprosarium, Japanese patients were forbidden from cohabitating or marrying and provided their own nursing care, food, and fire brigades because ordinary people feared the disease. Monetary currency that was valid only inside each leprosarium, harsh detention facilities, and persistent prejudice on the outside deterred escapes. Starting in the 1930s, doctors also routinely subjected patients to vasectomies and abortions in the mistaken belief that leprosy was heritable. As Japan headed to war, patients' allegedly subversive attempts to

---

7. Eunjung Kim, "Cultural Rehabilitation," *Wagadu* 4 (Summer 2007): 114–15.
8. Interview with Chae Gyu-tae, doctor, Seoul (January 30, 2009).

campaign for better conditions within the leprosaria received increasingly harsh punishment, and patients' writings were censored.

Japanese colonial authorities subjected Korean leprosy sufferers to these and even greater indignities. Staff at the Sorokdo leprosarium, which housed six thousand patients by 1935, used vasectomies to punish disobedient patients. Doctors also conducted medical experiments on patients without their consent and forced them to perform hard labor for construction projects.[9] One survivor of this period told me that he had lost parts of all four limbs—which were already weakened by his disease—after "being forced to work in icy conditions."[10] In 1942, a Sorokdo patient assassinated the Japanese leprosarium director, who had forced patients to erect a statue in his honor and bow to it. When Japanese staff left the island in 1945, they massacred eighty-four patients. Elderly Korean survivors of such colonial-era mistreatment applied for compensation from Japan in 2003.

After Promin: Postwar Leprosy Control Policies

Although segregating leprosy sufferers was standard public health policy in advanced nations during the first half of the twentieth century, the U.S. discovery that the sulfone drug Promin provided effective treatment rendered this policy medically unjustifiable. Promin became available in Japan and Korea by the early 1950s. As a result, some Japanese experts called for reforms that would allow treated patients to leave the leprosaria. To push for less restrictive policies, residents in Japan's leprosaria formed self-governing councils (*jichikai*), which officials permitted as democracy spread across Japan after 1945. In 1951 the councils united to form the National Council of Leprosarium Residents (NCLR, or Zenkankyō renamed Zenryōkyō in 1996). But most doctors and staff of Japan's thirteen national leprosaria favored continuing compulsory institutionalization and expanding their budgets. Hence, despite a twenty-day sit-in in Tokyo and hunger strikes by NCLR members, the Diet passed a new Leprosy Prevention Law (Rai Yobō Hō, or LPL) in 1953 that retained the prewar policy of forced institutionalization and had no provisions for discharges or outpatient treatment. Some cured patients were released in an ad hoc fashion after 1953, but the number of discharges fell from a peak of 216 in 1960 to just 47 in 1972.[11] Because of state-sanctioned vasectomies and abortions that continued until the 1980s, few Japanese leprosy survivors have offspring. After 2001, investigators discovered

9. HCA, *Hansenbyeongryeokja Gwonikbohoreul wihan Gwanryeon Jeongchaek Semina [Seminar on Policies Related to the Protection of Hansen's Disease Patients' Interests]* (Seoul: Hanseong Cooperative Association, March 15, 2002), 37.

10. Interview with Jang Gi-jin, Sorokdo resident, Sorokdo (August 14, 2009).

11. Fujio Ōtani, *The Walls Crumble* (Tokyo: Tōfu Kyōkai, 1998), 140.

scores of fetuses—often unlabeled and near full-term—preserved in formalde-
hyde in leprosaria.[12]

The NCLR restarted efforts to end forcible institutionalization in the early
1960s because the WHO began recommending outpatient care for anyone affected by leprosy. United States officials in Okinawa (which did not revert to
Japanese control until 1971) revised local policies regarding leprosy in accordance with the WHO's recommendation.[13] But the Japanese health officials and
leprosarium directors who determined leprosy-related policy had a vested interest in retaining the leprosarium system.[14] Facing such resistance, patients shifted
their focus toward improving conditions within the leprosaria through negotiations with the state. The NCLR achieved many small victories, and medical care
improved from the 1970s on. But regularly negotiating with the state tamed the
NCLR and reduced the impetus to repeal the LPL, as leprosarium residents came
to depend on the state and consider the leprosarium as their only home. Doctors
with knowledge of leprosy were also rare outside the leprosaria; the LPL ghet-
toized both patients and caregivers.[15]

In the early 1990s, however, the NCLR and its constituent self-governing
councils at each leprosarium once again began lobbying to bring Japanese leprosy policy in line with international medical practice by repealing the LPL. Their
demands were bolstered by Ōtani Fujio, who had overseen Hansen's disease policy as director of the National Leprosarium Division and later as Medical Affairs
Bureau director at the Ministry of Health and Welfare (MHW) until 1989. After
retiring, Ōtani had come to believe that "the only just course of action was to
repeal, rather than revise, the LPL."[16] Under pressure from the NCLR and Ōtani,
the MHW formed a committee, with Ōtani as chair, to reconsider the law. The
Japan Leprologists' Association (JLA) also succumbed to their pressure and issued an unprecedented public statement, saying,

> Any and all justifications for the current law have been lost. . . . From
> a medical perspective, [it] should be repealed. . . . The reason why the
> JLA has not taken a lead in the efforts to have the LPL repealed and has

---

12. Kenshōkaigi [Verification Committee], *Hansenbyō Mondai ni Kansuru Kenshōkaigi Saishū
Hōkokusho [Final Report of the Verification Committee on the Hansen's Disease Problem]* (Tokyo: Japan
Law Foundation, March 2005), 38–41, http://www.jlf.or.jp/work/hansen_report.shtml#higai.

13. Verification Committee, *Verification Committee concerning the Hansen's Disease Problem,
Final Report (English Summary Version)* (Tokyo: Japan Law Foundation, March 2005), 129, http://
www.mhlw.go.jp/english/policy/health/01/pdf/01.pdf.

14. Hajime Sato and Minoru Narita, "Politics of Leprosy Segregation in Japan," *Social Science &
Medicine* 56, no. 12 (2003): 2529–39.

15. Ōtani, *The Walls Crumble*, 145–46.

16. Interview with Ōtani Fujio, former MHW official, Tokyo (June 18, 2009).

failed to admit to the errors of the policies regarding Hansen's disease lies in the fact that the Association's core consisted of those involved in the leprosaria. . . . The Association deeply regrets that it has ignored the realities and permitted the existence of the LPL for so long.[17]

This campaign did successfully repeal the law in March 1996, but activism related to the repeal did not include calls for redress from the state.[18] In fact, in its negotiations with officials over repealing the LPL, the NCLR had apparently secretly agreed *not* to sue the state for compensation in order to ensure that the state would continue to provide homes and medical care for aging leprosarium residents.[19] State officials also calculated that offering onetime, no-fault payments of 2.5 million yen (about $24,000) to anyone who left the leprosaria might forestall potential efforts to hold the state accountable for maintaining a harsh and medically unjustifiable leprosy control policy for so long. But only seventeen of Japan's five thousand leprosy survivors accepted the payments. Health and Welfare Minister Kan Naoto—famous for his role in resolving the HIV-tainted-blood scandal that same year—visited leprosaria to apologize for the delay in repealing the LPL. But one leprosy survivor recalled being "stunned. . . . [Kan] did not say that the law itself was wrong at all. He didn't admit the government's fault."[20] Another leprosarium resident commented, "We must learn from the HIV redress movement and obtain a clear statement of the government's responsibility [for our suffering]."[21] Thus the LPL's repeal was a crucial precondition and became a catalyst for the ensuing redress movement.

The ROK's postliberation policies regarding leprosy were more complicated. After Japan's withdrawal from Korea, the colonial era's compulsory institutionalization policies remained in place, but enforcement proved beyond the capacity of the fledgling ROK government. In the late 1940s, therefore, Korean leprosy specialists and missionaries encouraged leprosy sufferers who did not enter leprosaria to form "hope villages" so they could support themselves by producing goods rather than by begging. Local communities resisted such settlements, to the point of killing leprosy survivors. Still, sixteen hope villages, inhabited by a total of about five thousand leprosy survivors, had formed by 1950. Proponents argued that the villages cost just 20 percent of what it cost to institutionalize someone in the Sorokdo leprosarium.[22] This belief that self-sufficiency could

---

17. Cited in Ōtani, *The Walls Crumble*, 4.

18. Rai Yobō Hō Haishi ni Kansuru Hōritsu (law no. 28, March 27, 1996).

19. Interview with Yahiro Mitsuhide, lawyer, Fukuoka (May 12, 2009).

20. Kunimoto Mamoru, *Ikite Futatabi [Alive Again]* (Tokyo: Mainichi Shimbunsha, 2001), 236.

21. Hansen's Disease Lawyers' Association (Hansenbyō Iken Kokubai Soshō Bengodan, hereafter Bengodan), *Hirakareta Tobira [The Opened Door]* (Tokyo: Kodansha, 2003), 31.

22. For a proponent's glowing assessment, see Joon Lew, "Leprosy in Korea, Past and Present," *Korea Observer* 23, no. 2 (Summer 1992): 204.

restore leprosy survivors' dignity and inexpensively promote social order motivated the "resettlement villages" (*jeongchakchon*), which relatively able-bodied leprosy survivors founded in remote parts of the country after the Korean War.

As part of efforts to build a modern public health system, however, the ROK enacted the Infectious Disease Prevention Law (IDPL) in 1954, mandating that anyone affected by leprosy be registered and institutionalized.[23] The state lacked the resources to fully implement the law, but it had registered about twenty-four thousand leprosy patients by 1960. Many were subjected to vasectomies and abortions, as in Japan. Others, especially outside the leprosaria in resettlement villages, were largely neglected by the authorities. Local residents of Bittori Island, for instance, killed twenty-six and injured seventy leprosy survivors who wanted to settle there in 1957. The people responsible for these killings received only two- and three-year sentences.[24]

By contrast with Japan's failure to repeal the LPL in accordance with the WHO's 1960 recommendation to end institutionalization, the ROK did revise the IDPL in 1963. But the ROK government did not enforce these revisions consistently, rendering the state's culpability more complex than that in Japan. Even after 1963, people afflicted with leprosy were still forced into leprosaria. The Hanseong Cooperative Association (HCA)—the organization of leprosy survivors that governed the resettlement villages and operated credit and business services until its bankruptcy in 2002—worked with the state to round up vagrants with leprosy until the 1980s.[25] And until the 1980s some doctors and health authorities continued to force leprosy patients to undergo vasectomies and abortions.[26] The government also did not educate citizens about Hansen's disease to curb discrimination. Few leprosy survivors were even aware of the 1963 reforms, "whereas *everyone* in Korea's Hansen's disease community knew about the repeal of Japan's LPL in 1996."[27]

While nearly all Japanese leprosy survivors endured similar conditions in state-run leprosaria, the diverse situations Korean leprosy survivors faced, especially

---

23. Jeonyeombyeong Yebang Beop (law no. 308, February 2, 1954).

24. NHRCK, *Hansen's Disease Human Rights Report*, 58–61.

25. First called the Korean Hansen's Federation when formed in 1969, the HCA was registered with the MOHW in 1975 as the leprosy community's representative. The group started animal feed and fertilizer factories in the late 1980s to supply the chicken and pig farms that sustained the resettlement village economy. Economic liberalization in the 1990s undermined the financial viability of these factories, despite government assistance and donations from wealthy leprosy survivors. Many went bankrupt soon thereafter. Hence the leadership of the Hansen's disease community was reshuffled, and Hanvit Welfare Association was formed in 2003 after the HCA dissolved in 2002.

26. NHRCK, *Hansen's Disease Human Rights Report*, 67–83.

27. Interview with Kim Jeong-haeng, Sorokdo Self-Governing Council president, Sorokdo (August 14–15, 2009).

after 1963, render the nature of the Korean government's responsibility for their suffering more complicated and their community more segmented.[28] Consider, for example, the resettlement village system. Its proponents contend that it "fostered independence, financial security, and dignity."[29] A 2004 survey of leprosy survivors revealed that 84 percent of respondents saw these villages as a "means of escaping social prejudice."[30] Under the leadership and considerable influence of HCA, villagers established successful poultry and pig farms, and subsequently furniture manufacturing firms. Indeed, by the 1980s, roughly one-third of all eggs in Korea came from resettlement villages. In 2012, there were ninety-one such villages, and 34 percent of Korea's leprosy population lived in them. The predominantly Christian Hansen's disease community has also exported the resettlement village model to leprosy populations in poorer countries through its missionary work.[31]

Other Hansen's disease survivors and observers contend that the resettlement villages "cemented leprosy survivors' marginalized status" and "prolonged their suffering."[32] More than 40 percent of Korean leprosy survivors received no formal schooling, and three-quarters live below the poverty line today.[33] Stigma against the disease also persists: in a 2005 survey, 86 percent of ordinary Koreans said that they would oppose a family member's marrying a leprosy survivor.[34] Unlike their Japanese counterparts, many Korean leprosy survivors have offspring and know that prejudice often extends to their children, though they do not have the disease. Consequently, most of the seven thousand survivors who live in ordinary society hide their disease. Though Japanese and Korean leprosy survivors endured different forms of hardship during the twentieth century, both communities mobilized around the turn of the millennium to hold their governments accountable for violating their basic rights.

---

28. Interview with Jung Keun-sik, Seoul National University professor, Seoul (January 19, 2009).

29. Interview with Jeong Sang-gwon, former HCA president, Seoul (July 24, 2009).

30. Gil Yun-hyeong, "Hansenbyeonghwanja . . . Sawoichabyeol eun Bulchiinga [Hansen's Disease Patients . . . Is Social Prejudice Incurable?]," *Hankyoreh Sinmun*, January 31, 2005.

31. Western missionaries' early commitment to serving leprosy sufferers led to many Christian converts in the leprosy population. Kim Jae-hyeong, "Hanguk Hansenindanche ui Haeoe Wonjo Saeop Model ui Hyeongseong e Gwanhan Sahoehakjeok Yeongu [A Sociological Study of the Formation of Models for Foreign Aid Projects among Korea's Organizations of People with Hansen's Disease]" (master's thesis, Seoul National University, 2007).

32. Interview with Park Chan-un, lawyer, Seoul (June 4, 2008). Interview with Jung Keun-sik, professor.

33. "Gamgeum, Haksal, Gangje Noyeok Hansenin Pihaeja 6,462myeong: Samang 1,754 myeong . . . Gicho Chasangui 4,000myeong Wol 15 Man Won Jigeup [6,462 Hansen's Disease Patients Victims of Imprisonment, Massacre, Forced Labor: 1,754 of Them Deceased . . . 4,000 Low-Income Patients to Receive 150,000 Won per Month]," *JoongAng Ilbo*, July 18, 2013.

34. NHRCK, *Hansen's Disease Human Rights Report*, 134.

Mobilizing to Claim Redress

New windows of opportunity opened for Hansen's disease survivors in the late 1990s in Japan and several years later in Korea. The repeal of Japan's Leprosy Prevention Law in 1996 both enabled and emboldened survivors to seek redress. In Korea, elderly survivors' transnational campaign in 2003–6 for restitution from Japan for colonial-era abuses ignited a domestic movement for redress from the ROK government in 2004. Yet the organizations at the core of each movement and the extent of victims' participation differed, contributing to their divergent receptions by third parties in each country.

Stepping outside the Leprosaria: The Origins of Japan's Hansen's Disease Movement

The movement to hold the Japanese government accountable for mistreating leprosy victims began with a letter that Shima Hiroshi—a resident of the leprosarium near Kumamoto in Kyūshū and an author whose works had been banned for being critical of the leprosaria—wrote to the Kyūshū Bar Association in September 1995. Shima's letter challenged the legal profession by asking whether the leprosaria were "places where the Japanese constitution [did] not apply, [and whether] persons affected by Hansen's disease [were] not human."[35] After receiving this criticism, a group of Kyūshū lawyers conducted an unprecedented survey of about 1,300 leprosarium residents and provided free legal counseling at the two Kyūshū leprosaria. They began building a case against the state after Shima and a few other residents indicated that they wanted to file suit.

Accordingly, thirteen initial leprosy survivors set foot in a court of law for the first time in July 1998, when they filed a collective civil suit against the Japanese government in the Kumamoto District Court. Scores of lawyers, who were mobilized through personal networks and the Kyūshū Bar Association, represented these plaintiffs as the Western Japan Lawyers' Group (Nishinihon Bengodan). Separate legal teams later formed in Tokyo and Okayama, as parallel lawsuits were filed there in 1999. Shima's original framing of Japan's leprosy control policies as violations of the constitution became the core legal argument. The plaintiffs sought 100 million yen (about $952,000) each in compensation and 15 million yen (about $143,000) for the lawyers. Their key legal challenges included proving that the government (and the Diet) should have ended the forced institutionalization policy decades earlier, persuading the court to waive the twenty-year

---

35. Association to Support the Hansen's Disease Lawsuits (hereafter ASHDL), ed., *Hansen Byō Mondai [The Hansen's Disease Problem]* (Tokyo: Nihon Hyōronsha, 2002), 31.

statute of limitations for claiming damages from the state (*kokka baishō*), and conveying the nature and extent of leprosy survivors' suffering. The lawyers also worried about expanding the number of plaintiffs.

Many leprosarium residents initially balked at the idea of suing the state because it provided them with food, shelter, and medical care. After an average of more than forty years in the leprosaria, residents worried about being forced to leave or reigniting prejudice against their relatives.[36] Some residents even tried to hamper the lawyers' work by denying them access to leprosarium photocopiers or meeting rooms.[37] In deference to its members' divergent opinions, the NCLR maintained a position of "watchful waiting" (*seikan*) toward the lawsuits until early 2001, although some NCLR leaders personally supported the litigation.[38]

Thus the plaintiff groups (*genkokudan*), which were formed at each court site and most leprosaria to provide mutual support in the face of such criticism from fellow leprosarium residents, remained distinct from and sometimes even in conflict with the leprosaria's self-governing councils and the NCLR. Without access to the NCLR's organizational resources, the plaintiff groups initially depended on their lawyers for tactical advice, encouragement, and logistical support. Yet they gained their own voice as the numbers of plaintiffs and lawsuits grew and as activism outside the courtrooms began to bear fruit in 2000. Even though the separate groups created divisions in the Hansen's disease community, they were free from the constraints imposed by the NCLR's mandate to represent all Japanese leprosy survivors and by the NCLR's longtime working relationship with the state. The plaintiff groups and their lawyers became the core of the Japanese redress movement, and citizens living near leprosaria or the court sites mobilized specifically to support the plaintiffs.

From the Side:
The Origins of Korea's Hansen's Disease Redress Movement

Whereas the Japanese Hansen's disease movement originated with Shima's letter, the impetus for a redress movement in Korea came not from below or above but from the side—from Japan.[39] Several Japanese lawyers, emboldened by their 2001 victory in Japan's Hansen's disease movement (described below), stimulated redress-related activism in Korea when they helped elderly Korean leprosy

---

36. Bengodan, *Hirakareta Tobira*, 51 ff.

37. ASHDL, *Hansen Byō Mondai*, 40.

38. NCLR, *Fukken e no Nichigestu [The Years to the Restoration of Our Rights]* (Tokyo: Kōyō, 2001), 133.

39. Interview with Gil Yun-hyeong, *Hankyoreh Sinmun* journalist, Seoul (January 22, 2009).

survivors file claims for compensation from the Japanese government in 2003.[40] After hearing about Japan's mistreatment of leprosy sufferers in its colonies prior to 1945 from a leftist Japanese historian who had conducted research on Sorokdo since 1995, several Japanese lawyers traveled to Sorokdo in 2003. They informed elderly residents who had survived colonial-era mistreatment that Japan's 2001 Hansen's Disease Compensation Law presented a unique opportunity because the law did not require that compensation recipients be citizens or residents of Japan.[41] As one lawyer explained, this "oversight was surprising since Korean atomic bomb survivors had already sued the Japanese government for denying medical coverage to *hibakusha* who were not Japanese nationals or denizens."[42] Moreover, Tokyo had a history of citing the statute of limitations or international treaties when refusing to compensate other colonial-era victims, such as Korean comfort women or forced laborers.

With Japanese lawyers' help, however, elderly Korean leprosy survivors used the opportunity created by the 2001 Japanese Hansen's disease law to apply for compensation from Japan. After the Japanese Ministry of Health, Labor, and Welfare (MHLW) rejected their applications—as the lawyers had predicted it would—117 claimants filed an administrative lawsuit in Tokyo in August 2004 to challenge that decision. Twenty-five elderly Taiwanese leprosy survivors, who had been mobilized by the same Japanese lawyers, simultaneously filed an analogous lawsuit. Plaintiffs' Japanese lawyers publicized both lawsuits and reactivated small groups of Japanese citizens who had supported Japanese Hansen's disease plaintiffs. Hanvit Welfare Association (Hanbit Bokji Hyeophoe, or Hanvit), Korea's main Hansen's disease organization, also threw itself behind this transnational redress campaign by helping to identify potential plaintiffs and gather evidence in Korea.

Previously, leaders within Korea's resettlement villages and leprosaria had encouraged leprosy survivors to pursue self-reliance and dignity rather than redress for past suffering. Yet when news of Japan's Hansen's disease movement reached Korea, it sparked new discussions about rights and past suffering. Citing the Japanese movement as their inspiration, for example, seventy academics, activists, journalists, and former leprosy patients formed the Group of People who Love Sorokdo (abbreviated Sosamo) in March 2001 to advance leprosy survivors'

---

40. For more on this transnational movement, see Celeste L. Arrington, "Leprosy, Legal Mobilization, and the Public Sphere in Japan and South Korea," *Law & Society Review* 48, no. 3 (September 2014): 563–93.

41. Text of Tokuda Yasuyuki's speech on Sorokdo, http://www5b.biglobe.ne.jp/~naoko-k/soroktorepo2.htm.

42. Interview with Kunimune Naoko, lawyer, Kumamoto (May 15, 2009).

well-being and restore their honor (*myeongye hoebok*).[43] Sosamo members traveled to Japan in July 2001 to meet with and learn from key players in Japan's Hansen's disease movement.[44] When they returned to Korea, they issued the first calls for state compensation for leprosy survivors' postwar suffering and urged the state to turn Sorokdo into a human rights education center.[45] But Sosamo ceased its activities shortly thereafter. Reasons for its demise are unclear, but they include internal dissension and possible discouraging signals from the Hanseong Cooperative Association, which wanted to ensure that only one organization represented Korea's Hansen's disease community. Meanwhile, the television station MBC Gwangju produced and aired a documentary called "Ah, Sorokdo!" in late 2001 and early 2002. After showing scenes of Japanese leprosy survivors celebrating their victory in Kumamoto, the documentary detailed both the colonial history of Sorokdo and Korean leprosy sufferers' postwar hardships.[46] The HCA also held a conference on welfare programs for leprosy survivors in March 2002, just before it declared bankruptcy and was replaced by Hanvit. Many former Sosamo members participated in the seminar, at which a Korean leprosy survivor listed examples of how the ROK government had harmed former patients like him since 1948. While acknowledging that the state's responsibility for leprosy survivors' past suffering was clearer in the Japanese case, the speaker specified instances of ROK government wrongdoing and negligence, as well as societal prejudice, to justify his call for the state to "repent" to the Hansen's disease community.[47] In addition, an ethnically Korean resident of a Japanese leprosarium explained why he had joined one of the Japanese lawsuits and urged Korean leprosy survivors to mount an analogous redress movement.[48] No domestic Korean redress movement formed, however, until after Japanese lawyers mobilized elderly leprosy survivors to claim redress from Japan for colonial-era abuses.

Not only did the Japanese movement's success raise Korean leprosy survivors' rights consciousness, but Japanese lawyers also first convinced Korean lawyers to take up the issue of redress for Korean Hansen's disease survivors. Park Chan-un, a key founder of the Korean Hansen's Human Rights Lawyers' Group

43. Interview with Lee Se-yong, leprosy survivor, Chungcheongbukdo (July 23, 2009). See Lee Sang-il, "Sorokdo Sarang Haneun Areumdaun Saramdeul [Beautiful People Who Love Sorokdo]," *Kookmin Ilbo*, March 31, 2001.

44. Kim Deok-mo, "Ilbon Hyeonji Hwaldong Gyeolgwa reul Bogo Hamnida [Reporting on Local Japanese Activism]," *Sorokdo reul Sarang Haneun Saramdeul ui Moim*, January 9, 2003, http://cafe.daum.net/ilovesosamo/5QHF/19?docid=1yqf5QHF1920030109153906.

45. Na Gwon-il, "Sorokdo reul Ingwon Jaehwal ui Ddang Euro [Turning Sorokdo into a Land of Rehabilitating Human Rights]," *Sisa Jeoneol*, December 30, 2001.

46. Kim, "Cultural Rehabilitation," 116, 119–122.

47. HCA, *Hansenbyeongryeokja Gwonikbohoreul wihan Gwanryeon Jeongchaek Semina*, 33.

48. Ibid., 9–18.

(Hansen Ingwon Byeonhodan, or HHRLG), recalled that "Korean society had so marginalized Hansen's disease survivors that almost no human rights lawyers or activists even knew about their situation."[49] He first found out about the issue after lawyers from the Gwangju branch of Minbyeon—who had provided initial translation and legal assistance to the Japanese lawyers on Sorokdo but could not commit to a protracted legal battle in Japan—suggested that the Japanese lawyers contact him.[50] Park Chan-un had worked on human rights cases since the 1990s and happened to be vice-chair of the Korean Bar Association's (KBA) Human Rights Committee in 2003. In early 2004, Japanese lawyers persuaded him to visit Sorokdo. "Transformed by the visit," he spent the return trip to Seoul convincing the committee to investigate the issue. He also formed the HHRLG, which would support both the campaign for redress from Japan and the ensuing indigenous Korean redress movement. Another key member of the HHRLG recalled that he had "joined out of embarrassment: not only had Korean lawyers neglected the rights of Korea's leprosy survivors, but it had also been Japanese lawyers who first mobilized this marginalized community in Korea."[51] By 2005, roughly forty lawyers, with an active core of about twenty, were members of the HHRLG. While researching colonial-era survivors' claims against Japan, the group amassed evidence of the ROK's mistreatment of Korean leprosy survivors and became convinced of the need for a domestic redress movement.[52]

Whereas Hanvit had played a supporting role to the Japanese lawyers in the transnational movement for colonial-era redress from Japan, it assumed a central role in the campaign for redress from the ROK that began with a symposium in the National Assembly building in October 2004. Hanvit officers decided that leadership in the domestic movement would help "maintain unity among leprosy survivors and preserve Hanvit's position as the voice of Korea's Hansen's disease community."[53] In 2003, the association (under the leadership of Lim Du-seong) had succeeded the HCA as the sole organization of leprosy survivors in Korea. Much as Japan's NCLR had, however, the HCA had sacrificed some autonomy during decades of negotiating with the state. Even after Hanvit replaced the HCA, more than half of its budget came from the state, with the rest coming from donations by corporations or individuals, often themselves leprosy survivors. Like the HCA, Hanvit exerted considerable influence and centralized authority within Korea's resettlement villages and leprosaria

---

49. Interview with Park Chan-un, lawyer.
50. Interview with Kunimune Naoko, lawyer.
51. Interview with Park Yeong-rip, lawyer, Seoul (August 20, 2009).
52. Interview with Lee Jeong-il, lawyer, Seoul (July 13, 2012).
53. Interview with U Hong-seon, director general of Hanvit Welfare Association, Seoul (January 30, 2009).

(but less over leprosy survivors residing in ordinary society), which some leprosy survivors criticized. One compared Hanvit to an extended family: "You may not always get along with everyone and may resent them at times, but it is still good that they exist."[54] Hanvit could effectively mobilize leprosy survivors if it chose to do so. As a state-recognized organization, it also enjoyed ready access to political elites and was able to work with the HHRLG to organize the 2004 symposium that launched the domestic redress movement.

Thus, Korean Hansen's disease survivors began their quest for redress with Hanvit's organizational resources, whereas Japan's plaintiff groups had to establish their organizational legitimacy and access without the NCLR's assistance and sometimes in the face of hostility from other leprosarium residents. Hanvit's central role in the redress movement and leprosy survivors' understandable suspicion of outsiders, however, also relegated lawyers in the HHRLG to a lesser role than the one played by Japanese Hansen's disease lawyers. Moreover, rank-and-file Korean leprosy survivors participated less in activism than their Japanese counterparts because, with Hanvit at the helm, they sensed little potential gain from exposing themselves to public scrutiny. These differences suggest that a movement's unity does not necessarily guarantee its effectiveness. As we shall see in the next section, divisions in the Japanese leprosy community helped activate third parties to redress claimants' side.

Claiming Redress and Shaming the State

From the time the Japanese and Korean Hansen's disease communities began their quests for redress, they sought to both pressure the state and recruit supporters who could help them in this effort. But the order in which diverse actors joined each redress movement—the sequencing of conflict expansion—differed. Spearheaded by the new plaintiff groups and their lawyers, the Japanese movement gained local supporter groups and local media coverage through legal mobilization before attracting elite political allies and national media coverage. Korea's movement, on the other hand, began with Hanvit's drafting redress legislation with a sympathetic lawmaker and only later involved litigation and attempts at grassroots mobilizing. By analyzing the nature of victims' participation, supporting groups' activism, media coverage, public opinion polls, and politicians' interest, this section traces how these different patterns of conflict expansion generated distinctive pressures on the state for redress.

---

54. Interview with Kang Chang-seok, leprosy survivor, Sorokdo (August 14, 2009).

Japanese Victims' Litigation and Bottom-Up Conflict Expansion

Japan's Hansen's disease redress movement, initiated by thirteen plaintiffs in July 1998, struggled in obscurity at first. After covering the initial filing of this historic lawsuit, national and local media lost interest. Leprosaria self-governing councils also barred journalists' entry to protect residents' privacy. Plaintiffs and their lawyers, therefore, focused on trying to turn particularistic grievances related to an obscure disease into a social issue and gradually incite public outrage over the government's treatment of Hansen's disease sufferers. About 140 lawyers in Kyūshū had worked pro bono to bring the lawsuit to court, although not all stayed equally active. Many of them had previously represented victims of industrial pollution and HIV-tainted blood products and drew on those experiences. Specifically, they had learned that "relying on litigation alone could allow the state to minimize the challenge from redress claimants."[55] They thus aimed to mobilize citizen supporters to fill seats in the courtroom and attract publicity by holding rallies outside the court.[56] A handful of local citizen groups, who had originally gained interest in state accountability by working with the movement of methyl mercury victims in previous decades in the nearby city of Minamata, and University of Kumamoto students became the Hansen's disease plaintiffs' earliest supporters.[57] The lawyers also prioritized increasing the number of plaintiffs. Yet without NCLR backing and with hostility toward the lawsuit in some leprosaria, the lawyers' goal of mobilizing five hundred plaintiffs—10 percent of Japan's leprosy population—"seemed impossible."[58]

MOBILIZING FELLOW VICTIMS AND GRASSROOTS SUPPORT

The first breakthrough in Japanese leprosy survivors' activism occurred in March 1999, when more than a hundred plaintiffs joined the lawsuit in Kumamoto and filed a parallel lawsuit in Tokyo. Both developments resulted from Kyūshū lawyers' efforts to build solidarity among leprosy survivors. The lawyers deliberately enlisted Sogano Kazumi, who had been president of the NCLR from 1983 to 1991, had traveled to all of Japan's leprosaria to convince residents to support the LPL's repeal, and was therefore a respected leader within the Hansen's disease community. From his home at the Ōshima leprosarium—where he led the self-governing council until 1999—Sogano had watched the Kumamoto lawsuit with ambivalence, because he knew of the NCLR's tacit agreement not

---

55. Interview with Yahiro Mitsuhide, lawyer.

56. Shimura Yasushi, *Watashi no Tomurai Gassen [My Avenging Battle]* (Kumamoto, 1999), 65.

57. Interview with Komatsu Hiroshi, professor and activist, University of Kumamoto (May 13, 2009).

58. Bengodan, *Hirakareta Tobira*, 53.

to sue the state after the LPL was repealed. Yet five Kyūshū lawyers visited him in late 1998 and showed him the government's court statements denying any wrong-doing in retaining the LPL for such a long time. The lawyers also argued that, in this case, "greater numbers of plaintiffs would give the claimants a strategic advantage in court."[59] Apparently incensed at the state's denials, Sogano decided to become a plaintiff and even broadcast his change of heart over the Ōshima PA system.[60] He declared that he wanted to "augment the voice of those demanding that the state take responsibility."[61] Ultimately, most of the eighty-two plaintiffs who joined the Kumamoto lawsuit in March 1999 did so because Sogano Kazumi had decided to back the suit.

In Kyūshū, the Western Japan Lawyers' Group for the Hansen's disease case believed that launching a lawsuit in Tokyo was also essential. Although a favorable ruling from the notoriously conservative Tokyo District Court was unlikely, the lawyers calculated that "a lawsuit in Tokyo would capture the attention of the national media, bureaucracy, and Diet."[62] As one journalist who wrote about the movement noted, "The judicial reporters' club was sure to give national coverage to any lawsuit filed in Tokyo."[63] Kyūshū lawyers also "contacted attorneys in Tokyo whom they knew from past work on lawsuits related to victim redress movements in order to activate the legal profession in Tokyo."[64] The selection of Toyoda Makoto—a veteran lawyer who had been involved in earlier redress movements—as the leader of the new Eastern Japan Lawyers' Group (Higashini-hon Bengodan) in Tokyo further ensured that the Hansen's disease movement could access networks and resources from these prior movements. With support from Tokyo and Kyūshū lawyers, therefore, twenty-one leprosy survivors filed a second lawsuit in Tokyo in March 1999, timed to coincide with Sogano and his fellow plaintiffs' joining the Kumamoto suit. Plaintiffs in wheelchairs led a phalanx of plaintiffs and lawyers into the Tokyo court past many reporters and cameras, reflecting lawyers' philosophy of "putting the victims first" to win public sympathy.[65]

Despite continued opposition from some fellow leprosarium residents, eleven plaintiffs filed a third collective lawsuit at the Okayama District Court in September 1999. As the litigation spread, lawyers divided tasks among themselves, forming teams to manage legal argumentation and communications with the

59. Interview with Yahiro Mitsuhide, lawyer.
60. Bengodan, *Hirakareta Tobira*, 62–65.
61. NCLR, *Fukken e no Nichigestu*, 137.
62. Much of this paragraph is based on my interview with Yahiro Mitsuhide, lawyer.
63. Interview with Esashi Masayoshi, *Mainichi Shimbun* journalist, Tokyo (June 17, 2009).
64. Interview with Kobayashi Yōji, lawyer, Fukuoka (May 12, 2009).
65. Interview with Itai Masaru, lawyer, Kumamoto (May 15, 2009).

plaintiffs, as well as to prepare for future interactions with the national media and political elites.[66] Lawyers also "introduced plaintiffs to their personal contacts and local organizations to help them recruit supporters and boost attendance at public events and court proceedings."[67] The local and issue-specific tendency of Japanese activist groups facilitated such grassroots mobilizing. Near each of the three court sites, citizens who had volunteered in a leprosarium as part of religious or other service or who were concerned about human rights issues formed local supporter groups (*shien dantai*) to aid the plaintiffs. Although the roughly twenty supporter groups started coordinating nationwide in mid-1999, they remained "locally rooted."[68] Yet national publicity proved elusive amid continued state denials of wrongdoing.

LEVERAGING THE COURT PROCESS

Several developments in the Kumamoto trial in 1999 and early 2000 encouraged Japanese Hansen's disease survivors and their supporters to become increasingly active. First, plaintiffs began testifying in court about their own sufferings, and these accounts shocked observers.[69] Second, Dr. Ōtani (who had helped repeal the LPL) surprised the Kumamoto court in August 1999 by declaring—*as the state's witness*—that the LPL had been "a mistake." Third, the three judges from the Kumamoto court took the unusual step of agreeing to visit the nearby leprosarium in November 1999, as requested by plaintiffs' lawyers.[70] These judges saw some leprosarium horrors firsthand, including unlabeled urns of cremated victims' remains, unclaimed by their families. Eventually judges in Kumamoto, Tokyo, and Okayama visited all thirteen national leprosaria. Close coordination among plaintiffs' lawyers in the three lawsuits helped convince the judges to accede to their requests for site visits. Indeed, one lawyer claims that the Hansen's disease movement marked the "first truly nationwide coordination among lawyers" in such litigation, and that "e-mail particularly aided the exchange of information exchange and the building of trust."[71]

Plaintiffs, the lawyers, and the supporter groups used such court testimonies and the judges' site visits as examples in seminars they organized to inform ordinary citizens about the redress movement and mobilize additional plaintiffs. For example, the second major increase in the number of plaintiffs occurred after a Ryūkyū University professor and his students explained the plaintiffs' progress in

---

66. Interview with Ayukyo Machiko, lawyer, Tokyo (May 30, 2008).
67. Interview with Kunimune Naoko, lawyer.
68. ASHDL, *Hansen Byō Mondai*, 77.
69. For descriptions of each plaintiff's testimony, see Bengodan, *Hirakareta Tobira*, 132–91.
70. Ibid., 16.
71. Interview with Noma Kei, lawyer, Tokyo (May 29, 2008).

the Kumamoto court at a leprosarium in Okinawa. Sixty-four of the 82 plaintiffs who filed in Kumamoto in December 1999 and 107 of the 110 plaintiffs who filed in April 2000 were from Okinawa. By the end of April 2000, the three lawsuits included more than 500 plaintiffs—meeting the lawyers' original goal. As one journalist recalled, many plaintiffs had "initially feared negative repercussions for or from family members, but more and more began to speak out in 2000."[72] On each day in court in Kumamoto, Tokyo, and Okayama, plaintiffs using their real names (*jitsumei genkoku*) also held press conferences to appeal for public sympathy. Japan's local media and relatively autonomous regional branches of national news companies thus gained greater access to plaintiffs, whose stories of suffering increasingly captivated local audiences. Media coverage and public attention remained greatest in Kyūshū, where the movement had started, but one plaintiff remembered "feeling momentum on our side."[73] By late 2000, those who wanted a seat in one of the courtrooms where leprosy cases were being heard had to take turns because demand was so high. Public support had risen so much in Kumamoto that a rally to mark the end of the court's hearings in December 2000 drew one thousand people, a number the lawyers and local supporters had thought impossible.[74] As the plaintiffs realized the moral leverage they had as victims, elected leaders of the three plaintiff groups also began participating more as equals with the lawyers' groups in tactical decision making.

GAINING ATTENTION FROM THE NATIONAL MEDIA AND LAWMAKERS

On the basis of such grassroots mobilizing, the Hansen's disease movement made several organizational changes to seek national attention more effectively in spring 2001, as the Kumamoto hearings ended and the court moved toward a ruling. First, the three lawyers' groups started planning how to achieve a "comprehensive resolution" (*zenmen kaiketsu*) to the Hansen's disease issue in late 2000 and elected the seasoned Tokyo cause lawyer Yasuhara Yukihiko to lead a newly constituted national organization of lawyers. The following month, lawyers and plaintiffs also voted to form a national plaintiff organization (Zenkoku Genkokudan Kyōgikai) and elected Sogano Kazumi to lead it. The plaintiffs realized that they "would have to speak with one voice when negotiating with the MHLW."[75] Until then, plaintiffs and their lawyers and supporters had shared evidence and tactical advice but had not yet coalesced into a truly *national* movement. Second, the lawyers and plaintiffs voted to redouble their efforts to gain

---

72. Interview with Kitano Ryūichi, *Asahi Shimbun* journalist, Kumamoto (May 9, 2009).
73. Interview with Shimura Hiroshi, leprosy survivor, Kumamoto (May 14, 2009).
74. Bengodan, *Hirakareta Tobira*, 256–59.
75. Interview with Morimoto Miyoji, leprosy survivor, Tama Zenshōen (July 3, 2009).

national media attention and pursue redress legislation through the Diet.[76] Frustrations with the lack of national news coverage before early 2001—despite concerted efforts to feed material to reporters—stemmed from the high barriers to entry created by the mainstream media's organizational structure and norms. As one lawyer commented, "local reporters from national news outlets frequently attended court hearings and visited leprosaria, but editors in Tokyo didn't run the stories they filed."[77] In February 2001, however, coordination between the lawyers and a sympathetic journalist produced an unprecedented series of articles on the lawsuits in the national edition of the *Mainichi Shimbun*, catalyzing broader national coverage of the issue by April 2001. And the NCLR—which had maintained a position of watchful waiting toward the lawsuits—threw its weight into the fight in April 2001 by voting to "do everything possible to bring about a favorable ruling."[78] Earlier grassroots mobilization facilitated these structural changes, which positioned the movement to pursue elite allies more effectively.

Indeed, the movement gained its first elite allies with the formation of the Parliamentarian Group to Advance a Final Resolution to the Hansen's Disease Issue (Hansen Gikon) on April 5, 2001.[79] The plaintiffs' lawyers had been briefing Diet members on the lawsuits since fall 2000, and plaintiffs began using their personal experiences in a sustained lobbying campaign in early 2001. The fact that the courts had already acknowledged their standing bolstered their claims. Several months later, their lobbying convinced 101 legislators from all opposition parties and the ruling LDP's junior coalition partner, Kōmeitō, to form the Hansen Gikon. Two members of the main opposition party, DPJ, spearheaded the group. Politicians joined for various reasons. For example, Fujī Hirohisa, who later led the group, first became interested in Hansen's disease while supervising budget negotiations between the NCLR and MHW in the 1970s as a Ministry of Finance bureaucrat. He personally visited ten leprosaria at the time, even though they were not directly his responsibility and unfounded fears of leprosy deterred even MHW officials with jurisdiction over the leprosaria from visiting the facilities. His "firsthand knowledge of leprosy survivors' suffering" apparently stayed with him after he became a legislator in 1977.[80] Since the preexisting lawmakers' group that focused on leprosy policy[81]—dominated as it was by LDP politicians who had

---

76. Bengodan, *Hirakareta Tobira*, 271.
77. Interview with Kunimune Naoko, lawyer.
78. Bengodan, *Hirakareta Tobira*, 205–7, 279–80.
79. Hansenbyō Mondai no Saishūkaiketsu wo Susumeru Kokkai Giin Kondankai, or Hansen Gikon for short.
80. Interview with Yamamoto Shimpei, lawyer, Tokyo (November 11, 2008).
81. The older group is called the Hansenbyō Taisaku Giin Kondankai and had monitored the state's implementation of the LPL since the 1960s. Originally led by a socialist lawmaker, it became LDP-dominated.

leprosaria in their districts—did not support the plaintiffs' claims, the Hansen Gikon's formation marked the first elite backing for the redress movement. Prominent politicians, seven plaintiffs, and a dozen lawyers attended the new group's first meeting, where a lawyer urged lawmakers to pursue a "comprehensive resolution," support the lawsuits, and acknowledge the Diet's responsibility for prolonging leprosy survivors' suffering. Supportive Kōmeitō politicians also pressured the LDP—from within the ruling coalition—to respond to victims' demands.

THE KUMAMOTO DISTRICT COURT'S RULING

Such societal and then political backing for redress claimants amplified the impact of the Kumamoto District Court's historic ruling, which came down in the plaintiffs' favor on May 11, 2001. The court ruled that the LPL had become unconstitutional in 1960 and found the MHW and the Diet negligent for having failed to repeal the LPL accordingly. The ruling called on the state to pay 1.82 billion yen (about $17 million) in compensation to 127 plaintiffs. Rejecting the state's attempt to impose a statute of limitations on redress claims, the judges also noted that the plaintiffs had suffered ongoing harm until 1996. The Kumamoto ruling was the first in Japanese history to specifically hold the Diet responsible for a legislative omission. The court process was also unusually short; the court reached a ruling in just two years and ten months—within the lawyers' promised three years.[82] Plaintiffs rejoiced, with one announcing, "This ruling confirms that we are humans!"[83]

The ruling further energized redress claimants and their supporters. On the eve of the ruling, for instance, an anticipatory rally in Kumamoto, entitled "I Want to Return to My Hometown," drew more than two thousand people. Twenty supporter groups from around the country sent representatives, and local civic groups filled the audience. Legislators from every party also attended. On the day the ruling was handed down, more than three hundred people gathered to try to watch the courtroom proceedings, even though there were just forty-six observers' seats in the courtroom. All national media outlets covered the ruling, prompting one lawyer to comment that "no sentient Japanese citizen could claim ignorance about the Hansen's disease issue."[84] Indeed, a government survey of Japanese citizens in early 2003 revealed that 97 percent of respondents had heard of Hansen's disease.[85]

---

82. Interview with Yahiro Mitsuhide, lawyer.

83. "'Ningen Toshite Ikirareru,' Nagasugita Kurayami ni Hikari, Hansenbyō Kōso Dannen ['I Will Be Able to Live as a Human Being,' A Light in the Darkness, Declining to Appeal the Hansen's Disease Lawsuit]," *Asahi Shimbun*, May 24, 2001.

84. Interview with Kunimune Naoko, lawyer.

85. MHLW, "Hansenbyō Mondai wo Tadashiku Tsutaeru Tameni: Hansenbyō no Mukōgawa [Correctly Communicating the Hansen's Disease Issue: The Other Side of Hansen's Disease]," 2003, http://www.mhlw.go.jp/houdou/2003/01/h0131–5.html.

PREVENTING AN APPEAL AND LEVERAGING
PUBLIC OUTRAGE

Despite success in court and in efforts to turn Hansen's disease into an issue, the plaintiffs remained wary. The ruling applied only to the 127 earliest plaintiffs in Kumamoto—not the nearly 650 other plaintiffs in the three lawsuits—and the state was likely to appeal it. Moreover, there were still thousands of other victims who were not party to the lawsuits, and the courts could not enact redress. The movement focused, therefore, on pressuring the state not to appeal the ruling. They began by demanding a meeting with Health and Welfare Minister Sakaguchi Chikara of the LDP's junior coalition partner, Kōmeitō. The lawyers believed that meetings with such high-level officials would give plaintiffs legitimacy in the eyes of other officials and help them articulate their demands more forcefully. Indeed, in the meeting, Sogano (as leader of the national plaintiffs' group) preempted the state's effort to "appease claimants with a cabinet-level apology" by declaring that "the plaintiffs would not accept Sakaguchi's apology without first receiving the government's pledge not to appeal the Kumamoto ruling."[86] Plaintiffs also used such meetings to cultivate politicians' sympathy: one plaintiff told the minister how she had been forced to have an abortion while seven months pregnant and had heard the baby's crying as leprosarium doctors killed it. Sakaguchi grew tearful recounting that story to me but also recalled that he had "personally come to support the victims' crusade against his own ministry in early 2001 after speaking with Dr. Ōtani, whose perspective as a retired bureaucrat formerly in charge of leprosy policy [Sakaguchi] respected."[87] Still, Sakaguchi had had to inform the plaintiffs that the Ministry of Justice (MOJ) intended to appeal the Kumamoto ruling.

Throughout May, therefore, about fifty plaintiffs and their lawyers also lobbied for a legislative solution, often noting that they had Minister Sakaguchi's backing. They demanded a "comprehensive resolution" that included an official apology, compensation, pensions, permanent medical care, a fact-finding commission, public education campaigns, and regular consultations with the state.[88] Plaintiffs' lawyers focused on countering MOJ officials' calls for an appeal.[89] Emphasizing that victims' average age was near eighty, the lawyers advocated settlement negotiations that covered *all former patients* (not just plaintiffs) to start before year-end. Meanwhile, the Hansen Gikon swelled to include 123 Diet members who unanimously announced their opposition to an appeal.[90] The plaintiffs also

---

86. Interview with Kobayashi Yōji.
87. Interview with Sakaguchi Chikara, Kōmeitō legislator and former health minister, Tokyo (July 9, 2009).
88. ASHDL, *Hansen Byō Mondai*, 49.
89. Bengodan, *Hirakareta Tobira*, 308.
90. Ibid., 305.

gained two influential allies: the LDP lawmakers Hashimoto Ryūtarō and Nonaka Hiromu. Hashimoto probably took up the cause because he had a leprosarium in his district. Nonaka framed his support for Hansen's disease survivors as natural because he had endured discrimination as a member of Japan's outcast Buraku-min population. Both politicians helped redress claimants put direct pressure on Prime Minister Koizumi Jun'ichirō to forgo an appeal. Nonaka, for example, arranged a meeting for the plaintiffs with LDP Policy Bureau chairman Aso Tarō, with the expectation that Aso would give their printed list of the pros and cons of not appealing the Kumamoto ruling directly to Koizumi.[91]

At the same time, public opinion in favor of redress for leprosy survivors became increasingly impossible to ignore because of the movement's multipronged activism. Movement leaders encouraged citizens to contact the government and urge against appealing the Kumamoto ruling. Plaintiffs, many of whom had "developed confidence through the lawsuits and associated activism," appeared on television to plead their case.[92] A further 923 plaintiffs also joined the lawsuits en masse on May 21, 2001, more than doubling the number of plaintiffs. On the same day, hundreds of leprosy survivors, few of whom had been outside the leprosaria in decades, held a sit-in outside the prime minister's residence to demand a meeting. One plaintiff even held a weeks-long hunger strike. And all of Japan's five main newspapers ran editorials calling for the state to forgo an appeal and compensate leprosy survivors.

COMPREHENSIVE REDRESS

By late May 2001, the movement's grassroots mobilizing had created a situation in which appealing the ruling would have been too politically costly for the government, though Prime Minister Koizumi's own calculus actually precipitated the political breakthrough that opened the door to redress. Plaintiffs and their lawyers had targeted Koizumi throughout mid-May because they believed that "his leadership was essential to overcoming the bureaucracy's opposition to the Kumamoto ruling."[93] Several factors contributed to Koizumi's decision on May 23, 2001, to forgo an appeal and then meet with nine of the plaintiffs who had been demonstrating outside his residence for days. News reports had spread the potent (but false) rumor that Minister Sakaguchi had threatened to resign if the government appealed the ruling.[94] Several reporters, emphasizing the depth

---

91. Interview with Noma Kei, lawyer, Tokyo (May 29, 2008). Interview with Itai Masaru, lawyer.
92. Interview with Itai Masaru.
93. Interview with Yasuhara Yukihiko, lawyer, Tokyo (May 26, 2008).
94. Sakaguchi denies ever explicitly threatening resignation, but the media reported it widely and it shaped the course of political discussions. Interview with Esashi Masayoshi, *Mainichi Shimbun*.

of public sympathy for Hansen's disease survivors, had also apparently personally urged Koizumi not to appeal the ruling the evening before he agreed to meet with plaintiffs.[95] Koizumi, as the head of a precarious new government, probably concluded that the potential gains in public approval—for meeting Hansen's disease survivors' demands and, more generally, for challenging the bureaucracy—outweighed the risks of alienating the MOJ and MHLW bureaucrats who favored an appeal. In fact, public approval ratings for Koizumi's cabinet jumped to 80 percent after he announced his decision not to appeal the ruling.[96]

Two days after this announcement, Koizumi offered a sweeping official apology to Japanese Hansen's disease survivors, declaring that state policies had violated their human rights and that the government would redress these wrongs. In addition to compensation, the state would provide health care, launch an educational campaign to "restore honor and dignity to the victims of the disease," remodel the national Hansen's disease museum, and hold regular discussions between MHLW officials and Hansen's disease survivors.[97] This historic apology closely mirrored the list of demands that plaintiffs and their lawyers had used while lobbying. Koizumi's statement also guided subsequent efforts to draft redress legislation, although plaintiffs and their lawyers canvassed lawmakers repeatedly to monitor the bill's content.

Within a month, the Diet unanimously passed a law granting leprosy survivors full redress.[98] The law pledged medical care and 8–14 million yen (roughly $76,000 to $133,000) in compensation to each of Japan's 4,500 leprosarium residents. The law included a clear statement of the government's wrongdoing, and in July 2001 the MHLW minister and vice minister visited each leprosarium to apologize to victims directly, echoing Koizumi's apology. In order to restore the dignity of those affected by Hansen's disease, the government created public advertisements and lesson plans about the human rights violations and prejudice that people with the disease had suffered. An independent fact-finding commission, which included lawyers and victims, also began meeting in October 2002 with a broad mandate to investigate past policies regarding Hansen's disease.

Through the newly established Council on the Hansen's Disease Issue (Kyōgikai), moreover, the MHLW, plaintiffs, the NCLR, and the lawyers' group

---

95. Interview with Yahiro Mitsuhide, lawyer.

96. Ikuo Kabashima and Gill Steel, "The Koizumi Revolution," *PS: Political Science & Politics* 40, no. 1 (2007): 81.

97. Koizumi Jun'ichirō, "Hansenbyō Mondai no Sōkikatsu Zenmenteki Kaiketsu ni Mukete no Naikaku Sōridaijin Danwa [Prime Ministerial Statement Concerning the Swift and Comprehensive Solution of the Hansen's Disease Issue]," May 25, 2001, http://www.kantei.go.jp/jp/koizumispeech/2001/0525danwa.html.

98. Hansenbyō Ryōyōjo Nyūshosha nado ni taisuru Hoshōkin no Shigo nado ni kansuru Hōritsu [Law Concerning the Compensation of Hansen's Disease Sanatoria Residents] (law no. 63, June 22, 2001).

settled all lawsuits with the Basic Agreement in July 2001 and began implementing the law. The national plaintiffs' organization, the NCLR, and the national lawyers' group had formed the Unified Negotiating Team (Tōitsu Kōshōdan) to present a united front vis-à-vis the state in this process. Through early 2002, working groups from this team fought to extend compensation to the relatively small number of Japanese leprosy survivors who had either never lived in leprosaria (*hinyūshosha*) or had left the leprosaria before 1996 (*taishosha*) and to the families of deceased leprosarium residents.

The tenor of interactions in the Kyōgikai reveals the extent to which the principles of policymaking related to Hansen's disease changed as a result of plaintiffs' activism.[99] In particular, the leprosarium self-governing councils and NCLR developed a more assertive and independent relationship with the state alongside the plaintiffs. For example, the Unified Negotiating Team forced the MHLW to hold a plenary Kyōgikai at least once yearly and issue a written confirmation (*kakunin jikō*) of everything discussed at these meetings.[100] Before each meeting, the stakeholders on the victims' side met to hammer out a coherent set of demands, which were drafted by lawyers but debated by the NCLR and plaintiffs. Since 2002, Kyōgikai subcommittees have tackled issues concerning commemoration activities, protections for those still in the leprosaria, leprosy survivors' social reintegration, fact-finding, and the future of the leprosaria. As residents' average age surpassed eighty, preserving the leprosarium as a home for anyone who wanted to remain became a particular priority. Thus, the Unified Negotiating Team proposed that the leprosaria—often oases of lush greenery with advanced medical amenities—be gradually converted into multiuse or medical facilities for the adjacent communities. Despite community support for the plan and calls for reductions in public spending, the MHLW argued that the 1996 law that repealed the LPL permitted only the dwindling Hansen's disease population to remain in the leprosaria, precluding broader uses for these facilities.

The NCLR, former plaintiffs, and their lawyers decided in 2007 to pursue an entirely new law—"a legislative solution to such bureaucratic intransigence," as one lawyer put it.[101] They lobbied both the lawmakers in the Hansen Gikon, which had formed in 2001 to help realize redress, and the older leprosy-related lawmaker group that had more ruling-party members. At the same time, they remobilized public support for their cause, collecting 930,000 signatures in favor of the proposed Hansen's Disease Basic Law in spring 2008. The Hansen Gikon and the older lawmakers' group signaled support for such new legislation by

---

99. Author's observation at the annual Kyōgikai meeting, Tokyo (June 22, 2009).
100. Interview with Yasuhara Yukihiko, lawyer (May 7, 2009).
101. Interview with Yamamoto Shimpei, lawyer.

holding an unprecedented joint public hearing in April 2008. With backing from all of Japan's political parties, the movement still faced the challenge of ensuring that the bill was enacted before the Diet's anticipated vote of no confidence against Prime Minister Fukuda Yasuo brought all government activity to a halt. Ultimately, it passed just hours before the no-confidence vote.[102] The new law further clarified the government's responsibility for leprosy survivors' past suffering and included measures by which the leprosaria would remain open and be used by localities as needed. It also formalized arrangements worked out in the Kyōgikai during the previous seven years. According to one lawyer, the law contained an "unprecedented 80 percent of the Hansen's disease community's goals," which lawyers had spelled out in a draft bill submitted to both lawmakers' groups.[103] Following on the 2001 law, the 2008 Basic Law rendered redress even more comprehensive for Japan's Hansen's disease survivors.

The Top-Down Expansion of the Korean Hansen's Disease Conflict

The domestic Korean Hansen's disease movement gained political attention and publicity comparatively quickly. Unlike the Japanese movement, it began with a symposium in October 2004 in the National Assembly building in Seoul, not in a courtroom far from the capital. In coordination with Hanvit, Park Chan-un and fellow members of the Hansen's Human Rights Lawyers' Group organized the event. They had been "shocked by the plight of leprosy survivors in Korea" while visiting leprosaria and resettlement villages to help Japanese lawyers prepare elderly Korean victims' applications for redress from Japan.[104] At the symposium, lawyers described the ROK government's and society's mistreatment of leprosy survivors since 1948, and several victims testified (albeit anonymously) about their experiences of discrimination and forced vasectomies. One of the main objectives of the organizers was to frame "Hansen's disease as a social issue, not just a medical issue."[105] The symposium drew several hundred leprosy survivors and interested citizens, as well as reporters. MBC television's investigative program, *PD Sucheop*, also broadcast a segment on Hansen's disease, illustrating the relative ease with which new issues can gain media coverage in Korea. Although Hanvit and the HHRLG did hope to raise public awareness through such publicity,

---

102. Hansenbyō Mondai no Kaiketsu no Sokushin ni Kansuru Hōritsu [Law to Promote a Resolution of the Hansen's Disease Issue] (law no. 82, June 11, 2008), nicknamed the Hansen's Disease Basic Law.

103. Interview with Kobayashi Yōji, lawyer.

104. Interview with Park Chan-un, lawyer.

105. Interview with Jo Yeong-seon, lawyer, Seoul (February 11, 2009).

the symposium was mainly geared toward placing the Hansen's disease issue on the political agenda, as is evident from the location in which it was held. Indeed, rather than marking the beginning of legal action against the ROK government like the Japanese lawsuits, the symposium catalyzed two independent initiatives, one legislative and the other investigatory.

REDRESS LEGISLATION AND A HUMAN RIGHTS INQUIRY

The symposium gave the Hansen's disease community a chance to articulate a rationale for redress, but its main impact was to spur one politician to take up the Hansen's disease issue and begin crafting legislation to help leprosy survivors. The progressive lawmaker Kim Chun-jin had volunteered in a resettlement village as a student, and his electoral district included such a village. But he did not become aware of the ROK government's role in perpetuating leprosy survivors' hardships until he and his staff prepared a speech for the symposium, which he had agreed to attend and speak at only because another colleague had had to cancel. Still, the issue gave him a chance to enhance his credentials as a health and welfare expert.[106] In the symposium's wake, Kim's staff met regularly with Hanvit officers from November 2004 to April 2005 while researching and drafting the bill. Hanvit requested compensation, an official apology, and public measures to restore the victims' honor.[107] Consequently, they looked to Japan's 2001 law as an example. They also proposed using as models the ROK government's allowances to comfort women and the April Third Incident Special Law of 1999, which provided recognition and financial assistance to victims of the ROK's counterinsurgency campaign on Jeju Island from 1948 to 1954. But Korean society had not expressed the kind of widespread public outrage against the government that had facilitated Japan's sweeping redress legislation, and the Hansen's disease issue was far less salient in Korea than the Jeju or the comfort women's movements. Aware of this fact, some HHRLG members used a public hearing about the bill in February 2005 to urge Kim to wait and use evidence from the anticipated National Human Rights Commission of Korea (NHRCK) report on Hansen's disease to mobilize greater public support for a stronger redress law.[108]

But Kim Chun-jin ultimately disregarded this advice in order to accelerate the process of submitting the bill to the National Assembly. With minimal public interest or even awareness among leprosy survivors, Hanvit could not prevent

---

106. Interview with Yu Gyeong-seon, Seoul (August 19, 2009).
107. Interview with U Hong-seon, Hanvit.
108. Gil Yun-hyeong, "Hansenin Teukbyeolbeop Jejeong Nonui Hwalbal [Lively Debate about the Proposed Hansen's Special Law]," *Hankyoreh Sinmun*, February 20, 2005.

Kim and his staff from curtailing the bill's content. The Ministry of Health and Welfare (MOHW) had raised concerns over the bill's potential cost, the way it portrayed the state's liability, and the use of the term "forced institutionalization" (*gangje gyeongni*). To increase its likelihood of passing, therefore, Kim's office decided to omit specific budgetary stipulations and statements of state liability.[109] In September 2005, Kim Chun-jin and sixty-two other legislators formally proposed the Law Concerning the Investigation of Hansen's Disease Victimization Incidents and Living Assistance for the Victims, nicknamed the Special Law for Hansen's Disease Victims (Hansenin Teukbyeolbeop).

During this legislative process, but separately from it, the lawyer Park Chan-un became director general of the NHRCK's Human Rights Policy Bureau and in the spring of 2005 commissioned a study of Hansen's disease survivors' human rights. The fact that Park could call for an inquiry as an insider in the NHRCK—a quasi-governmental watchdog institution of a type that does not exist in Japan—indicated that Korean cause lawyers such as Park had "become the establishment," particularly during Roh Moo-hyun's administration (2003–8).[110] Park also used his position at the NHRCK to persuade the NHRCK chairman to visit Sorokdo in 2005 and apologize for the ROK's inconsistent, harmful, and negligent policies. Although political figures had previously visited Sorokdo to express sympathy for leprosy sufferers, this was the first official apology in history, even if the chairman did not speak on behalf of the state. More important, the NHRCK report released in December 2005 documented for the first time a dozen massacres of leprosy survivors, forced institutionalization, forcible abortions and vasectomies, and other violations of leprosy survivors' rights.[111]

Whereas Japan's inquiry into abuses of leprosy survivors came *after* the Kumamoto ruling and legislation that acknowledged the state's wrongdoing and thus had a substantial mandate, the NHRCK report straddled the line between official inquiry and activism. The Japanese inquiry was designed to help the state learn from past wrongs, prevent future victimization of this kind, and educate the public about Hansen's disease. The NHRCK report aimed to publicize leprosy survivors' hardships for the first time and recommend appropriate measures for the government to take. Indeed, Park told me he had "hoped that the NHRCK investigation would catalyze redress legislation."[112] Although the NHRCK report

---

109. Interview with Yu Gyeong-seon.

110. Tom Ginsburg, "Law and the Liberal Transformation of the Northeast Asian Legal Complex," in *Fighting for Freedom*, ed. Terrence Halliday, Lucien Karpik, and Malcolm Feeley (Oxford: Hart, 2007), 54–55; Patricia Goedde, "From Dissidents to Institution-Builders," *East Asia Law Review* 4 (2009): 63–90.

111. NHRCK, *Hansen's Disease Human Rights Report*.

112. Interview with Park Chan-un, lawyer.

explicitly proposed text for legislation,[113] Kim Chun-jin had already submitted his bill to the National Assembly by the time the report was released. While Kim's Special Law proposed including government officials on its truth-finding (*jin-sang gyumyeong*) commission, the NHRCK draft recommended setting up an independent committee to conduct truth-finding activities. Such lack of coordination between the legislative and investigative initiatives in 2005 limited the impact of both. Moreover, the Hansen's disease issue had already been framed as a question of *Japanese* wrongdoing in the Korean public sphere. Indeed, elderly Korean leprosy victims' quest for compensation from Japan almost eclipsed the Special Law's submission to the National Assembly and the NHRCK report's release in late 2005.

PROTESTING THE UNEVEN RULINGS IN TOKYO

Hansen's disease-related activism did briefly capture widespread public attention as it had in Japan, but Koreans focused on leprosy survivors' transnational campaign for redress from Japan. The main catalyst, moreover, was less claimants' activism than the contradictory rulings that judges in the Tokyo District Court handed down in cases regarding compensation for survivors of leprosaria in Japan's former Korean and Taiwanese colonies. On October 25, 2005, one set of judges ruled that Japan was *not* responsible for compensating plaintiffs. On the same day, another set ruled that the twenty-five Taiwanese leprosy survivors who had brought identical claims against the Japanese government *were* eligible for compensation under Japan's 2001 Hansen's disease law. Before these rulings, Korean public awareness of the transnational redress movement had been relatively limited. Earlier in 2005, while Kim Chun-jin's bill and the NHRCK report were being drafted, Japanese lawyers had orchestrated petition drives in Japan, Korea, and Taiwan to urge the Japanese government to acknowledge colonial-era leprosy survivors' claims to compensation.[114] In Korea, they collected about 135,000 signatures. More than 142,000 Japanese citizens also signed the petition, revealing the Japanese public's continuing sympathy toward leprosy survivors—even non-Japanese ones. Similarly, the uneven rulings elicited criticism from all Japanese media outlets, interest groups, opposition parties, the LDP's coalition partner Kōmeitō, the NCLR, and the Union of Korean Residents in Japan.[115] Back in Korea, Hanvit and the HHRLG planned a demonstration in Seoul to "capitalize on indignant media coverage and pressure the Japanese and ROK governments"

---

113. NHRCK, *Hansen's Disease Human Rights Report*, 389–97.
114. Kunimune Naoko, "Signature Petition Report," http://www15.ocn.ne.jp/~srkt/syomei.htm.
115. Statements opposing the uneven rulings are available at http://www15.ocn.ne.jp/~srkt/syodantaiseimei.html.

on the issue.[116] More than a thousand people affected by Hansen's disease converged on Seoul just two days after the rulings in Tokyo. Many of them had not been in public for decades, but they came to "protest the injustice of the Tokyo rulings."[117]

This period marked the peak of public awareness of the Hansen's disease issue in Korea, but public outrage was directed at the Japanese rather than the Korean government. All Korean news outlets covered the victims' protest in Seoul, and editorials accused Japan of reopening colonial wounds. An editorial in the left-leaning *Kyunghyang* newspaper, for instance, denounced the inconsistent rulings as another of Japan's "petty tricks" (*jankkoi*) over history but made no mention of the ROK's postliberation mistreatment of leprosy sufferers.[118] Nationalist resentment toward Japan pervaded public perceptions of the Hansen's disease issue. As one lawyer noted, the transnational leprosy movement was more of an "anti-Japanese" movement than a "Hansen's disease" movement.[119] Even the Korean Bar Association's letter to the Tokyo court used nationalistic rhetoric to criticize the uneven rulings as discriminatory. Yet "since leprosy-related activism in Korea initially focused more on the Japanese government's past wrongs than on leprosy survivors' actual conditions," one leprosy doctor complained, "people don't understand the disease or believe that leprosy survivors deserve respect."[120] Rather than clarifying that the disease was fully treatable and not contagious, the transnational movement reinforced and resonated with widespread public criticisms around 2005 of Japan's handling of its colonial history and its territorial dispute with Korea over Dokdo/Takeshima. Hence, public interest in the transnational movement did not readily translate into support for leprosy survivors' claims against the ROK government.

EMPOWERMENT:
JAPANESE COMPENSATION ARRIVES IN KOREA

Nonetheless, the arrival of Japanese compensation in Korea empowered the domestic redress movement in three ways: by providing an example of a successful redress movement, by adding impetus to Kim Chun-jin's still-pending Special Law, and by supplying funds for future legal mobilization in Korea. In early 2006, the Japanese Diet capitulated to domestic and international pressure to politically resolve the impasse created by the uneven rulings from the Tokyo District Court by

---

116. Interview with Park Yeong-rip, lawyer.
117. Interview with Kim Jeong-haeng, council president.
118. "Hansenin Pihae Bosang eun Ingweon Munje Ida [Compensation for Hansen's Disease Victims Is a Human Rights Issue]," *Kyunghyang Sinmun*, November 7, 2005.
119. Interview with Park Yeong-rip, lawyer.
120. Interview with Chae Gyu-tae, doctor.

amending the country's Hansen's disease law to clarify that colonial victims were eligible for compensation. The Japanese government's first payments arrived on Sorokdo in March 2006. Korean lawyers noted that speaking with the elderly claimants became "more like talking with equals" after these survivors each received 8 million yen (about $76,000) from Japan.[121] Many people affected by Hansen's disease also felt "empowered because [they] could use [their] newfound wealth to help relatives and the church."[122] Some members of the community worried about "the influx of money to an otherwise impoverished and undereducated group of individuals, who had forged a simple way of life."[123] But the impact has been mostly positive. Furthermore, since most of these older leprosy survivors were deprived of the ability to reproduce, they could speak publicly without exposing their offspring to stigma. They did so increasingly, as Korean journalists sought interviews with compensation recipients, who were—after the Korean atomic bomb survivors—just the second group of Korean victims of Japanese historic abuses to receive compensation. The interviews gave elderly leprosy survivors opportunities to also describe the hardships they had endured after 1945, and the elderly redress recipients encouraged younger leprosy survivors to assert their right to redress.

In addition, victory in the transnational movement "added impetus to Kim Chun-jin's efforts to see his Special Law enacted," even though it did not affect the content of the already-pending bill.[124] Since Japan had redressed elderly Korean leprosy patients' pre-1945 suffering, Kim and Hanvit argued, the ROK government should do something for younger Korean leprosy survivors. To promote the Special Law, Hanvit organized an exhibit of leprosy-related paintings at the National Assembly, contacted lawmakers, and hosted a visit by the National Assembly's Health and Welfare Committee members to Sorokdo in June 2006. These activities foregrounded Hanvit and its leaders more than the testimonies of leprosy survivors, in contrast to the role that plaintiffs' personal stories played in the Japanese movement. And Hanvit's centralized management of such activities, while ensuring a unified message for the movement, deterred participation by rank-and-file leprosy survivors. Whereas in Japan plaintiffs and lawyers had lobbied lawmakers together, Hanvit officers were rarely accompanied by lawyers or ordinary leprosy survivors when they met with lawmakers. One journalist also commented that Hanvit "seemed reluctant to let other organizations help champion leprosy survivors' rights."[125] Indeed, the small group of scholars, journalists,

---

121. Interview with Park Chan-un, lawyer (February 13, 2009).
122. Interview with Jang Gi-jin, Sorokdo resident.
123. Interview with Kim Jeong-haeng, council president.
124. Interview with Yu Gyeong-seon.
125. Interview with Gil Yun-hyeong, *Hankyoreh Sinmun* journalist.

and lawyers involved in the movement stopped supporting Kim's bill in 2006 because it "fell short of Japanese and Taiwanese Hansen's disease legislation."[126] In addition, there was little media or public interest in the bill. Hanvit's leader complained that Korean society could "get behind us on the Hansen's disease issue to 'settle the past' with Japan, but then ignore the Hansen's disease issue in Korea—our own history!"[127] Despite Hanvit's lobbying and Kim's efforts to persuade fellow lawmakers to pass the bill, therefore, it languished, receiving "virtually no attention from the president or other lawmakers."[128]

PASSING AND REVISING THE SPECIAL LAW

Despite these obstacles, the National Assembly did finally pass the Special Law for Hansen's Disease Victims in October 2007, probably, according to someone closely involved, because it "required little financial outlay and no official apology."[129] It came into force a year later.[130] An official from the Ministry of Budget and Planning had also testified to the National Assembly's Health and Welfare Committee in April 2007 that the cost of enacting the law would be trivial and that "people would be protected equally" whether or not it passed.[131] Without acknowledging governmental wrongdoing, the law recognized the Korean leprosy community's past suffering, highlighting several incidents of violence against leprosy survivors. Victims of these incidents could apply for recognition from a fact-finding commission established by the law and receive stipends, but only if they did not already receive state assistance. Moreover, two-thirds of the 71 billion won (about $65 million) in the law's budget was designated for memorial activities on Sorokdo rather than aid for victims. The law's passage signaled the ROK's willingness to provide at least partial redress to victims of past abuses, but the legislation was disappointing. One leprosy doctor noted that his patients had had "little sense of how they would benefit from the Special Law."[132] Even the Hanvit officer most closely involved in drafting the bill called it "insufficient."[133]

Before the law went into force, therefore, Hanvit began campaigning to revise it. Hanvit president Lim Du-seong's election to the National Assembly in May 2008 from the conservative Grand National Party's (GNP) proportional

126. Interview with Park Yeong-rip, lawyer.

127. Gil Yun-hyeong, "Gongheohada, Hansenin Teukbyeolbeop [The Hansen's Disease Special Law Is Empty]," *Hankyoreh 21*, May 25, 2007.

128. Interview with Jo Yeong-seon, lawyer.

129. Interview with Yu Gyeong-seon.

130. Hansenin Pihaeja Sageon ui Jinsang Gyumyeong mit Pihaeja Saenghwal Jiwon deunge Gwanhan Beopryul (law no. 8644, October 17, 2007). It went into force October 18, 2008.

131. Gil, "Gongheohada, Hansenin Teukbyeolbeop."

132. Interview with Chae Gyu-tae, doctor.

133. Interview with U Hong-seon, Hanvit.

TABLE 3.1 Survey of the Korean Hansen's disease community on revision of the Special Law

PREFERRED REVISIONS TO THE LAW (RESPONDENTS COULD SELECT MULTIPLE ANSWERS)	NUMBER OF RESPONSES	PERCENTAGE OF RESPONDENTS WHO CHOSE THIS OPTION
Designate resettlement village living as victimization	5,855	93.6%
Increase aid for medical and welfare facilities	4,589	73.4%
Provide compensation (*bosang*)	4,546	72.7%
Grant assistance to bereaved families	1,952	31.2%
Delete the prohibition against double-dipping	851	13.6%
Change the term *Hansenin* (Hansen people) in the law	595	9.5%

representation candidate list signaled an important advance in the status of leprosy survivors in Korea and gave the movement an insider position from which to push for revisions. He was the first legislator in Korea, and indeed the world, to have survived Hansen's disease. As with the first legislative initiative in 2005, however, the availability of this "elite ally" lowered incentives for mobilizing ordinary leprosy survivors. Rather than encourage buy-in from rank-and-file leprosy survivors by having them tell their own stories to lawmakers to persuade them to vote for a revised bill, as Japanese plaintiffs had, Hanvit surveyed six thousand leprosy survivors and presented the results at an event unveiling Lim Du-seong's revised bill in February 2009. The event drew 60 National Assembly members, 420 Hansen's disease survivors, and about 280 ordinary citizens but received little publicity.[134] According to the survey, leprosy survivors overwhelmingly favored designating the resettlement village system as a form of victimization, awarding compensation, and increasing state aid for medical and welfare facilities (see table 3.1)[135] Eighty-five percent of respondents supported enhanced medical subsidies, and 27 percent sought increased subsidies for the disabled among them. These pressing day-to-day concerns make sense for the community. Most leprosy survivors (88 percent) are unemployed and almost all (91 percent) reported having no savings.[136] In addition, more than two-thirds of respondents thought that state-sponsored public education campaigns would help reduce

---

134. Hanvit, "Hansenin Pihae Sageon Pihaeja Myeongye Hoebok mit Bosang deunge Gwanhan Beopryul Ipbeop Gongjeonghoe Gechoe [Hosting a Public Hearing for the New Law Concerning the Honor Restoration and Compensation of Hansen's Disease Victims of Incidents]," *Hanvit Magazine*, February 2009, 12.

135. Hanvit, *Public Hearing on the Revised Law*, 170.

136. Ibid., 143.

social prejudice.[137] But fewer than 15 percent of respondents understood that one of the 2007 Special Law's main weaknesses was its prohibition against double-dipping, which rendered the nearly 90 percent of Korean leprosy survivors who receive welfare or disability aid from the state ineligible for assistance.[138] Such results indicate the degree to which rank-and-file leprosy survivors were, as one man put it, "pretty uninvolved in efforts to revise the 2007 law" just as in the campaign for Kim Chun-jin's original Special Law.[139]

Lim Du-seong had heeded advice from HHRLG members to include in the revised bill calls for an official apology, public education campaigns to reduce prejudice against leprosy survivors, and a broader official inquiry, elements that had been lacking in the 2007 Special Law but not in the Japanese and Taiwanese laws.[140] But the Korean movement still lacked the lawsuits and grassroots mobilization that had enabled the Japanese Hansen's disease community to obtain such elements of redress. Hence, whereas Japan's prime minister had apologized in 2001 in response to broad-based mobilization, Korea's prime minister told me he had made a historic visit to Sorokdo in 2009 to express condolences to the leprosy community "because Lim Du-seong [who was also from the ruling GNP] had personally asked [him] to."[141] Although unprecedented, the prime minister's statement drew criticism from leprosy survivors for "having been made in a room that was not accessible to the handicapped" and having failed to acknowledge the state's role in prolonging their suffering.[142] Another Hansen's disease survivor—who had participated in Sosamo in 2001—derided the prime minister's 2009 statement, saying that "an official apology should have an impact on society's perceptions of Hansen's disease."[143] Meanwhile, the revised bill was submitted to the full assembly in August 2009. It became void before being voted on, though, because Lim Du-seong was arrested later that year for taking millions of dollars in bribes and "donations" to Hanvit from local developers. His arrest could have damaged the movement's image more than it did, but media attention was low. The main impact of his arrest was to spark a leadership shuffle in Hanvit, which was welcomed by some after his long tenure. Since Lim had been both a leader in the movement and then an elite ally of sorts in the National Assembly, his

---

137. Ibid., 165–66.
138. The original law would not have passed without this prohibition on double-dipping. Interview with Yu Gyeong-seon.
139. Interview with Gang Chang-seok, leprosy survivor, Sorokdo (August 15, 2009).
140. Testimony from Jo Yeong-seon, in Hanvit, *Public Hearing on the Revised Law*, 61–66.
141. Interview with Han Seung-su, former ROK prime minister, Cambridge (October 22, 2010).
142. Interview with Kim Yeong-deok and Han Doek-ja, leprosy survivors, Sorokdo (August 14, 2009).
143. Interview with Lee Se-yong, leprosy survivor.

departure alleviated some of the liabilities of elite access and may have facilitated the movement's shift toward litigation.

A SHIFT TO THE COURTS

When efforts to revise the law failed in 2009, Hanvit officers and the HHRLG began discussing the possibility of suing the ROK government for state compensation (*gukka baesang*), as Japanese Hansen's disease survivors had. While the impetus for Japan's lawsuits against the state came from a rank-and-file leprosy survivor, however, Korea's leprosy litigation began from the top down (i.e., from the HHRLG) and it postdated efforts to achieve redress through legislation. Although the fact-finding commission (Hansenin Pihaeja Sageon Jinsang Gyumyeong Wiwonhoe in Korean) established by the 2007 Special Law had started reviewing applications for victim status in late 2008, its progress was slow and victims were aging. The commission was composed of experts, government officials, and several leaders in the Hansen's disease community, and its meetings were more bureaucratic and less adversarial than the Kyōgikai meeting in Japan. Still, disagreements and a small staff hobbled its progress. By 2011, the commission had processed only a fraction of the applications it had received, and the MOHW had not distributed any funds to recognized victims. The proximate cause of leprosy survivors' lawsuits against the state, though, was reportedly a Supreme Court ruling in another case of state wrongdoing that helped HHRLG members realize that they could argue that the statute of limitations on seeking state compensation—set at three years from when claimants discover their injury—could be interpreted as starting when the Special Law recognizing leprosy survivors as "victims" had gone into force in late 2008.[144] The group therefore prepared to sue before the three-year time frame ended in late 2011.

Like the rest of the movement, litigation was centrally organized, but the HHRLG assumed a more equal role with Hanvit. Hanvit used its organizational reach to help the lawyers identify potential plaintiffs and arranged meetings for the lawyers at resettlement villages and leprosaria. Despite interest from survivors of other human rights violations suffered by Korea's leprosy community (such as forced institutionalization, forced labor, and discrimination), the lawyers focused on mobilizing only victims of forced vasectomies and abortions because such damages "were easier to prove."[145] The lawyers already had some evidence from depositions taken for the lawsuit in Japan. Hanvit and the Sorokdo leprosarium supplied further medical records, though few victims had documentation because of the semilegal nature of the medical procedures at the time and because

---

144. Interview with Jo Yeong-seon, lawyer (July 13, 2012).
145. Interview with Park Yeong-rip, lawyer (July 5, 2012).

many records had been destroyed by a fire in Sorokdo's archives in the 1970s.[146] The HHRLG subsidized the transportation, research, and per diem expenses of its members with a fund it had created by pooling the commissions that its members had received for their work on the Sorokdo lawsuit. According to an agreement with the Japanese lawyers, HHRLG members involved in that suit had received 4 percent of each claimant's compensation, while Japanese lawyers and Hanvit had collected 4 percent and 2 percent, respectively. By the time the first lawsuit against the ROK government was filed in 2011, Korean lawyers' pooled commissions amounted to nearly $2 million and allowed the HHRLG to hire an administrator to support the pro bono work of about ten HHRLG members on leprosy-related lawsuits.[147]

Citing the shortcomings of Korea's 2007 Special Law and the state's unwillingness to acknowledge past wrongdoing, an initial 207 plaintiffs filed a lawsuit in October 2011 seeking 30 million won (about $27,000) for each vasectomy victim and 50 million won (about $45,000) for each victim of a forced abortion. The plaintiffs' lawyers persuaded the government to waive the filing fee. By 2013, more than 650 victims of forced vasectomies and abortions had filed four additional suits against the state. Whereas Japanese litigation had begun far from the capital, in Kumamoto near a leprosarium, all but one of the Korean suits were filed in Seoul. To make up for this, HHRLG members traveled to resettlement villages and leprosaria every few weeks to meet with plaintiffs, answer questions about the lawsuits, and try to "empower leprosy survivors to be actively involved in reclaiming their rights."[148] They also encouraged plaintiffs to testify in court. After doing so, one plaintiff told me she felt that "her grievances were finally heard."[149] Ultimately, however, distance and physical infirmity prevented many plaintiffs from becoming actively involved. Although HHRLG members tried to avoid the elite model of cause lawyering that predominates in Korea (described in chapter 2), many plaintiffs seemed to feel "little personal role in the legal battle and preferred to entrust it to the experts—the lawyers."[150]

Without much participation from plaintiffs, members of the HHRLG struggled to sustain media attention, the power of which they had witnessed during the Sorokdo lawsuit in Tokyo. Most Korean media covered the press conference announcing the first suit in 2011. For example, an editorial in the left-leaning *Hankyoreh* newspaper highlighted the shortcomings of the 2007 Special Law,

---

146. Interview with U Hong-seon, Hanvit(July 11, 2012).
147. Interview with O Ha-na, HHRLG administrator, Seoul (July 1, 2012).
148. Interview with Lee Jeong-il, lawyer.
149. Interview with Mrs. Kim, leprosy survivor and plaintiff, by telephone (July 13, 2012).
150. Interview with U Hong-seon, Hanvit (July 11, 2012).

pointed out how much more comprehensive Japanese redress policies had been, and urged the ROK government to apologize and compensate Hansen's disease survivors.[151] Several plaintiffs also gave interviews to major news outlets after reporters agreed to conceal their names to protect them from stigma. One woman described being forced to abort her first pregnancy in 1972 and then forced to have tubal ligation surgery when she became pregnant a second time.[152] On their first day in court, plaintiffs' lawyers expressed hope that the lawsuit would help mobilize grassroots support by forging "a bond of sympathy [*gonggam daega*] with ordinary citizens . . . and thereby make it possible for those who were harmed by the state to recover their human rights and improve their basic welfare."[153] Yet one lawyer noted that most media lost interest because of the dearth of "new news from the sluggish court process."[154] Court hearings occurred only once every few months (as had been the case in Japan), but the Korean movement lacked the supporter groups that had helped the Japanese movement organize events between court dates. Even additional lawsuits filed by hundreds more plaintiffs, whose average age was seventy-six, failed to incite broader interest. And even when the HHRLG hosted the annual international symposium with Japanese and Taiwanese lawyers in 2012 and focused it on issues related to the forced vasectomies and abortions that leprosy survivors had endured in all three countries, the Korean media largely ignored it.

The lawsuits received little attention in Korea but appeared to prod the state to make some concessions. In early 2012, just after the first suit was filed, the MOHW doubled the number of staff working for the fact-finding commission established under the 2007 law. It also extended the period during which the commission would accept applications and expanded the range of incidents that it classified as victimization. Especially important, it removed the prohibition on double-dipping by announcing that anyone recognized as a victim—whether or not he or she was already receiving welfare benefits from the state—would receive 150,000 won per month (about $136). Although the MOHW official in charge of Hansen's disease issues denied any connection between lawsuits and these changes,[155] members of the HHRLG and Hanvit officers believe the impact of

---

151. "Hansenin Tanjong Naktae Haksal, Gukka Seuseuro Chaekim Jeoya [The State Should Take Responsibility for Hansen's Disease Survivors' Vasectomy and Abortion Massacres]," *Hankyoreh Sinmun*, October 18, 2011.

152. Shin Gwang-yeong, "'Sum Suiryeoneun Ne Agi Reul Geudeuleun Binile Dama Beoryeotda' ['They Threw Away My Still Breathing Child in a Plastic Bag']," *DongA Ilbo*, October 19, 2011.

153. Hanvit, "Hansenin Gangje Danjong, Naktae Gukka Baesang Sosong Cheot Jaepan [First Court Date in the State Compensation Lawsuit for Hansen's Victims of Forced Vasectomies and Abortions]," *News*, February 1, 2012, www.ehanvit.org/board.php?db=news&mode=view&idx=290&page=2.

154. Interview with Jo Yeong-seon, lawyer (July 13, 2012).

155. Interview with an MOHW official, Seoul (July 9, 2012).

litigation was considerable. By mid-2013, the commission had finished reviewing about ten thousand applications and had recognized about 6,500 individuals as victims, of whom about 4,000 were still alive.

Yet the Korean Hansen's disease movement has yet to achieve the level of redress that the Japanese movement achieved. And Korean leprosy survivors' legal battle continues. In October 2014, the Gwangju High Court upheld an April 2014 decision from a lower court in Suncheon, which had ruled in favor of nineteen leprosy survivors' claims for compensation from the state for the forcible vasectomies and abortions they had endured. The Suncheon court, which has jurisdiction over Sorokdo, found that the state had acted illegally and violated leprosy survivors' rights to reproduce and live with dignity. The HHRLG welcomed the ruling because it clearly articulated the state's liability and accepted the lawyers' interpretation of the statute of limitations. All local media outlets and several national outlets covered the landmark ruling. Even the conservative newspaper *Chosun Ilbo* published an editorial urging the state to forgo an appeal of the Suncheon ruling "as Japan had and compensate Hansen's disease survivors."[156] Subsequently, in the first half of 2015, lower courts in Seoul ruled in most of the plaintiffs' favor in three parallel cases, and media coverage "was better than with the 2007 Special Law because reporters could interview plaintiffs (albeit without revealing their names) and the lawyers."[157] Especially in the Suncheon lawsuit, plaintiffs also participated more actively than had been the case in the Hanvit-led campaign for the 2007 Special Law. But the state appealed all the rulings, arguing that the statute of limitations had expired and that the 1963 revision to the IDPL formally ended the practice of forced vasectomies and abortions. In the face of such resistance, Hanvit, which was renamed the Korean Federation of Hansen Associations (Hanguk Hansen Chong Yeonhaphoe) in 2013, continues to work with the HHRLG on the lawsuits.[158] It also organizes activities to raise awareness about Hansen's disease and reduce prejudice.

The distinctive ways in which the Japanese and Korean conflicts over redress for leprosy survivors expanded contributed significantly to their divergent outcomes. In Japan, a broad network of activist lawyers, local citizen groups, and sympathetic journalists helped redress claimants gain support from the attentive public. Indeed, nearly every Japanese person had heard of Hansen's disease by the time the government started granting redress in 2001. Three lawsuits also gave leprosy survivors a new identity as plaintiffs that was separate from the NCLR,

---

156. "Jeongbu, Hansenin Pihae Kkalkkeumhage Ilgwal Bosang eul [The Government Should Give Hansen's Disease Survivors Neat Onetime Compensation]," *Chosun Ilbo*, May 1, 2014.

157. Interview with Park Yeong-rip, lawyer (May 29, 2015).

158. The group's website is http://www.hansenkorea.org.

Japan's existing leprosy patient organization that had secretly pledged not to sue the Japanese government during negotiations over repealing the country's Leprosy Prevention Law. The lawsuits attracted media coverage, especially of the Kumamoto ruling, and public outrage against the state gave lawmakers reason to pressure the prime minister and bureaucracy to make extensive concessions from 2001 onward. Table 3.2 summarizes how the Japanese and Korean Hansen's disease movements score in terms of the components of redress introduced in chapter 1.

TABLE 3.2 Redress outcomes in the Hansen's disease movements

	JAPAN: COMPONENTS OF REDRESS	KOREA: COMPONENTS OF REDRESS
Official inquiry	2—Yes (with victim representation on independent inquiry committee)	2—Extensive NHRCK report; curtailed inquiry into specific incidents (with victims on committee)
Apology	2—Yes and public education campaigns	1—Expression of condolence only
Compensation and other assistance	2—Compensation, pensions, free medical care	1—Living stipends for victims of specific incidents
Institutional reforms	2—Victims involved in decision making through regular consultations with officials	1—More consultation with Hanvit; but leprosy still treated as an infectious disease
TOTAL	**FULL REDRESS (8)**	**PARTIAL REDRESS (5)**

Note: The scores reflect the extent to which state actions fulfill each component of redress: fully (2), partially (1), or not at all (0).

Lower redress outcomes for Korean Hansen's disease survivors stem from the fact that the movement first attracted an elite political ally rather than first mobilizing the leprosy community and support from societal actors. In addition, Korea's media and activist sectors emphasized the elderly leprosy survivors' campaign for redress from Japan more than the campaign to hold the ROK government accountable for more recent abuses. The dearth of public and political interest in the domestic redress movement reduced Hanvit's leverage over the lawmaker who championed their cause and drafted special legislation for leprosy survivors. When that legislation proved disappointing, the movement resorted to litigation against the state, which has produced rulings affirming plaintiffs' claims. To date, however, the ROK government has granted only partial redress to leprosy victims. Comparing the Japanese and Korean Hansen's disease movements illustrates the downsides of early access to elite allies and the ways in which initial political closure can spur the kinds of movement building and grassroots mobilizing that render more useful those politicians who subsequently take up the movement's cause.

4

THE POLITICS OF HEPATITIS C–TAINTED BLOOD PRODUCTS

Asakura Mitsuko had suffered from hepatitis C for more than a decade before she realized that she could "blame the government and drug manufacturers, rather than [herself]" for this chronic liver infection, which she had developed a month after giving birth to a son in 1988.[1] Through an investigative television series in 2003, Asakura learned that thousands of Japanese had, like her, contracted hepatitis C from blood products designed to treat hemophilia or stop bleeding during labor and surgery. She also discovered that some of these victims had already filed two collective lawsuits against the government and manufacturers. After calling the lawyers' phone number mentioned on the broadcast, Asakura consulted two lawyers, who cried with her as she recounted how she had been unable to care for her newborn son because of her hepatitis. Although symptoms vary from person to person and chronic infections often develop slowly, the hepatitis C virus (HCV) causes inflammation of the liver cells and can lead to liver failure or liver cancer. Treatment took about one year, caused severe side effects, and cured only about one-third of patients until 2011, when new drugs increased the cure rate to about 60 percent.[2] To claim redress for such suffering alongside scores of other victims, Asakura joined one of the ongoing HCV lawsuits in 2003 because she realized that she "could not allow the government and drug makers to get away with this!"

---

1. Account based on interviews with Asakura Mitsuko, HCV plaintiff, Tokyo (May 21 and June 9, 2009).

2. Based on correspondence with Dr. Jerry Powell, UC Davis (April 2010, February 2012).

More than a hundred Koreans filed an analogous lawsuit in 2004. A call for Korean hemophilia patients—nearly half of whom were infected with HCV—to join the suit argued that victims' infections stemmed from government regulators' and the producer's "moral laxity" and urged plaintiffs to band together "to defeat the authoritarian medical administration and make the medical environment better for future generations."[3] With guidance from the patient-run Korea Hemophilia Association (KOHEM), the plaintiffs' lawyers researched how HIV-tainted blood products had ravaged hemophilia communities across the developed world in the 1980s and learned that HCV was similarly transmitted through blood or its derivatives.[4] They also read about effective campaigns for redress by HIV-infected hemophiliacs in the United States, France, United Kingdom, Germany, and Japan, as well as about HCV-related activism in Canada and Europe. But few of the Korean plaintiffs were "confident [they] could win against such powerful government and pharmaceutical adversaries."[5]

Despite the Japanese and Korean HCV movements' parallel claims and contemporaneity, their quests for redress proceeded quite differently. Japan's HCV plaintiffs struggled to achieve national attention and sympathy from legislators for nearly four years, while Korea's HCV movement gained support from a lawmaker within a year of filing suit. Initially lacking national visibility or elite political allies, Japan's movement invested in grassroots mobilization by encouraging plaintiffs to attend court dates and participate in extrajudicial activism, collaborating with small supporter groups at the five court sites to raise citizens' awareness of the HCV issue, and leveraging aspects of the court process to gain media attention. In addition, Japanese plaintiffs formed an independent organization devoted to holding the government and pharmaceutical companies accountable, whereas Korean victims pursued redress primarily through the country's existing hemophilia patient organization. Early access to an elite political ally in the Korean case reduced the impetus for grassroots mobilization such that officers of the patient-run KOHEM and the plaintiffs' lawyers handled most lobbying, media relations, and court-related activism with relatively less involvement from rank-and-file plaintiffs or other civic groups. Consequently, while the Japanese conflict over HCV expanded from the bottom up, the scope of the parallel conflict in Korea barely expanded at all.

As a result of these differences, the Japanese HCV movement elicited more redress. In late 2007 and early 2008, it used several partially favorable court

---

3. KOHEM, "C-Hyeong Ganyeom (HCV) Sosong Indan Annaemun [Announcement about the HCV Lawsuit Group]," KOHEM Announcements, no. 122, June 30, 2004, http://www.kohem.net.

4. Based on interviews with U Gweng-pil, lawyer, Seoul (August 21, 2009), and Kim Yeong-ro, KOHEM, Seoul (February 27 and July 27, 2009).

5. Interview with Kim Tae-il, KOHEM, Seoul (July 10, 2012).

rulings, national media coverage, and public indignation to gain politicians' support and wring concessions from the government. Redress measures included an apology, an official inquiry, medical subsidies and financial assistance from the state and the manufacturers, and measures to include victims in future policy decisions related to hepatitis. In Korea, legislative efforts to achieve even independent oversight of the nation's blood supply—let alone compensation—have failed. Moreover, although a high court found the defendants liable for thirteen of the plaintiffs' HCV infections in February 2013, none has received redress because the case was appealed to the Supreme Court. KOHEM must still balance redress-related goals with other priorities, such as subsidies for hemophilia treatment and access to new drugs. At this writing, the Korean movement has yet to achieve redress. This chapter summarizes the problem of contaminated blood products and then analyzes the divergent form and efficacy that the Japanese and Korean HCV movements took, highlighting the downsides of gaining an elite ally early on.

Naming and Blaming:
The Etiology of Tainted Blood Products

Like many advanced industrialized countries, Japan and Korea suffered blood-borne hepatitis C epidemics in an era of rapidly changing scientific knowledge and technology. Across the developed world in the 1970s and 1980s, patients with hemophilia and other bleeding disorders began receiving concentrated forms of clotting factor as part of their treatment. These new blood products had several benefits, even if scientists later discovered that they caused mass HIV and HCV infections. Before factor concentrates were available, hemophilia patients, who have a congenital lack of coagulation factor, had to use whole blood, fresh-frozen plasma, or cryoprecipitate to treat bleeds. All these treatment options were inconvenient and time-intensive and required the patient to be in or near a hospital. Factor concentrates, first developed in the late 1960s, were more costly but also portable, easy to prepare, and effective. As such, they dramatically improved hemophilia patients' quality of life. For patients with other illnesses, clotting factor reduced some of the bleeding risks associated with labor or surgery.

But because producing factor concentrates involved pooling thousands of units of whole blood, one unit of virus-tainted blood could contaminate an entire batch of factor (usually tens of thousands of doses). Contamination of whole blood and its derivatives, particularly with the different types of hepatitis, had been a concern since World War II. Although scientists had not yet developed tests to detect viral contamination, they suspected a common etiology for hepatitis infections among people who received blood transfusions or were vaccinated en masse with the same needle. Indeed, Japan stopped purchasing and pooling blood for transfusions (but, notably, not for making blood derivatives) in 1964, after U.S. ambassador Edwin O. Reischauer contracted hepatitis while being treated in Tokyo for a knife wound. In the early 1970s, U.S. regulators also stopped approving pooled plasma because of concerns about hepatitis contamination.[6]

Around the same time, pharmaceutical companies started developing factor concentrates and increasing the number of units of blood they pooled to reduce the new drugs' production costs. Some U.S. scientists raised concerns about epidemiological evidence of rising hepatitis rates among hemophiliacs because the producers often used blood purchased from "high risk" populations such as prisoners, drug addicts, and poor people.[7] In 1974, scientists also uncovered a new pathogen in blood: non-A non-B hepatitis, which was renamed hepatitis C when the virus was identified in 1989. Yet in the 1970s and early 1980s, hepatitis was widely seen as an "acceptable risk" for patients because of the effectiveness of factor concentrates in treating hemophilia.[8]

Addressing contamination in blood products did not gain international urgency until the early 1980s, when Western experts discovered a previously unknown disease, HIV/AIDS, in gay men and in hemophilia patients who had infused factor concentrates. By 1985, 74 percent of Americans with severe hemophilia, or nearly ten thousand people, had contracted HIV. About 40 percent of Japan's hemophiliacs were similarly infected with HIV. There were fewer HIV cases among Korean hemophiliacs because Korea's relative poverty made expensive factor concentrates a less common form of treatment. Yet nearly all of the twenty-five HIV infections among Koreans with hemophilia appear to trace to factor IX made domestically with improperly implemented virus inactivation procedures in 1990, years after the developed world knew about and had addressed viral contaminants in blood products.[9]

---

6. Douglas Starr, *Blood* (New York: Knopf, 1998), 225.

7. J. G. Allen, "Letter: The High Cost of Cheap Blood," *New England Journal of Medicine* 294, no. 12. (March 18, 1976): 675.

8. The Institutes of Medicine et al., eds., *HIV and the Blood Supply* (Washington, DC: National Academies Press, 1995), 8.

9. Most hemophiliacs have hemophilia A, which is usually treated with factor VIII. The few who have hemophilia B treat with factor IX. Factor IX is sometimes also used for nonhemophiliacs, as it was in Japan. Young-Keol Cho et al., "Molecular Epidemiologic Study of a Human Immunodeficiency Virus 1 Outbreak in Hemophiliacs B Infected through Clotting Factor 9 after 1990," *Vox Sanguinis* 92, no. 2 (2006): 113–20.

In the early 1980s, however, experts around the world debated various coun-
termeasures to viral contamination—often without full information, as scientific knowledge evolved rapidly. The conflicts over restitution for victims of
tainted blood products, which subsequently played out in many developed nations (often in the courts), centered on competing interpretations of how much
governmental and industry decision makers knew or should have known about
HIV or HCV in blood products. These interpretations tried to delineate the actions and inactions for which governments and pharmaceutical companies could
be held responsible. Yet, as the 1995 Institute of Medicine (IOM) report in the
United States warned, "The risk of hindsight is unfairly finding fault with decisions made by people who had to act long before scientific knowledge became
available to dispel their uncertainty."[10] Consider, for example, producers' and regulators' decisions to introduce, approve, and mandate virus inactivation procedures in the 1980s. With hindsight, these decisions seem straightforward. As early
as the 1970s, some scientists had argued that detergent or heat treatment could
inactivate the hepatitis B virus in blood products.[11] Yet only after the discovery
of AIDS did the main Western producers begin implementing heat treatment
processes in 1983. Japanese producers began using heat treatment over the next
few years. Korea's main producer of blood products started heat-treating in 1990,
a year after it began distributing Korea's first domestically made clotting factor.
Introducing virus inactivation procedures earlier might have curtailed the spread
of HIV and HCV through blood products.[12] But experts did not identify the
AIDS and hepatitis C viruses until 1985 and 1989, respectively, and devised tests
for these viruses thereafter. They had also debated the value of virus inactivation
procedures until the early 1980s, because these techniques were expensive and
difficult to implement. Indeed, from the time that researchers started investigating virus inactivation technologies in the 1960s, their main challenge had been
to find those that would not damage the delicate proteins that made blood and
its derivatives effective. Furthermore, most governments did not require such
safety procedures until the extent of AIDS contamination became apparent in
the mid-1980s.

Amid global fears of blood-borne HIV, Korean and especially Japanese hemophilia patients and doctors worried about the safety and potential side effects
of imported factor, whether heated or not, because the first HIV infections had

---

10. The Institutes of Medicine et al., *HIV and the Blood Supply*, vi.

11. Starr, *Blood*, 297.

12. William Foege, "The National Pattern of AIDS," in *The AIDS Epidemic* ed. Kevin M. Cahill
(New York: St. Martin's, 1983), 7–17; The Institutes of Medicine et al., *HIV and the Blood Supply*,
chap. 4.

occurred in the West. Since AIDS was still rare in East Asia, Japanese and ROK regulators decided in the mid-1980s to promote factor made from domestic blood, which was theoretically less likely to be tainted.[13] These decisions also benefited Japanese and Korean pharmaceutical firms as they tried to compete with the dominant Western producers. Japan's Green Cross, which split into Mitsubishi Pharma and Benesis after the HIV lawsuits, had long been the country's primary producer of plasma derivatives. In 1974, it helped Korea's Green Cross Corporation (GCC)—which is not related to the eponymous Japanese company—start producing blood derivatives. GCC became Korea's main maker of blood products. At first it distributed them through local Red Cross blood centers free of charge, but it began selling more advanced blood derivatives in the late 1980s in an effort to forestall Western suppliers' dominance in the emerging Korean market.

Retrospective studies have concluded that Japanese (and thus perhaps Korean) suspicions of imported factor delayed regulators' approval of heat-treated factor from the West, even though it was safer than the unheated domestic products available at the time.[14] While officials weighed new scientific information, patient safety, cost considerations, and the interests of domestic producers, therefore, HCV-tainted domestic and foreign blood products continued to circulate. In fact, some Western producers sold surplus unheated factor in Asia and Latin America even after they had begun heat treatment for Western markets. One such firm defended its actions by noting consumers' doubts about heated factor and the difficulty of gaining approval to sell it in countries such as Japan.[15] Japanese producers likewise sold excess unheated and potentially HCV-tainted stock through the mid-1980s as they introduced heat treatment. Both imported and Korean-made factor may explain the similar rates of HCV infections among Korean hemophiliacs. In the mid-1980s, U.S. scientists finally confirmed some experts' suspicions that HCV was infecting people through blood products, just as HIV/AIDS had.

Thus, while the developed world was preoccupied with the much-publicized AIDS crisis, hepatitis C spread. About 60 percent of Korean and Japanese hemophilia patients who received factor before 1992 are infected with HCV. Table 4.1 summarizes the current rates of HIV and HCV infections among hemophilia patients in both countries.[16] An estimated ten thousand nonhemophilic Japanese,

---

13. Awaji Takehisa, "HIV Litigation and Its Settlement (in Japan)," trans. Keisuke Mark Abe, *Pacific Rim Law & Policy Journal* 6 (1997): 581.

14. Eric A. Feldman and Ronald Bayer, *Blood Feuds* (Oxford: Oxford University Press, 1999), 72.

15. Walt Bogdanich and Eric Koli, "2 Paths of Bayer Drug in 80's," *New York Times*, May 22, 2003.

16. AIDS Prevention Foundation, "Ketsueki Gyōko Ijōbyō Zenkoku Chōsa [National Coagulation Disorders Survey]," 2012, 3, 33, http://api-net.jfap.or.jp/library/alliedEnt/02/images/h24_research/h24_research.pdf; Korea Hemophilia Foundation, *Hyeolubyeong Baekseo [Hemophilia White Paper]*, 2012, 23, http://www.kohem.org/_data/board_list_file/8/2013/1305040914501.pdf.

TABLE 4.1   HIV/AIDS and hepatitis C infections among living hemophilia patients in Japan and Korea (2012)

COUNTRY	LIVING WITH HIV (total HIV infections, incl. deaths)	INFECTED WITH HCV (percentage of total)	NOT INFECTED WITH HCV (percentage of total)	INFECTION STATUS UNKNOWN (percentage of total)	TOTAL
Japan	743	2,545	3,072	—	5,617
	(1,412)	(45.3%)	(54.7%)		
Korea	19	583	1,279	82	1,944
	(25)	(30.0%)	(65.8%)	(4.2%)	

most of whom were women, also contracted HCV from blood products that were prescribed unusually often in Japan in the 1970s and 1980s for use during labor or surgery. Since the ROK has yet to conduct a nationwide epidemiological study of blood-borne HCV, the extent of infections beyond the hemophilia community is unknown. As will be discussed below, Japanese victims who sought redress beginning in 2002 included only nonhemophilic HCV victims, whereas Korean redress claimants included only HCV-infected hemophilia patients.

The Legacies of HIV-Related Activism

Japanese and Koreans infected with HIV from blood derivatives mobilized to seek redress before victims of HCV-tainted blood products did. A full comparison of these HIV movements is beyond the scope of this book, but they constitute an important backdrop for each country's HCV movement. Japanese HIV victims filed two collective lawsuits against the pharmaceutical companies and the state in 1989, and Korean HIV-infected hemophiliacs and their families similarly sued GCC in 2003. Both sets of victims used litigation, media coverage, and conventional lobbying to claim redress. Because of the differing scale of the HIV epidemics in Japan and Korea and the timing of victims' mobilization, however, HIV-related activism had divergent legacies for the Japanese and Korean HCV movements.

The Japanese *yakugai* (drug-induced) AIDS movement began when a lawyer with hemophilia assembled a group of fellow lawyers who were concerned about patients' rights in Japan.[17] In the late 1980s, two groups of about fifty lawyers each—many of whom would later also represent HCV victims—recruited

---

17. See Eric A. Feldman, *The Ritual of Rights in Japan* (Cambridge: Cambridge University Press, 2000).

HIV-infected hemophiliacs to file lawsuits in Tokyo and Osaka. More than two hundred plaintiffs (of whom nearly a third died) had joined the lawsuits by the time a settlement was brokered in 1996. Concerns about discrimination led the lawyers to persuade the courts to pioneer the use of numerical identifiers in all court documents and proceedings to protect plaintiffs' privacy under Article 92 of the Civil Code.[18] The opportunities these privacy protections provided for anonymous plaintiffs (*tokumei genkoku*) to participate in the movement without fear of exposure and for real-name plaintiffs (*jitsumei genkoku*) to appeal for public sympathy became a model for the subsequent HCV movement, as well as for the Hansen's disease movement discussed in the previous chapter.

As the Japanese HIV legal battle seemed to stall in 1994, a teenage plaintiff's decision to come out as a *yakugai* victim in 1995 helped turn the issue into a public scandal. Kawada Ryūhei was not the first HIV plaintiff to "reveal his real name" (*jitsumei kōhyō*), but his youthfulness attracted sympathy from fellow university students and much media attention.[19] The head of the Tokyo plaintiffs' legal team recalled "the importance of a symbolic [*shōchōteki*] figure like Kawada for the movement to connect with bystanders."[20] The plaintiffs' lawyers also leveraged the political fluidity created by the LDP's fall from power in 1993 for the first time since 1955 to urge politicians to support the plaintiffs. In response to mounting public indignation against the government in 1996, Kan Naoto, the new health minister from the LDP's small coalition partner, took the populist step of backing the claimants against his own ministry. Soon thereafter, the state concluded a court-mediated settlement with the HIV plaintiffs, providing 45 million yen (about $429,000) and medical subsidies to each victim—the largest award in HIV-related litigation worldwide.[21] Executives from the pharmaceutical companies sued in these cases also bowed their foreheads to the floor in what became an iconic apology to surviving victims. The government subsequently restructured regulatory agencies to enhance blood safety, and prosecutors successfully pursued criminal charges against a doctor, a government official, and three pharmaceutical executives.

Japan's HIV movement contributed knowledgeable lawyers, funding, and evidence for the subsequent HCV movement. In 2000, several lawyers who had represented HIV victims formed the Yakugai Hepatitis Study Group at the urging of the Japanese Federation of Liver Disease Patient Associations (Nikkankyō). They

---

18. See Koga Katsuhige, *Shūdan Soshō, Jitsumu Manual [A Practical Manual for Collective Litigation]* (Tokyo: Nihon Hyōronsha, 2009), 34–36.

19. Joanne Cullinane, "Tainted Blood and Vengeful Spirits," *Culture, Medicine and Psychiatry* 29, no. 1 (2005): 11–12.

20. Interview with Yasuhara Yukihiko, lawyer, Tokyo (May 26, 2008).

21. Feldman and Bayer, *Blood Feuds*, 75.

received data and institutional support from the NGO Yakugai Ombudsperson, which some lawyers had established in 1997 with their commissions from the HIV lawsuit.[22] Alongside Ienishi Satoru, a lawmaker from the opposition Democratic Party of Japan (DPJ) and a hemophiliac infected with both HIV and HCV, they successfully pressured the government to investigate "fourth route" HCV infections (i.e., not through sex, mother-to-child, or hemophilia-related routes). Although Ienishi might appear to have been an early elite ally for the HCV movement, his questions in the Diet predated the movement's emergence and made no references to redress. Instead, the government inquiry he had pushed for catalyzed the formation of an HCV redress movement because in mid-2002 the inquiry officially confirmed a link between blood products and mass HCV infections but denied any governmental wrongdoing.[23] In the wake of these findings and media coverage of them, the newly formed National HCV Lawyer Group was able to recruit plaintiffs by holding a thousand free legal consultations.[24] As detailed below, the resulting HCV movement drew on the HIV movement for ideas about issue framing, legal arguments, tactics, media contacts, and recruiting supporters and political allies. It also eventually tapped into reservoirs of public concern about *yakugai*, or drug-related damages, left over from the national scandal of HIV in 1996. While the HIV lawyer groups in Tokyo and Osaka had remained separate and only informally coordinated, the lawyers who mobilized for the HCV lawsuits "purposefully started out as one organization so as to better coordinate litigation with publicity, activism, and lobbying."[25]

By comparison, Korean HIV-infected hemophilia patients' campaign for redress was more recent and received less public attention. Still, it also helped catalyze an HCV movement. In autumn 2002, preparations for HIV-related litigation began shortly after the *DongA Ilbo* reported on new research linking nearly all Korean hemophiliacs' HIV infections to factor IX allegedly produced from blood purchased from two HIV-positive Korean men.[26] Using a new technique that assessed the genetic similarities between the hemophilia patients' HIV and the donors' viruses, the researchers hypothesized that Korea's Green Cross Corporation had failed to properly implement virus inactivation procedures when it started

---

22. Interview with Minaguchi Masumi, lawyer, Tokyo (May 30, 2008). See also http://www.yakugai.gr.jp.

23. MHLW, *Fibrinogen Seizai ni yoru C Gata Kanen Virus Kansen ni Kansuru Chōsa Hōkokusho* [*Report on the Investigation into Hepatitis C Infections from the Product Fibrinogen*], August 29, 2002, http://www.mhlw.go.jp/houdou/2002/08/h0829–3.html.

24. Yakugai Kanen Soshō Zenkoku Bengodan, website at http://www.hcv.jp/main.html.

25. Interview with Noma Kei, lawyer, Tokyo (May 29, 2008).

26. Shin Dong-ho, "Hyeolubyeong 10yeomyeong AIDS Gamyeom [About 10 Hemophiliacs Infected with HIV]," *DongA Ilbo*, September 13, 2002.

producing factor in 1989 and 1990.[27] In response to the story, KOHEM boycotted the corporation and elicited public statements of support from several regional legislatures. Most major Korean news outlets also covered the HIV issue, albeit with single stories. GCC, however, denied liability by arguing that imported factor or blood transfusions could have caused the infections. Reflecting the growing use of libel charges to silence opponents in Korea, GCC also filed a libel suit against the lead researcher on the study, Cho Young-keol. Later in 2002, the Korean government launched an ultimately inconclusive inquiry, as it had in 1992 after HIV infections among hemophiliacs were first discovered. Yet, unlike in Japan, neither Korean inquiry considered potential HCV contamination in blood products.

Whereas Korea's HIV victims had retreated to avoid the stigma associated with AIDS during the government's first inquiry in 1992, they took action after the research was reported in 2002. KOHEM contacted a lawyer, who worked pro bono to help sixteen hemophiliacs and fifty-three family members file a collective lawsuit against GCC in February 2003. By contrast with the approach taken in the Japanese HIV litigation, Korean plaintiffs' lawyers and KOHEM leaders decided that "listing the government as a defendant would make the lawsuit too difficult to win."[28] Moreover, since Korea lacks the procedural rule that enabled Japanese plaintiffs to hide their identities, plaintiffs generally avoided the courtroom and publicity for fear of discrimination. As one plaintiff's father later explained in court, "The family had feared for two decades that our son's HIV and HCV infections might be revealed before he could complete high school and college."[29] Instead, KOHEM handled most tactical decisions, lobbying, and media relations and relayed information between the lawyers and plaintiffs. This pattern persisted in Korea's HCV lawsuit that began the following year, before the first ruling in the HIV case.

Although Korea's HIV and HCV lawsuits overlapped temporally, developments in the HIV case still affected the HCV movement. On the positive side, the HCV movement benefited from the close working relationship that developed between KOHEM and the researcher Cho Young-keol and HIV plaintiffs' lawyers, who became ardent advisers and supplied evidence to bolster the HCV plaintiffs' claims. KOHEM and HCV plaintiffs' lawyers also stressed the severity of the HCV epidemic among hemophiliacs in all meetings with reporters and politicians, even if they often obtained such meetings primarily because of concern about HIV. Additionally, a district court's 2005 ruling in favor of one of the HIV plaintiffs'

27. Heungsup Sung et al., "Phylogenetic Analysis of Reverse Transcriptase in Antiretroviral Drug-Native Korean HIV Type 1 Patients," *AIDS Research and Human Retroviruses* 17, no. 16 (2001): 1551.

28. Interview with Kim Yeong-ro, KOHEM (February 27, 2009).

29. Author's observation of a court hearing in the HIV lawsuit, Seoul High Court (July 15, 2013).

claims gave the HCV plaintiffs "court-certified evidence that Green Cross's heat-treatment procedures were not fail-safe and deserved scrutiny."[30] Yet the judges hearing the HCV case did not accept this line of argument. More broadly, the HIV lawsuit strained KOHEM's relations with government officials, GCC, the Korea Hemophilia Foundation (KHF), and doctors. Possibly under pressure from GCC, the KHF demanded in 2007 that KOHEM vacate its offices in their shared building, which is owned by GCC. The plaintiffs in both lawsuits cited such "constraints" and "intimidation" when arguing that "there were objective reasons that they could not have exercised their right to seek compensation within the ten-year statute of limitations."[31] Fear of losing research funding or facing libel charges like those that GCC had filed against Cho Young-keol may have also had a chilling effect on journalists or potential expert witnesses.

Korea's HCV victims may have started their quest for redress without a model like the successful HIV movement, but Korea's HIV movement affected the parameters of HCV victims' claims making. Most significantly, the Korean Supreme Court recognized the need to relax the statute of limitations and evidentiary standards in the HIV case, overturned a high court's 2008 decision against the plaintiffs, and remanded the case to the high court. In the wake of this 2011 ruling, the plaintiffs began two fitful rounds of court-mediated settlement talks with GCC. In the settlement finally brokered in late 2013, the plaintiffs relinquished the right to pursue legal claims against GCC in the future in exchange for undisclosed payments of up to 220 million won (about $200,000) for each victim from the corporation, which did not admit liability. Although "not entirely satisfied with the settlement," plaintiffs and their families agreed on the desirability of "escaping the decade-old legal battle."[32] As detailed below, the settlement raised hopes of a resolution for the HCV movement.

Undeniably, the Korean HIV movement did not provide as deep a pool of resources, issue frames, and allies as the Japanese *yakugai* AIDS scandal had for Japan's HCV victims, but the distinctive legacies of HIV-related activism in Japan and Korea do not, on their own, account for the divergent outcomes of the two HCV movements. Rather, as the rest of this chapter will show, the HIV movements affected how the public, civic groups, the media, and lawmakers responded to HCV victims' claims, and thus the way in which the political conflicts over redress expanded.

---

30. Interview with U Gweng-pil, lawyer. Interview with Cho Young-keol, doctor, Seoul (August 11, 2009).

31. Kim Yeong-ro, "Hyeolaek Yurae Baireoseu (HIV, HCV) Sosong e Gwanhan Bogoseo (2) [Report on the Blood-Borne HIV and HCV Lawsuits (2)]," *Uri KOHEM [Our KOHEM]*, December 2009, 11.

32. Personal communication with Kim Yeong-ro, KOHEM (November 10, 2013).

Taking the Government and the Producers to Court

Starting in 2002 and 2004, respectively, individuals in Japan and Korea filed analogous collective lawsuits seeking redress for their drug-induced hepatitis C. The plaintiffs in both countries aimed to prove that the state and pharmaceutical companies had failed in their duties to monitor blood derivatives' safety and withdraw any products with safety or efficacy problems.[33] They also accused government officials and the producers of responding slowly to signs of mass HCV infections from blood products. The Japanese suits began in October 2002 with 16 anonymous plaintiffs (13 in Tokyo and 3 in Osaka) but gradually expanded to Fukuoka, Nagoya, and Sendai and included more than 200 plaintiffs by late 2007. By late 2004, 102 plaintiffs had joined Korea's single HCV lawsuit, filed in Seoul in July that year. Only 77 of them appealed the district court's unfavorable ruling in late 2007, and 44 plaintiffs remain on the case currently pending before the Supreme Court. As a proportion of the total HCV victims, however, more Koreans than Japanese mobilized to sue the state and the manufacturers.

Despite their analogous claims, the Japanese and Korean HCV movements took distinctive organizational forms. Since Korean plaintiffs were all hemophiliacs with HCV, they mobilized through and enjoyed organizational support from KOHEM. This patient association was founded by a group of patients' mothers in 1984 and renamed KOHEM when hemophilia patients took it over in 1989. Although KOHEM promotes the interests of all two thousand Koreans with bleeding disorders, it subsidized the HCV lawsuit. KOHEM staff also gathered medical records and coordinated publicity and lobbying with the plaintiffs' four lawyers, only one of whom remained on the case for the entire decade. Early on, the lawyers and KOHEM had discussed the idea of seeking help from Minbyeon, Korea's influential and progressive association of lawyers who had made litigation a popular tactic for activist groups in the 1990s.[34] But they deemed Minbyeon lawyers "too political" and worried that they might "take over the case for their own objectives."[35] Partly because KOHEM had more manpower and expertise and also because the lead lawyer moved his office to the southern city of Busan in 2008, the lawyers handling Korea's HCV suit, unlike those in the Japanese case, focused more on the court process, leaving broader activism to KOHEM. As will be detailed below, plaintiffs also entrusted most activities to KOHEM.

---

33. Japanese plaintiffs sued their government and Mitsubishi Tanabe Pharma Corp. (the successor to Japan's Green Cross), its subsidiary Benesis, and Nihon Pharmaceutical. Korean plaintiffs sued their government, the Korean National Red Cross (KNRC), and Korea's Green Cross Corporation.

34. Patricia Goedde, "Lawyers for a Democratic Society (Minbyun)," in *South Korean Social Movements*, ed. Gi-Wook Shin and Paul Y. Chang (London: Routledge, 2011), 224–44.

35. Interview with U Gweng-pil, lawyer.

As nonhemophiliacs, Japanese plaintiffs initially depended more on their lawyers because they had no other preexisting connections. Japanese lawyers had apparently "limited the scope of the lawsuits to nonhemophilic claimants to increase their chances of victory."[36] Japan's hemophilia community was also too wearied and divided from the difficult battle they had fought to redress their HIV infections.[37] As a result, the lawyers' free legal counseling proved essential for bringing together a critical mass of nonhemophilic HCV victims. When lawyers met with potential plaintiffs, they "helped them conceive of their suffering as *yakugai* and built relationships of trust with each plaintiff."[38] Nearly 150 Japanese lawyers signed onto the legal teams (*bengodan*) at the five court sites, though only a smaller core of lawyers was active. Such like-minded cause lawyers mobilized through diffuse networks centered in Tokyo, Osaka, and Kyūshū, starting with the Yakugai Hepatitis Study Group. For them, litigation was just one tactic to be coordinated with others, including publicity, lobbying, and demonstrations. Lawyers and plaintiffs developed closer relationships than did those in the Korean movement, especially through the plaintiff groups (*genkokudan*) they organized at each court site to provide plaintiffs with mutual support and raise local citizens' awareness of the issue. Japanese plaintiffs worked increasingly as coactivists alongside their lawyers inside and outside the courtroom through these organizations.

Yet neither the Japanese nor the Korean plaintiffs had an easy battle proving the defendants' negligence and the causal link between the defendants' actions and plaintiffs' HCV infections. Since Japanese law required doctors to keep patients' charts for only five years, many plaintiffs struggled to procure evidence that they personally had received tainted blood products (mostly fibrinogen and some factor IX), which the Japanese government acknowledged in 2002 had caused mass HCV infections—albeit without admitting negligence. The defendants also resisted releasing data about which hospitals had prescribed fibrinogen, so the lawyers used the "painstaking process" of freedom of information requests to force the defendants to release information.[39] Moreover, plaintiffs and defendants disagreed over *when* government and industry decision makers had had enough information about HCV contaminants that their inaction might be considered negligence. While the Japanese defendants claimed that they could not have known about or prevented contamination before 1988, the plaintiffs

36. Interview with Ōnishi Akahito, hemophilia patient, Tokyo (July 19, 2012).
37. Sano Ryūsuke, "Hemofilia Tomo no Kai Zenkoku Nettowaaku ni Tsuite [About the National Network of Hemophilia Associations]," comment no. 2998, CHPNet, September 30, 2008, http://log. chpnet.info/bbs3_pre/pslg2998.html#2998.
38. Interview with Sugiyama Shinichi, lawyer, Tokyo (May 22, 2008).
39. Interview with Ayukyo Machiko, lawyer, Tokyo (May 30, 2008).

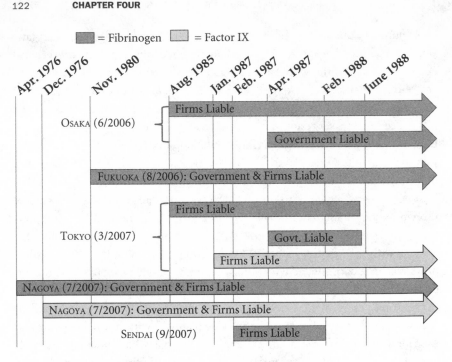

FIGURE 4.1   Japanese HCV court rulings 2006–7

argued that Japanese regulators and producers should have foreseen the dangers of hepatitis contamination in 1977, when the U.S. Food and Drug Administration (FDA) had withdrawn its approval of Japanese-made fibrinogen because of evidence of inefficacy and hepatitis contamination.[40] The plaintiffs also cited a Japanese doctor's March 1987 report to the Ministry of Health and Welfare that eight of his patients in Aomori had contracted hepatitis after receiving unheated fibrinogen. In response to this report, the producer had issued a voluntary recall of unheated fibrinogen and brought a heat-treated version of the drug to market two months later. Yet the MHW did not order the producer to issue warnings about fibrinogen or recall it until June 1988. As a result of these debates, the courts hearing HCV cases found the state and producers liable but for different periods of time. Figure 4.1 depicts the variation among the Osaka, Fukuoka, Tokyo, Nagoya, and Sendai courts' rulings in 2006 and 2007 regarding the defendants' liability for HCV infections from fibrinogen and factor IX.

In Korea, proving that domestic clotting factor caused HCV infections has been even more difficult. Unlike the Japanese government, the ROK government

---

40. "Kyū Midori Jūji no Ketsueki Seizai, Bei de Kinshigo mo 10nen Hanbai 'Yakugai Kanen' Meihaku ni [Drug-Induced Hepatitis Clear from Sales of Former Green Cross's Blood Product Ten Years after U.S. Prohibition]," *Yomiuri Shimbun*, March 21, 2002.

has not acknowledged a link between the two. Causation is further complicated by the fact that Koreans with hemophilia used combinations of blood transfusions, imported factor concentrates, domestic factor concentrates, and older blood products as treatment practices evolved in the 1980s and early 1990s. The plaintiffs' lawyer urged "the defendants to share the burden of proof with plaintiffs, as has become standard practice in Korean environmental and product liability cases."[41] But the Korean manufacturer (Green Cross Corporation) withheld documents regarding production dates and lot numbers that could be correlated with plaintiffs' medical charts. In addition, the plaintiffs have struggled to convince the court to waive the statute of limitations. By dismissing all plaintiffs' claims in 2007, for example, a district court sided with the defendants' argument that the plaintiffs lacked the legal right to seek damages because most were infected more than ten years before filing suit (i.e., beyond the statute of limitations). The plaintiffs' side countered by referencing rulings in recent lawsuits related to authoritarian-era state violence in which judges had waived the statute of limitations because plaintiffs had not been free to claim damages. The plaintiffs' lawyer emphasized that HCV victims could not have exercised their right to seek damages from the defendants within the ten-year time frame because they depended on GCC and state subsidies to treat their hemophilia. In early 2013, however, a high court in Seoul recognized a causal link between clotting factor and HCV infections for the first time. It found the defendants liable for thirteen plaintiffs' HCV infections but dismissed the sixty-three other plaintiffs' claims because they had either not yet developed symptoms or had been infected before May 1991, when the test for HCV contamination became available in Korea. Both sides appealed this ruling to the Supreme Court, where it is waiting to be heard.

Despite such legal debates over causation and liability, several factors indicate that the Japanese and Korean HCV epidemics had similar underlying causes. First, the high rates of HCV infection among Korean hemophiliacs (nearly 50 percent) relative to the general population (less than 1 percent) mirror the figures in other countries affected by tainted blood products. Second, although the causes of the blood-borne epidemics are complex and vary in specifics from country to country, official inquiries in Japan, the United States, Britain, and Canada have identified common factors that led producers and regulators to respond more slowly than they should have to signs of an epidemic. These include the slow diffusion of scientific awareness, profit considerations, lax regulations, and cozy ties between government and industry. For example, in order to implement medical drug

---

41. U Gweng-pil's report in Kim Yeong-ro, "Hyeolaek Yurae Baireoseu (HIV, HCV) Sosong e Gwanhan Bogoseo (3) [Report on the Blood-Borne HIV and HCV Lawsuits (3)]," *Uri KOHEM [Our KOHEM]*, January 2010, 11.

policy efficiently in Japan, LDP politicians with health policy expertise, health ministry officials, doctors' associations, and the main industry players formed close relationships.[42] In Korea there was also close coordination between and little oversight of industry players, doctors, and government officials.[43] Retired health officials in both countries joined the boards of pharmaceutical companies, facilitating medical drug advances but also impeding officials' ability to quickly grasp and address the spread of HCV among citizens. In court, as well as while meeting with lawmakers or seeking media coverage, Japanese and Korean HCV victims cited such similar structural factors when demanding redress from their governments and the producers for their infections.

Claiming and Shaming Inside and Outside the Courtroom

Alongside their lawsuits, Japanese and Korean HCV victims sought to raise public awareness of their cause and attract support from political elites in order to enhance their leverage over the state and industry actors they held accountable for their infections. While the Korean movement gained support from a lawmaker relatively quickly, the Japanese plaintiffs encountered less receptivity from political elites at first. Instead, the Japanese movement invested more in mobilizing victims, building local bases of societal support, and cultivating sympathetic coverage from local and regional news outlets. Even though both countries' HCV movements began with litigation, therefore, the Japanese conflict over redress for victims of HCV-tainted blood products expanded in a more bottom-up fashion. By examining the nature of victims' participation, supporting groups' activities, media coverage and editorials, public opinion polls, and lawmakers' actions in Japan and then Korea, this section analyzes how these patterns of conflict expansion created distinctive pressures that contributed to greater redress in Japan.

The Hepatitis C Issue in Japan

Although the two collective lawsuits filed in October 2002 marked the beginning of the Japanese HCV movement, HCV-tainted blood products—but not redress for HCV victims—had already attracted public and political attention. The government's lackluster response is what first motivated the movement for redress.

---

42. Feldman and Bayer, *Blood Feuds*, 61–63, 72–74.
43. Gang Geon-il, *Hanguk Jeyak ui Jipyeong [The Prospects for Korean Pharmaceuticals]* (Seoul: Cham Gwahak, 2011), chap. 13–14.

The *Yomiuri Shimbun* had revealed in March 2002 that Japan had continued to approve Japanese-made fibrinogen until 1988, even though the U.S. FDA had banned the blood product in 1977. One indicator of the impact of this scoop is that after March each of the main dailies ran nearly ten articles per month mentioning HCV.[44] Moreover, the Japanese government drafted a bill concerning the safety of blood products, which the Diet passed in July, and offered HCV testing even while repeatedly denying wrongdoing. Such denials amid what the plaintiffs considered clear evidence of wrongdoing and negligence emboldened plaintiffs and their lawyers to pursue legal action. Yet since many observers perceived that the government had already resolved the HCV issue in summer 2002, the nascent HCV redress movement struggled to sustain national visibility. Indeed, by late 2002, the number of articles mentioning HCV in the three main dailies had fallen to below five per month, and few referenced the lawsuits. Initial political closure and the successful model of grassroots mobilization provided by the *yakugai* AIDS and Hansen's disease movements drove Japan's HCV victims to focus instead on leveraging their lawsuits to expand the pool of redress claimants and cultivate local bases of support among ordinary citizens. They sought to "spread the realization that the government and the producers had committed a wrong."[45]

LAWSUITS, IDENTIFIABLE PLAINTIFFS, AND LOCAL SUPPORT BASES

Japan's HCV plaintiffs first started gaining support from civic groups and ordinary citizens when a personally identifiable plaintiff began to tell her story in April 2003. Yamaguchi Michiko revealed her name because a local lawyer had convinced her that "a personally identifiable plaintiff was crucial for appealing to the public and the media."[46] As they later would for each new real-name plaintiff, the lawyers choreographed her announcement to coincide with a batch of fifteen new plaintiffs and the start of litigation at a third court site—Fukuoka. All other plaintiffs—who numbered thirty at that point nationwide—however, had availed themselves of the pseudonym system developed in the HIV lawsuits to protect their privacy. Yamaguchi was initially wary of exposing herself and her family to the risks that publicity entailed, but she said she came to feel that she was "fighting for justice, not just for herself, but also for other victims and future generations of Japanese." She had researched Japan's HIV lawsuits and

---

44. Data from the digital databases of the *Yomiuri Shimbun, Asahi Shimbun,* and *Mainichi Shimbun,* counting articles in the national morning editions that mentioned "C gata kanen" (HCV).
45. Interview with Noma Kei, lawyer.
46. Based on an interview with Yamaguchi Michiko, lead HCV plaintiff, Tokyo (June 16, 2009).

other redress movements at her local library and recalled feeling "strongly that directly affected parties [*tōjisha*] gained power by standing at the front of the movement." The lawyers' experiences representing victims of industrial pollution or defective food products and medicine had taught them "the importance (and the challenges) of putting the plaintiffs first" in order to gain public sympathy.[47] Yamaguchi's example helped the lawyers recruit additional plaintiffs and strengthened their case. Several plaintiffs who later joined the suit in Fukuoka specifically noted how "inspiring Yamaguchi was" and how the lawyers, many of whom had recently won a historic victory against the state in the Hansen's disease case in nearby Kumamoto, had "awakened a legal consciousness in plaintiffs that helped [them] become active in the movement."[48] Another plaintiff also recalled realizing that "those of us who had medical records had to raise our voices for those victims who had no records."[49] The growing number of plaintiffs, even if they were mostly fighting under pseudonyms, lent credence to Japanese victims' claims in the eyes of potential supporters in the legal, media, activist, and political spheres. By 2008, the lawyers had convinced about 10 percent of the two hundred plaintiffs to use their real names, but this did not prevent anonymous plaintiffs from participating in activism and lobbying activities, as discussed below.

Yamaguchi's and subsequent plaintiffs' decisions to use their real names had several important effects on the movement's efforts to gain third-party support. They provided local citizens with a sympathetic focal figure, and their personal accounts attracted local media attention. An advocate of HCV victims in Tokyo noted that supporter groups (*shien dantai*), which concerned citizens often form around particular plaintiffs or accused persons in Japan, grew "especially active once Yamaguchi revealed her name because they could rally around an identifiable person."[50] Citizens who became supporters of HCV plaintiffs attended lectures that the real-name plaintiffs gave, informed themselves about drug-related disasters and drug safety, contacted their Diet members, and told their friends about the HCV issue. University students, initially mobilized through seminars with professors who were interested in social justice issues, organized events on campuses to raise awareness about HCV and folded flyers alongside real-name and anonymous HCV plaintiffs.[51] Even some leprosy survivors, along with

---

47. Interview with Itai Masaru, lawyer, Kumamoto (May 15, 2009).
48. E.g., Interview with Sakata Kazue, HCV plaintiff, Tokyo (June 25, 2009).
49. Personal communication with Fukuoka plaintiff no. 11 (March 15, 2011).
50. Tokyo HCV Supporter Group, *Yakugai Kanen Soshō wo Shien Suru Kai (Tokyo) Kirokushū [Collected Documents from the Tokyo Association to Support the Iatrogenic Hepatitis Lawsuit]*, March 1, 2012, 4, http://www.gaiki.net/yakugai/hc/lib/12318yha.pdf.
51. Interview with Yamaguchi Michiko, lead HCV plaintiff. Interview with Sakata Kazue, HCV plaintiff.

citizens who had backed the leprosy plaintiffs, attended rallies in support of the HCV plaintiffs because they were "outraged at the government's negligence" in the HCV case.[52] Through their activism, supporter groups accepted—and then propagated—the plaintiffs' and lawyers' framing of the HCV issue. Redress claimants emphasized their demands' relevance for all citizens and the government's failure. As one lawyer asserted, "We were not just doing this to get compensation for [our plaintiffs]. We [wanted] to ensure that everybody in this country who is suffering from hepatitis can get the help they need, and that a scandal of this kind never recurs."[53]

Although plaintiffs struggled until 2006 to break into the relatively homogeneous mainstream national media, which gave more coverage to the state and producers' denials of responsibility, they found local and regional news outlets more receptive. Real-name plaintiffs' accounts, told in the victims' "raw voices" (*nama no koe*), catered to local media outlets' desire for human interest in their stories and photo ops.[54] The movement aimed to have "the media convey images that convince ordinary citizens that they cannot permit [*yurusenai*] such victimization."[55] The HCV movement also emphasized its connection to the HIV scandal of the 1990s by invoking the term *yakugai* and suggesting that the government had not fully addressed the sources of that problem. In spreading this issue framing, it helped that the earlier HIV conflict had introduced journalists to the technical details of blood products. The lawyers reconnected with journalists they had known during the HIV conflict.[56] Since court hearings occurred only once every few months, maintaining a media presence, albeit local, through local activism was also crucial for sustaining the movement's momentum. Through such grassroots mobilizing, real-name plaintiffs became publicly recognizable figures, especially in Kyūshū supermarkets, as one plaintiff commented. But the fact that a reporter in Tokyo mistook Yamaguchi for a lawyer in 2006 revealed what Yamaguchi described as "a distressing lack of national media coverage."[57]

RULINGS AND A NATIONAL PLAINTIFF ORGANIZATION

The combination of grassroots mobilizing and a series of court rulings—albeit inconsistent ones—eventually enabled the Japanese HCV movement to break onto the national stage. The proximate cause of the movement's heightened

---

52. Interview with Naka Shuichi, leprosy survivor, Kumamoto (May 15, 2009).

53. Justin McCurry, "Japan Compensates Some of Its Hepatitis C Victims," *Lancet* 371, no. 9618 (2008): 1062.

54. Interview with Itai Masaru, lawyer.

55. Interview with Ayukyo Machiko, lawyer.

56. Interview with Shimizu Kenji, *Mainichi Shimbun* journalist, Tokyo (June 11, 2009).

57. Interview with Yamaguchi Michiko, lead HCV plaintiff (June 16, 2009).

national visibility was a journalist from the *Mainichi* newspaper, who knew the plaintiffs' lawyers from when he had covered Kyūshū in the 1990s, and had "convinced" his editor to run "an unprecedented series of five articles on the movement" in the paper's national edition in early 2006.[58] Until then, the defendants denied fault and brought considerable resources to bear in rejecting the plaintiffs' claims in the five lawsuits and related publicity. In addition to the fact that few plaintiffs still had charts to prove which blood products they had received, the plaintiffs' side also had trouble convincing doctors to testify on behalf of the victims. They apparently contacted more than a hundred doctors before they found their first expert witness.[59] To address such challenges, the lawyers from all five lawsuits shared research and evidence among themselves and sometimes even had the same witness go to multiple courts. One lawyer recalled that cell phone mailing lists helped them "share argumentation tips or evidence in real time."[60] In June 2006, however, the Osaka court handed down the first ruling in these cases, finding the state and producers responsible but only for some of the plaintiffs' infections.

In anticipation of a ruling from the Osaka court, plaintiffs from across Japan had met in Tokyo in May 2006 to strategize. Since the court battle could take years still, they decided they needed to adopt a political approach alongside the judicial one. As the Hansen's disease plaintiffs had, they decided to form a national plaintiff organization. Although their lawyers had had a national organization since the start of the movement, the plaintiff groups had remained decentralized, organized around each of the five court sites. The new national plaintiff organization elected Yamaguchi Michiko as their leader. Access to local media had helped them hone their public relations tactics and develop a loyal following at the local level. In mid-2006, though, they focused their activism on Tokyo, which still had no real-name plaintiffs, in order to "capture the attention of the national media and thus political elites."[61] They calculated (correctly) that stories coming from the press clubs attached to the Tokyo District Court and MHLW had higher chances of making it into the national news. Members of these press clubs also gradually warmed to redress claimants and would share useful inside information about politicians' calculations during the crucial phase of activism in December 2007 (described below). In 2006, the *Mainichi Shimbun* journalist who had engineered the series of articles on the movement also introduced Yamaguchi to his paper's

---

58. Interview with Esashi Masayoshi, *Mainichi Shimbun* journalist, Tokyo (June 17, 2009).

59. Iwasawa Michihiko, *Yakugai C Gata Kanen Onnatachi no Tatakai [The Battle of the Women Victims of Drug-Related Hepatitis C]* (Tokyo: Shogakukan, 2008), 136.

60. Interview with Noma Kei, lawyer.

61. Interview with Yahiro Mitsuhide, lawyer, Fukuoka (May 12, 2009).

editorial staffers, who were preparing editorials on the anticipated rulings from Osaka and Fukuoka.[62]

Focusing the movement on Tokyo, plaintiffs' lawyers arranged meetings with lawmakers so that they could urge lawmakers to support their cause. Although the defendants appealed the Osaka ruling, plaintiffs increasingly gained meetings with legislators after a surprisingly favorable August 2006 ruling in Fukuoka found that the state had failed to act in 1980 after the U. S. FDA withdrew approval for fibrinogen. But the minister of health, labor, and welfare refused to meet with plaintiffs, and the Fukuoka ruling was also appealed. Rulings in Tokyo in March 2007 and Nagoya in July 2007 similarly found the state liable for some plaintiffs' infections but were appealed. One of the plaintiffs' lawyers remembered feeling that "the multiple inconsistent rulings in the HCV case were a sign that the judiciary had regressed since the Kumamoto ruling [in the Hansen's disease case] and that [the HCV rulings] were hardening the bureaucracy's position" against redress claimants.[63] Ultimately, four of the five courts had ruled partly in plaintiffs' favor, but compared with the Kumamoto ruling in the Hansen's disease case, these rulings had a less decisive political effect because they differed.

ELITE ALLIES EMERGE

Instead, as a former cabinet minister recalled, "The lawsuits and plaintiffs' activism made hepatitis C a political issue."[64] The array of small supporter groups around each court site helped signal to political elites the breadth of societal concern about the HCV issue. And rulings in the cases in Osaka and Fukuoka put judicial pressure on these elites to address it. By fall 2006, there were about 130 plaintiffs, of whom 16 had revealed their real names. Even those who remained anonymous lobbied lawmakers for support and attended court-related events. As a result, the Japanese HCV movement gained elite allies in 2006. Soon after the Osaka ruling, the opposition DPJ formed the Hepatitis Headquarters to study the issue. Not to be outdone, the ruling LDP organized the Hepatitis Project Team.

Although the HCV plaintiffs strove to appear nonpartisan by lobbying all parties evenly, they benefited particularly from the early support of several DPJ lawmakers and the DPJ's ascendance in 2007. One DPJ legislator, Yamanoi Kazunori, decided to support the plaintiffs partly because he wanted to "bolster his credentials as a health and welfare expert" but also because a journalist friend predicted that the issue would become "a big political scandal."[65] In November 2006,

---

62. Interview with Yamaguchi Michiko, lead HCV plaintiff.
63. Interview with Yahiro Mitsuhide, lawyer.
64. Interview with Sakaguchi Chikara, former minister of health, labor, and welfare, Tokyo (July 9, 2009).
65. Interview with Yamanoi Kazunori, DPJ Diet member, Tokyo (May 20, 2009).

therefore, Yamanoi raised the HCV issue in a Diet subcommittee for the first time since the lawsuits had begun. From then on, he became an ardent ally and declared his small office "a home away from home for the plaintiffs," who came to Tokyo multiple times per month, often from Kyūshū.[66] Compared with the LDP, the DPJ also had a large number of actual victims, lawyers, and others with redress movement experience in its ranks. When the DPJ took control of the upper house after its victory over the LDP in the July 2007 election, the HCV issue gave the DPJ something on which to distinguish itself from the LDP. With this issue, it aimed to show that, according to one lawmaker, "the DPJ was, relative to the LDP, more open to citizens."[67] Like pension reform, the HCV issue highlighted the DPJ's pledge to reform the bureaucracy because the issue clearly illustrated the MHLW's failures.[68] Thus, particularly in fall 2007, the Hepatitis Headquarters held numerous public hearings and helped plaintiffs arrange meetings with key Diet members and officials. To increase pressure on the LDP-led coalition government to offer a political resolution to the HCV conflict, the DPJ-led upper house also proposed the HCV Assistance Measures Law in October 2007, though it did not pass.

Even with support from the DPJ, the movement continued to focus on activism in Tokyo to win third-party supporters who could give the movement leverage over key decision makers in the ruling coalition. As one plaintiff's mother explained, the plaintiffs had come to realize that the lawsuits "were not enough to move the government. . . . They needed the public on their side because the prime minister and cabinet seemed to pay close attention to public opinion and approval ratings."[69] After the Tokyo court's March 2007 ruling, therefore, plaintiffs staged sit-ins near the MHLW and the prime minister's residence. These events drew hundreds of plaintiffs and supporters, as well as several lawmakers, albeit mostly from the opposition parties.[70] Among them were Kawada Ryūhei, the poster child of the HIV movement, and the DPJ's Kan Naoto, who had facilitated a resolution to the HIV conflict. After one plaintiff died, the survivors also staged a "die-in," sprawling on the pavement in Hibiya Park to emphasize the high stakes in delaying redress. Then in June, more than four hundred plaintiffs, lawyers, and supporters marched on the prime minister's residence to demand a meeting with Prime Minister Abe Shinzō. Although officials had repeatedly refused to meet the plaintiffs, Abe mentioned hepatitis C in his daily press conference for the first time

66. Interview with Sakata Kazue, HCV plaintiff.
67. Interview with Matsuno Nobuo, DPJ Diet member, Tokyo (April 28, 2009).
68. Interview with a DPJ staffer, Tokyo (May 23, 2008).
69. Interview with mother of Fukuoka plaintiff no. 19, Tokyo (June 9, 2009).
70. Iwasawa, *Onnatachi no Tatakai*, 211–17.

that evening. Yet fiascoes related to the MHLW distracted journalists, especially in the MHLW press club, from the HCV issue. The health minister had to resign after referring to women as "baby-making machines," and then the MHLW was accused of having misplaced fifty million pension records. Abe's embattled government also faced a historic defeat by the DPJ in the upper house of the Diet in July 2007. Furthermore, even though the Nagoya ruling in July was the clearest articulation of the defendants' liability to date, a Sendai court ruled in the opposite direction, in the defendants' favor, in September. Abe's sudden but unrelated resignation several days after the Sendai ruling dealt a blow to the plaintiffs, who remember feeling that he "had personally betrayed them."[71] Thus the HCV movement's efforts to build momentum for a political resolution to its conflict, as the Hansen's disease movement had done in May 2001, were stymied several times in 2007.

To rectify this situation, the plaintiffs and their lawyers began a sustained lobbying campaign (*kokkai rōraa*) in fall 2007. They wanted to convince politicians to draft and pass legislation that would supply "uniform compensation [for all victims]" (*ichiritsu kyūsai*). Their first targets were lawmakers who belonged to each party's hepatitis task force. They carried spreadsheets listing targeted legislators and compared notes at the end of each day to make sure that they were pressuring all parties evenly.[72] The plaintiffs sought political but not partisan support. Teams of two or three plaintiffs, often accompanied by a lawyer, went door-to-door seeking meetings with lawmakers in order to relate their stories of hiding their disease from employers for fear of losing their jobs or of blaming themselves for their disease. All plaintiffs paid a small membership fee to help fund the most active plaintiffs' repeated trips to Tokyo. As a result of all this activity, legislators seemed "increasingly familiar with the small army of HCV plaintiffs, most of whom were women, roaming their office buildings."[73] But one journalist also recalled that there was a "palpable sense that something else was still needed to actually resolve the HCV issue."[74]

STOKING PUBLIC OUTRAGE

To give redress claimants' cause more momentum, several lawyers choreographed a publicity event that capitalized on the Japanese news media's penchant for competitive matching. In October 2007, they rereleased the so-called 418 list, which demonstrated that the producer and the MHLW had known about the HCV infections from tainted blood products in 2001 but failed to notify the 418

---

71. Interview with Yamaguchi Michiko, lead HCV plaintiff.
72. Author's participant observation of HCV plaintiffs' lobbying, Tokyo (May 20, 2009).
73. Personal communication with Kyūshū plaintiff no. 11 (March 15, 2011).
74. Interview with Esashi Masayoshi, *Mainichi Shimbun* journalist.

known victims. MHLW officials had given the list to members of the ministry's press club in 2002, after the government's inquiry into HCV infections. But the media had not publicized the list because it was part of a large number of documents, and officials had not explicitly flagged it. In 2007, however, the lawyers maximized its impact by alerting sympathetic journalists and making plaintiffs whose names appeared on the list available for media interviews. With lawyers' coaching, a DPJ politician also mentioned the list in the Diet, and the DPJ proposed special legislation for HCV victims.[75] Competing for the same story, Japan's main newspapers each published about thirty articles on the HCV issue in October, and that number had more than doubled by December.

The 418 list clearly embarrassed the month-old government of Prime Minister Fukuda Yasuo, who responded by calling on the government, producers, and plaintiffs to reach a resolution by the year's end. When Health Minister Masuzoe Yoichi met with plaintiffs and lawyers in November, however, he proposed that the state pay a onetime, lump-sum settlement to the national plaintiff group (without admitting government responsibility for the infections) and have the plaintiffs divide the money among themselves.[76] Plaintiffs' lawyers described this proposal as "unacceptable" and said it confirmed their "suspicions that the state was still trying to avoid or limit its liability, as it had in court."[77] In addition, in early December, the Osaka High Court proposed a settlement based on the Tokyo District Court's March 2007 ruling, which had defined defendants' liability most narrowly among the four rulings that favored the plaintiffs. The plaintiffs rejected the proposal because it discriminated among them according to when and how they had been infected, and they decried the state's attempt to "just throw money at [them]."[78]

In the face of continued government pushback, the plaintiffs redoubled their lobbying and activism. Many of them spent most of December in Tokyo, away from their families. With few plaintiffs using their real names, the burden of engaging the media and the public fell to five women, including Yamaguchi Michiko.[79] As December progressed, ignoring the HCV issue became less of an option because of the public outrage the movement incited. When plaintiffs were collecting signatures in the Ginza—Tokyo's central shopping district—to petition the state for comprehensive redress, for example, one plaintiff noticed that "passersby recognized [them] from TV and expressed more sympathy than at

75. Iwasawa, *Onnatachi no Tatakai*, 239.
76. Interview with Shimizu Kenji, *Mainichi Shimbun* journalist.
77. Interview with Yahiro Mitsuhide, lawyer.
78. Iwasawa, *Onnatachi no Tatakai*, 211–17.
79. Interview with Suzuki Toshihiro, lawyer.

previous petition drives."[80] In just one weekend, the plaintiffs gathered forty-five thousand signatures. Moreover, a march from the MHLW to the prime minister's office to demand a meeting with him failed to produce the desired meeting, but all the major TV stations covered the three hundred plaintiffs and their supporters live. And a survey conducted that month found that 87 percent of ordinary Japanese thought the prime minister should draft legislation to give restitution to all HCV victims.[81] He also faced pressure to do something about the issue from plaintiffs' elite allies in the DPJ, smaller opposition parties, the LDP's small coalition partner (Kōmeitō), and even his own party.[82]

REDRESS: A POLITICAL RESOLUTION

Redress claimants' activism had thus mobilized an array of third-party supporters who made the LDP and specifically Prime Minister Fukuda realize in late 2007 that they would suffer politically if they did not address the HCV issue. After Fukuda's approval ratings fell more than 10 percent between November and mid-December, one lawyer suggested that he might have remembered from his time as Prime Minister Koizumi Jun'ichirō's chief cabinet secretary during the Hansen's disease conflict that "decisive action could boost the prime minister's leadership image."[83] A more likely catalyst for Fukuda's decision to act was a note that the powerful LDP politician Yosano Kaoru apparently wrote to him outlining an HCV compensation law and urging the prime minister to save his government by taking action on this issue.[84] On December 25, 2007, the prime minister met with plaintiffs and admitted "the state's responsibility for causing immense harm to the victims and for failing to prevent the harm from spreading."[85] He also pledged to pursue redress legislation within the LDP. Echoing concerns within the HCV movement, the DPJ president, Ozawa Ichirō, criticized the prime minister's decision to have LDP lawmakers draft redress legislation, saying that the government should write the legislation since the infections were the government's responsibility.

---

80. Interview with Sakata Kazue, HCV plaintiff.

81. Hōdō Station-Asahi News Network Public Opinion Poll, reported in *Kanen Relay* (blog), December 11, 2007, http://kanenrelay.exblog.jp/i2/3.

82. Interview with Yahiro Mitsuhide, lawyer.

83. Interview with Ayukyo Machiko, lawyer. A *Nikkei Shimbun* poll showed that 46 percent of respondents did not support the Fukuda cabinet. "Nikkei Shimbun Opinion Polls (conducted December 14–16, 2007)," Mansfield Foundation translation, December 2007, http://www.mansfieldfdn.org/polls/2007/poll-07–34.htm.

84. Yumoto Hiroshi and Nakayama Shozo, "Poll Worries Prompted Government HCV U-Turn," *Daily Yomiuri*, December 25, 2007.

85. "Hepatitis C Bill Offering Aid, Apology Clears Diet," *Japan Times*, January 12, 2008.

Yet the different categories of people infected with HCV at different times and by different blood products made drafting such legislation difficult. As members of the Health, Labor, and Welfare Committee in the Diet discussed a draft bill in early January 2008, for example, they called on the leader of an emergent national network of hemophilia patient groups to present the views of the hemophilia community on HCV relief measures.[86] He criticized the bill, saying, "For us to be left out of the relief package is tantamount to being told that by having a congenital disease we should resign ourselves to being infected."[87] And Japanese hemophilia patients felt that their inclusion in the Diet hearing was "purely symbolic because the bill's content had already been decided."[88] Victims of hepatitis B-tainted blood also complained that the bill excluded them.[89] HCV plaintiffs negotiated with these related groups and publicly emphasized that they desired uniform compensation (*ichiritsu kyūsai*) for all persons infected with hepatitis because of faulty or negligent medical practices. Plaintiffs' lawyers emphasized this demand, even as they agreed with the bill's authors in the LDP's HCV task force to exclude HCV-infected hemophiliacs. One of the most visible real-name plaintiffs, Fukuda Eriko, summarized many victims' feelings about the bill thus: "This isn't the finish; it's just the start."

Despite the bill's limitations, both houses of the Diet unanimously passed the Hepatitis C Special Measures Law on January 11, 2008.[90] The law included an admission of government liability and stipulated amounts of monetary relief for people who had contracted HCV from contaminated blood products (12–40 million yen per person, or about $114,000–$381,000, depending on the severity of symptoms). Although its preamble contained important statements about the state's responsibility and an apology, the law provided financial relief (*kyūsai suru tame no kyūfukin*) to victims rather than the compensation (*hoshō*) provided in the Hansen's disease case, ostensibly to curtail the precedent that this law might set for other redress claimants. Furthermore, not all of Japan's estimated ten thousand HCV victims would be able to obtain redress because the

---

86. Sano, "Hemofilia Tomo no Kai Zenkoku Nettowaaku ni Tsuite."

87. McCurry, "Japan Compensates Some of Its Hepatitis C Victims," 1061.

88. Interview with a Japanese hemophilia patient, Tokyo (July 19, 2012).

89. The 2008 law did not include the estimated 1.4 million HBV victims, many of whom contracted hepatitis through blood transfusions or mass inoculations. In 2006 the Supreme Court found the state responsible for failing to prevent five victims' infections and for failing to respond appropriately. Thousands of HBV victims had filed lawsuits against the state, which were settled in in 2011.

90. The full title of this law is Tokutei Fiburinogen Seizai oyobi Tokutei Ketsueki Gyōko Dai9 Inshi Seizai ni yoru Cgata Kanen Kansenhigaisha wo Kyūsai suru tame no Kyūfukin no Shigo ni kansuru Tokubetsu Sochi Hō [Act on Special Measures concerning the Payment of Benefits to Relieve the Victims of Hepatitis C Infected through Specified Fibrinogen Concentrates and Specified Coagulation Factor XI Concentrates] (law no. 2, 2008).

government stipulated that victimhood had to be proven in court with medical charts or pharmacy records, which many victims lacked. The government did, however, reveal the names of hospitals where tainted blood products were used so that other victims could apply for state aid during an initial five-year window, which HCV victims successfully lobbied to extend in 2012. Especially important, the law established an independent commission with plaintiff representation that is tasked with investigating the epidemic's causes and the government's negligence. The producers also admitted liability in settlement negotiations in fall 2008, after plaintiffs relinquished the right to bring further claims, and began contributing to a fund managed by the MHLW.[91] About two thousand victims were receiving financial relief by 2013.

To reform policymaking processes, the MHLW also established regular meetings with the HCV victims, as well as with hemophiliacs and individuals who had contracted hepatitis B after being inoculated with the same needle as other people during vaccination drives. Through these meetings and other activism and lobbying efforts, HCV victims and other hepatitis sufferers achieved passage of the Hepatitis Policy Basic Law under the newly inaugurated DPJ government in 2009.[92] This law provided more comprehensive subsidies for the treatment of all forms of hepatitis and established a policy advisory panel that includes victims. As the leader of Japan's first non-LDP government since 1994, Prime Minister Hatoyama Yukio also apologized to HCV victims again. Despite facing many challenges early in their movement, the Japanese HCV plaintiffs managed to amass broad public support before persuading politicians to join their battle for redress. Largely as a result of this pattern of conflict expansion, which was facilitated by Japan's mediating sectors, the victims received comprehensive redress.

Hepatitis C-Related Claims in Korea

Korean hepatitis C victims began their quest for redress amid public concern about HIV-tainted blood. The Korean government's independent watchdog agency, the Board of Audit and Investigations (BAI), and the Health and Welfare Committee of the National Assembly had launched inquiries into the safety of the blood system in 2003, after several whistle-blowers had exposed evidence of

---

91. See Mitsubishi Tanabe Pharma Corporation, "Standard for Our Company's Payment Burdens Related to Fees Required for Benefit Payments and Other Operations, Based on the Special Relief Law Concerning the Payment of Benefits to the Patients of Hepatitis C," April 10, 2009, http://www. mt-pharma.co.jp/e/release/nr/2009/pdf/eMTPC090410.pdf.

92. Participant observation at the DPJ Hepatitis Headquarters' meeting, Tokyo (May 21, 2009). Kanen Taisaku Kihon Hō [Basic Law on Hepatitis Measures], (law no. 97, December 4, 2009).

viral contamination.[93] The Korean National Red Cross (KNRC) had started using a national computer database to enhance its management of the blood system in 2003, but several KNRC employees exposed the agency's indifferent response to signs from the database that tens of thousands of units of HIV- and HCV-tainted blood had been distributed for transfusions or the manufacture of clotting factor. One of the whistle-blowers detailed lax safety standards within the KNRC on the KBS news magazine *Chujeok 60bun* and would later become a supporter of the country's HIV and HCV redress movements.[94] For KOHEM, concerns about viral contamination were not new. In 1999, for example, KOHEM compelled the national health insurance system to cover part of the cost of foreign-made clotting factor because GCC's factor was tainted with hepatitis A.[95]

Yet in 2003 concerns regarding blood safety and the hemophiliacs' lawsuit over HIV-tainted blood products spurred the HCV victims to take legal action and helped their new lawsuit gain initial media coverage. About a dozen reporters attended the press conference launching the suit in July 2004. The plaintiffs' lawyer, U Gweng-pil, explained the case, and a representative plaintiff offered a heartfelt appeal for support, which one KOHEM staffer said "seemed to move some of the reporters in attendance."[96] Yet media coverage varied across outlets. The article in the progressive daily, *Hankyoreh*, was four times longer than the article in the conservative daily, *Chosun*.[97] *Hankyoreh* also reported the plaintiffs' point about the abnormally high HCV infection rates among Korean hemophiliacs, compared with the rest of the Korean population.[98] The online newspaper *Pressian* ran a sympathetic piece that drew parallels with factor-borne HCV epidemics abroad.[99] On TV, though, KBS reported on the safety of the blood supply without mentioning HCV. Thereafter, media attention fizzled because of the sluggish pace of the court process and the lack of other activism by plaintiffs. But

---

93. BAI, "Hyeolaek Anjeon Gwalli mit Hyeolaek Geomsa Sisutem unyong Bujeokjeong [Improprieties in the Operations of the Blood Safety Management and Inspections Systems]" (February 2004).

94. Interview with Kim Yong-hwan, KNRC whistle-blower, Seoul (February 13, 2009).

95. Shin Hye Son, "KFDA to Destroy 22 Batches of Tainted Hemophilia Drug," *Korea Herald*, January 29, 2000.

96. Kim Tae-il, "HCV Sosong Gijahoegyeon Hyeonjang Seukkechi [A Sketch of the Press Conference for the HCV Lawsuit]," *Uri KOHEM [Our KOHEM]*, July 2004, 3.

97. Kang Hun, "Hyeolubyeong Hwanja 23myeong 'Hyeolaek Gwanli Chal Mot' 10eok Sonbaeso [23 Hemophilia Patients File a Billion Won Lawsuit for 'Faulty Blood Management']," *Chosun Ilbo*, July 30, 2004.

98. Gil Yun-hyeong, "Hyeolubyeong Hwanjadeul Jipdan Sonbaeso Jegi [Hemophilia Patients Collectively File Damages Lawsuit]," *Hankyoreh Sinmun*, July 31, 2004.

99. Kang Yang-gu, "Hyeolubyeong Hwanja 23myeong, Jeoksipjasae 10eok Gyumo Sonhaebaesang Cheonggu [23 Hemophilia Patients File a Damages Lawsuit against the KNRC for 1 Billion Won]," *Pressian*, July 30, 2004.

concerns about blood safety created an opening for the nascent redress movement to contact political elites.

EARLY ACCESS TO AN ELITE ALLY

The Korean HCV movement gained backing from the conservative legislator Ko Gyeong-hwa within months of filing its lawsuit. As the lawmaker Kim Chun-jin had in the Korean Hansen's disease case, Ko found out about the HCV issue partly by happenstance, but she saw in the cause a way to boost her credentials as a health and welfare expert in the National Assembly and to criticize the progressive administration.[100] A journalist had introduced her secretary to the KNRC whistle-blower, who was looking for a legislator to pursue reforms to the blood system. The legislator he had previously worked with had stepped down from the National Assembly but agreed to deliver numerous documents related to viral contamination in whole blood and blood derivatives to Ko's office. This research and discussions with the whistle-blower and KOHEM officers formed the basis of Ko's efforts in 2005 to raise awareness about tainted blood products and to draft related legislation. Since Ko Gyeong-hwa's Grand National Party was in the opposition at the time, she "faced resistance from the bureaucracy when she requested official documents and evidence."[101] But KOHEM officers and especially the whistle-blower advised her staff on which documents to demand from the government and KNRC.

As a result, in September 2005, during the annual legislative audit of the government, she revealed that Green Cross had distributed clotting factor made from contaminated blood, even though GCC and government regulators had known that the blood was tainted.[102] GCC claimed that its virus inactivation procedures would have rendered the blood products safe. The revelation spawned isolated articles in several national newspapers but had limited impact on the attentive public. Its most significant outcome was to give the HCV movement a platform from which to appeal for other lawmakers' support and to directly pressure the state. Whereas a DPJ lawmaker's questions in the Diet in 2000 had predated and were separate from the country's HCV redress movement, Ko's revelations came after the Korean redress movement had begun. She therefore invited the secretary general of KOHEM, who is also a plaintiff, to testify in the National Assembly about HCV among persons with hemophilia. In his testimony, the secretary

---

100. Interview with Jeon Gyeon-su, former secretary of Ko Gyeong-hwa, Seoul (August 6, 2009).

101. Interview with Ko Gyeong-hwa, former GNP legislator, Seoul (August 4, 2009).

102. "AIDS Gamyeomja Hyeolaek, 26 se Yeoseongege Suhyeol . . . Yakpumeurodo Panmae [Blood from an HIV-Positive Person, Transfused to a 26-Year-Old Woman, Even Sold as a Drug]," media materials from the office of Assemblywoman Ko Gyeong-hwa (September 5, 2005).

general emphasized the unusually high rates of HCV infection (48 percent) among hemophiliacs, compared with 1 percent in the rest of the population. He also argued that the distribution of contaminated blood for use in making factor concentrates worried the hemophilia community because "there is no way to guarantee that the manufacturing process is 100 percent safe."[103] He mentioned the HCV lawsuit, but politicians' questions focused more on the safety of whole blood than on the state's responsibility for hemophiliacs' HCV infections.

Even though contaminated blood and blood products were on the political agenda in 2005, achieving policy changes that benefited the HCV-infected hemophilia population proved impossible. Ko Gyeong-hwa had proposed revisions to the Blood Management Law in early 2005 in response to her research about the KNRC. Based on recommendations from KOHEM and scholars, her bill called for an independent Citizens' Blood Management Agency—composed of people unconnected to the health ministry, pharmaceutical industry, or KNRC—to oversee the safety of the blood supply. The MOHW and KNRC opposed the revision, however, because the Comprehensive Blood Safety Policy of 2003 had already created an oversight committee, albeit not an independent one.[104] The 2003 policy had also established a compensation system for people infected as a result of the KNRC blood centers' errors with whole blood for transfusions. Yet the policy deemed the hundreds of hemophilia patients who had contracted HCV from tainted blood derivatives ineligible for compensation. Ko's 2005 bill also did not address the question of compensation for such victims of tainted blood products (as opposed to whole blood), but had it passed, it might have injected more transparency into the decision-making processes that had contributed to plaintiffs' HCV infections. When Jeon Hyeon-hee—the HIV plaintiffs' lead lawyer who also had medical expertise as a former dentist—was elected to the National Assembly from Korea's main progressive party in 2008, she used the Supreme Court 2011 ruling in favor of the HIV plaintiffs to try to revive Ko Gyeong-hwa's blueprint for revisions to the Blood Management Law.[105] But Jeon's bill became void when she failed to win reelection in 2012.

These ultimately unsuccessful efforts to enact legislation related to tainted blood and blood derivatives reveal some of the downsides of gaining elite allies early on. KOHEM's direct access to Ko Gyeong-hwa lowered incentives to mobilize plaintiffs, cultivate media coverage, form coalitions with like-minded civic

---

103. Kim Yeong-ro, KOHEM, testimony to the National Assembly's Health and Welfare Committee (September 23, 2005).

104. Interview with Jeon Gyeong-su, secretary.

105. Yang Hye-In, "10nyeonkan Muryo Byeonron Beopjeong Tujaeng . . . Hyeolaekgwanri Jaejeongbi Gihoiro Samaya [After Giving Pro Bono Legal Services to a 10-Year Long Legal Battle . . . We Must Use This Opportunity to Revise Blood Management]," Medical Today, October 4, 2011.

groups, or appeal for sympathy from the attentive public. KOHEM did organize a rally in conjunction with Ko's revelation in 2005. About 150 hemophiliacs, joined by members of a health policy NGO (Geongang Sesang Network) and the Korean Coalition of Disease Associations (Hanguk Jilhwan Danche Chongyeonhap), demonstrated outside the MOHW. They called for the government to accept responsibility for the blood-borne HIV and HCV epidemics, for the health minister to resign, for criminal charges to be filed against the director of the Korean FDA, and for safer blood products.[106] Yet the coalition proved fleeting and had no impact on the lawsuits. Whereas supporter groups in Japan had formed solely to back plaintiffs, these Korean organizations had agendas of their own. Without evidence of broad societal backing for her 2005 bill, Ko Gyeong-hwa struggled to persuade other National Assembly members to vote for it. Moreover, KOHEM did not marshal multiple voices in favor of redress for HCV victims when it was discussing tainted blood products with Ko. Her bill therefore focused more on issues related to the safety of whole blood (which anyone might need) than on blood products for Korea's two thousand people with genetic bleeding disorders. In fact, Ko does not recall spending much time discussing the HCV lawsuit with KOHEM officers.[107] Media coverage of her revelations in 2005 thus also failed to make the link to the HCV lawsuit, and her efforts did little to mobilize other third parties.

CLAIMING AND SHAMING IN OBSCURITY

After this spate of legislative activity in 2005, the Korean HCV movement received little support from any third parties for several years. Instead, it faced outright opposition from powerful actors and struggled in obscurity. The defendants stalled in the process of allowing the court to commission medical appraisals of the plaintiffs to determine their condition and potentially help establish when they were infected. They also rejected the plaintiffs' proposal to have the state conduct an epidemiological study of HCV to statistically show the extent of HCV infections in Korea relative to infections among hemophiliacs.[108] Meanwhile, Korea's largest newspaper, the *Chosun Ilbo*, did not publish a single article mentioning HCV for six months after Ko's efforts to raise the issue in the 2005 legislative audit. And in September 2007, the court ruled that the statute of limitations had expired for all 102 HCV plaintiffs, preventing any from

---

106. Protest flyer, KOHEM, "Hyeolaek Oyeomsago Jaebalbangjireul wihan Gukmingyutan Daehoe [Citizens' Rally to Call for the Prevention of a Reoccurrence of Tainted Blood Disasters]" (September 13, 2005), on file with the author.

107. Interview with Ko Gyeong-hwa, former GNP legislator.

108. Interview with U Gweng-pil, lawyer.

claiming damages. The court also accepted the defendants' argument that GCC production processes did not merit investigation because GCC had been using heat treatment. This contradicted the 2005 ruling in the HIV lawsuit, which had recognized a causal relationship between GCC-produced factor (which was allegedly heat-treated) and the HIV infections.[109] Signaling a nadir in both the HIV and HCV redress movements in 2007, the GCC-funded Korea Hemophilia Foundation also tried to evict KOHEM from its offices in the GCC-owned building that both organizations occupied. One KOHEM staff member summarized the extent to which redress claimants felt overpowered, saying that he "got the sense that GCC employees would follow him and buy a fancier drink for any journalist he met with. Then the journalist would call the next day and apologize for not being able to write a story."[110] Such opposition and the effects of having gained access to an elite ally early on hampered grassroots mobilizing in Korea.

Efforts to gain support from the attentive public through media coverage were further limited by several other dynamics. Initially, hemophilia patients were wary of publicity. KOHEM's former director recalled that in 2005, "many mothers [of hemophilia patients] called to complain about KOHEM being in the news . . . or stopped coming to the KOHEM offices"—visible from the Korea Hemophilia Foundation office—because they worried about how it would affect their sons' medical care.[111] Yet such fears faded over time amid the relatively low level of publicity the hemophilia community received. Online newspapers specializing in medical issues covered the HCV issue and the lawsuits. But most mainstream media coverage of HCV came from stories about the mismanagement of the blood supply and HIV infections from blood transfusions, which mentioned HCV-tainted factor for hemophiliacs only occasionally as a side note because it concerned fewer people. One KOHEM member described some news articles as outright hostile, "focusing on the high costs of blood products for hemophiliacs rather than the injustices patients endured."[112] And another quipped that "it seems like you can't get media attention without money."[113] Fear of libel suits—a growing phenomenon in Korea—may also have deterred reporters from covering the HCV issue in detail. Between 2000 and 2011, therefore, the number of articles in any given month mentioning hepatitis C in Korea's largest paper, *Chosun Ilbo*, peaked at six in July 2004, when the victims filed their lawsuit. To

---

109. Kim Yeong-ro, "Hyeolaek Yurae Baireoseu (HIV, HCV) Sosong e Gwanhan Bogoseo (1) [Report on the Blood-Borne HIV and HCV Lawsuits (1)]," *Uri KOHEM [Our KOHEM]*, November 2009, 10.

110. Interview with Han Jae-gyeong, former KOHEM staff, Seoul (July 19, 2013).

111. Interview with Kim Yeong-ro, KOHEM (July 27, 2009).

112. Interview with Han Jae-gyeong, former KOHEM staff.

113. Interview with a person affiliated with KOHEM, Seoul (July 6, 2012).

rectify this situation, KOHEM hired a press agency in 2006 and 2010, collected donations from its members to purchase ads in major papers, and contacted any journalist its members knew. KOHEM and its press releases gave journalists an obvious and credible source of information about tainted blood, the HCV lawsuit, and hemophilia.[114] Yet, since Korean news outlets compete for market share by becoming more diverse in the topics they cover and targeting narrow subaudiences, the average Korean citizen would have had difficulty piecing together a coherent picture of the plaintiffs' claims about the government and producer's liability for their HCV infections.

Compared with their Japanese counterparts, Korean HCV victims were also less involved in the movement, which further hampered efforts to use redress claimants' moral authority to raise awareness of the issue and build grassroots support. For instance, HCV-related lobbying in Korea normally involved just a few KOHEM officers but no rank-and-file plaintiffs or lawyers.[115] Although the HCV plaintiffs became bolder over time, only a dozen regularly appeared in court and fewer were available for media interviews.[116] One explanation for this lack of involvement is that Korean plaintiffs lacked the court-enforced privacy protections that Japanese plaintiffs had enjoyed. Their lawyer could request that journalists refrain from revealing plaintiffs' names but could not guarantee privacy. In addition, while Japanese HCV plaintiffs had had to build organizations and legitimacy from scratch, Korean plaintiffs started their quest for redress with an established representative organization, KOHEM. They could thus rely on KOHEM to coordinate publicity and activism surrounding the lawsuit. KOHEM's approach gave rank-and-file plaintiffs more ownership than Hanvit's did in the Hansen's disease case. Yet KOHEM's secretary general described the "dilemma with raising societal awareness" as being a trade-off between fears of discrimination and the need for hemophiliacs to "raise their voices in order to get public sympathy, which puts effective pressure on the state."[117]

Activating other civil society groups in support of redress was also more difficult in Korean than in Japan. KOHEM, as an established patient organization, had the resources and legitimacy to be able to contact other NGOs. But the fact that the plaintiffs did not form a separate organization from KOHEM may also have impeded efforts to gain backing from other activist groups. KOHEM exists primarily to advance the particularistic interests of its members—people with bleeding disorders. Historically, it achieved a number of successes. For example, in the

---

114. Interview, Kim Tae-il, KOHEM, Seoul (July 25, 2013).
115. Interview with Ko Gyeong-hwa, former GNP legislator.
116. Interview with U Gweng-pil, lawyer.
117. Interview with Kim Tae-il, KOHEM (July 10, 2012).

early 1990s it pressured the Kwangju Red Cross blood center to stop using plasma from paid donors, who were more likely to be HIV- and/or HCV-positive.[118] Yet KOHEM also negotiates regularly with the state for continued insurance coverage, medical subsidies, and drug approvals. Newer, more independent civil society groups in Korea sometimes criticize such cooperation. The HCV movement did try to tap into issue framings that resonated with the Korean activist sector's battles to roll back authoritarianism after 1987 and to fight *chaebeol* dominance. Calls for plaintiffs to join the HCV lawsuit had decried Korea's "authoritarian medical administration" and claimed to promote the rights of all who have suffered from a "medical world distorted by money."[119] Unlike Japanese efforts to enlist grassroots supporter groups, however, KOHEM's one-off collaborations with other organizations—such as the Korean Leukemia Patients' Association, the AIDS Patients' Association, and the Blood Donors' Association—were initiated by the groups' leaders and did nothing concrete to support the ongoing HIV and HCV lawsuits.[120] Instead, these other groups remained focused on their own priorities because they had staff, constituents, and influence to maintain. And, as had happened in 2005, the HCV plaintiffs' demands were usually subsumed within a more diffuse agenda that fit the concerns of all groups involved. The organizational structure and norms of Korea's activist sector at least partially encouraged such coalitional activism organized by NGO leaders. In Japan, by contrast, the norms in civil society had facilitated the formation of supporter groups that explicitly backed redress claimants.

PRESSING THE STATE IN OTHER VENUES

As the wheels of justice ground to a virtual standstill in 2008, KOHEM continued to press the government for non-redress-related benefits for HCV victims in other venues. Most important, it lobbied the government to expand patients' access to synthetically produced recombinant factor, which is much less likely to be contaminated than factor made from human plasma.[121] In the wake of

---

118. Interview with Kim Cha-hyeon, former director of the Kwangju Blood Center, Kwangju (August 15, 2009).

119. KOHEM, "C-Hyeong Ganyeom (HCV) Sosong Indan Annaemun."

120. Interview with a person affiliated with KOHEM.

121. Recombinant factor is synthetically produced using recombinant DNA technology rather than by purifying clotting factor from human blood. The U.S. FDA first approved two recombinant proteins in the early 1990s. New developments have refined recombinant technology, so that by 2008 recombinant-factor preparations contained no human-derived proteins, thus eliminating any potential for future viral transmission. Plasma-derived factor is safe today, but hemophilia patients still worry about the next virus that could contaminate their coagulation-factor preparations. Jerry S. Powell, "Recombinant Factor VIII in the Management of Hemophilia A," *Therapeutics and Clinical Risk Management* 5 (May 2009): 391–402.

the 2002 revelations regarding HIV-tainted domestic clotting factor, the state had approved imported recombinant factor but only for young hemophiliacs because they would not already be infected with HIV and/or HCV. National Health Insurance officials resisted covering recombinant factor for all hemophiliacs for two reasons. First, it is more expensive than plasma derivatives. Second, GCC lobbied the government to protect its near-monopoly market share of plasma-derived factor in Korea until it could develop its own recombinant factor production capabilities.[122] Yet 70 percent of hemophilia patients nationwide thought that the age limit on recombinant factor should be abolished.[123] Accordingly, KOHEM filed complaints with the National Human Rights Commission in 2007 and the Anti-Corruption and Civil Rights Commission in 2010 over such age discrimination. About a dozen National Assembly members also signed a KOHEM petition calling for the abolition of the age limit on recombinant factor. Then, in 2009, the movement gained another elite ally when the GNP legislator Shin Sang-jin used information from KOHEM to argue, during the legislative audit of the government, that the age limit violated constitutional clauses about citizens' equality and right to welfare protections. Finally, KOHEM members filed a case with the Constitutional Court in November 2010, alleging that the age limit on who could receive recombinant factor was unconstitutional. In what one KOHEM leader called "a major victory for Korea's hemophilia community," the Constitutional Court ruled in hemophiliacs' favor in June 2012.[124] And National Health Insurance started covering recombinant factor for all hemophiliacs the next day.

In this process of pursuing nonredress objectives, Korea's HCV movement tried, albeit largely in vain, to recover from the effects of gaining early access to an elite ally. For example, KOHEM organized a demonstration in 2011 in conjunction with the suit filed in the Constitutional Court over the age limit on coverage for recombinant factor. Yet "only about fifty people showed up and the demonstration felt much weaker than the one in 2005."[125] The movement also tried to downplay perceptions that the HCV issue was associated with any political ideology. Although a conservative GNP legislator raised the issue of the age limit in 2009, KOHEM also emphasized its relationship with the HIV plaintiffs' main lawyer, who had been elected to the National Assembly from the progressive Democratic Party in 2008. Yet both left the National Assembly in 2012. One

---

122. The KFDA approved the GCC's recombinant factor VIII, Greengene, in 2008. It came to market in July 2009.

123. KOHEM, "Hyeoluhwanu Wonwecheobang Hoetsu e daehan Seolmunjosa [Survey about the Prescription Benefits of Hemophilia Patients]," *Uri KOHEM [Our KOHEM]*, June 2006, 9.

124. Interview with Kim Yeong-ro, KOHEM, Seoul (July 15, 2013).

125. Interview with a person affiliated with KOHEM.

of the downsides of gaining elite allies before mobilizing broader societal concern is that there is little incentive for other politicians to take up the cause if the allies lose their seats or resign. Meanwhile, the high court to which HCV plaintiffs had appealed the 2007 ruling ended up scheduling few court hearings, on the premise that it was awaiting a ruling in the HIV case that was pending before the Korean Supreme Court. One HCV plaintiff complained, "If this case cannot be won, let's not continue with something that will hurt plaintiffs a second time."[126] By comparison with the Japanese case, Korean plaintiffs' efforts to leverage litigation to expand public awareness of the HCV issue and pressure the government into granting redress were frustratingly noncumulative. Litigation seemed to be going nowhere, and virtually no third parties still supported victims' demands for redress.

HEADWAY IN COURT

In fall 2011, however, the Korean Supreme Court issued a surprisingly favorable ruling in the HIV case, which had significant implications for the HCV lawsuit. The court relaxed the burden of proof, reinterpreted how the statute of limitations should be calculated, acknowledged the high likelihood (but not actual causality) that Green Cross's product had caused HIV infections, and remanded the case to a high court. As a result, the same high court judges heard the HIV and HCV lawsuits from late 2011 to early 2013, when a routine rotation of judges landed these cases before different panels of judges. Just before they rotated, however, the judges handed down the first favorable ruling in the HCV case. They found GCC and the KNRC liable for thirteen of the seventy-six plaintiffs' HCV infections. The ruling said nothing about the state's responsibility. Like the HIV ruling, the HCV decision won some media attention, which KOHEM tried to capitalize on. But it seemed that "individual reporters, rather than the news organizations they worked for, were interested in the movement."[127] And few plaintiffs were available to be interviewed. To facilitate communication among patients and their families, KOHEM had set up a private discussion forum ("café") on Daum in 2005, but the plaintiffs rarely used it to discuss the lawsuit and met infrequently in person.[128] Even on the day the high court handed down its ruling in the HCV case in 2013, only four plaintiffs and five relatives of plaintiffs attended the court hearing.[129] And although the high court supervised a settlement in the HIV case in late 2013, the Supreme Court has yet to hear the HCV case. At this

126. KOHEM, "Interview with a HCV Plaintiff," *Uri KOHEM [Our KOHEM]*, December 2009, 11.
127. Interview, Kim Yeong-ro, KOHEM, Seoul (July 3, 2012).
128. Interview with Han Jae-gyeong, former KOHEM staff.
129. Interview with Kim Tae-il, KOHEM (July 25, 2013).

writing, therefore, Korean HCV plaintiffs have almost no societal or political support and continue to wait for redress.

The comparison of the Japanese and Korean hepatitis C redress movements highlights how different patterns of conflict expansion create different incentives for politicians who consider taking up a victim group's cause and thus affect redress outcomes. Whereas most politicians in Japan came to support comprehensive redress because the plaintiffs had amassed broad public backing, Korean politicians supported the HCV victims out of personal concern and a desire to bolster their reputations as health and welfare experts. In Japan, HCV plaintiffs and their lawyers coordinated five lawsuits, albeit with inconsistent rulings, with activism and publicity to mobilize grassroots support that rendered the government politically vulnerable, much as the prior Hansen's disease movement had. The mainstream national media's tendency toward homogeneity also helped the movement eventually reach wide swaths of the public with a consistent narrative. By late 2007, nearly 90 percent of Japanese citizens in one survey favored granting redress to victims of HCV-tainted blood products. Such bottom-up pressure enabled the movement to attract elite allies who pushed through policy changes that amounted to full redress. Table 4.2 compares redress outcomes in the Japanese movement with those in the Korean movement, as they would score on the scale described in chapter 1.

By contrast, in the Korean case, having an elite ally early on diminished the impetus to mobilize plaintiffs and broader societal support around HCV victims' lawsuit against the state and a pharmaceutical company. It also left the movement's

TABLE 4.2   Redress outcomes in the HCV movements

COMPONENTS OF REDRESS	JAPAN	KOREA
Official inquiry	2—Yes: Victims on inquiry committee	0—No: Government dallying on epidemiological study
Apology	2—Yes	0—No
Compensation and other assistance	1—No compensation but monetary relief and medical care; better insurance coverage	0—No compensation, but expanded insurance coverage for safer drugs
Institutional reforms	2—More transparent decision making; victims hold regular meetings with officials	1—No change to decision-making process, but better testing and storage of blood products
TOTAL	FULL REDRESS (7)	NO REDRESS (1)

Note: The scores reflect the extent to which state actions fulfill each component of redress: fully (2), partially (1), or not at all (0).

elite ally with little leverage to realize policy changes. Since redress claimants had little support beyond Korea's two thousand-strong hemophilia community, their elite allies put more effort into advocating for policies that would affect a greater number of people, such as blood transfusion recipients, instead of just for redress for victims of HCV-tainted blood products. Korea's HCV plaintiffs also relied on KOHEM, the country's existing hemophilia patient association, and did not establish an independent organizational identity as Japanese HCV plaintiffs had done. The Korean media's diversity and the politicization of advocacy further hampered the movement's efforts to gain third-party support. A settlement in the lawsuit may still yield partial redress, but Korean HCV victims are unlikely to gain widespread attention and redress, as their Japanese counterparts did. Thus a comparison of HCV-related litigation and activism in Japan and Korea draws our attention to the effects of the dynamic web of interacting relationships among redress claimants, their supporters, a society's mediating institutions, and the state they seek to hold accountable.

5

THE NORTH KOREAN ABDUCTIONS AND ABDUCTEE FAMILIES' ACTIVISM

Since the Korean War, North Korea (the Democratic People's Republic of Korea, DPRK) has purportedly kidnapped thousands of foreign nationals. Some were literally abducted on foreign soil by North Korean agents. Others were captured and detained against their will after unwittingly venturing into North Korean territory or waters. The DPRK's apparent reasons for abducting foreign nationals were to obtain foreign language teachers, secure foreign identities for its spies, and gain propaganda fodder. In all, the country has allegedly abducted or detained nearly four thousand South Koreans, at least seventeen Japanese, and individuals from a dozen other countries since 1953. These abductions and detentions broke international norms, violated other nations' sovereignty, and caused pain to thousands of families, who had little information about their loved ones' whereabouts.

In the late 1990s, families of suspected abductees began organizing in Japan and South Korea. They wanted to discover whether their missing relatives were still alive and press for their return. The abductions issue and families' activism are usually considered in terms of foreign policy or inter-Korean relations. But besides blaming the DPRK, the associations of abductee families in Japan and South Korea also held their own governments accountable. The Japanese families faulted their government for failing to protect its citizens, thoroughly investigate suspected abductions, and pressure the DPRK into releasing abductees. South Korean abductee families made analogous accusations and contended that their government had also subjected them to systematic discrimination, police surveillance, interrogations, and even torture in the 1970s and 1980s because a family member was or had been in the North. From their own governments, the family associations in both countries sought full inquiries into the abductions, official recognition of their suffering, compensation and financial assistance, and more proactive measures to rescue abductees still believed to be in North Korea. Despite being deeply intertwined with thorny foreign policy questions, therefore, these movements provide interesting parallels with wholly domestic redress movements such as those analyzed in the previous chapters.

If considered through the lens of conflict expansion, both movements gained elite allies early on, which had implications for the redress outcomes each movement achieved. Within several weeks of the formation of Japan's abductee family association in 1997, more than 120 Diet members organized to tackle the abductions issue. Similarly, South Korea's conservative party formed a committee to handle abductee-related policy in July 2000, several months after the progressive president Kim Dae-jung's policy of rapprochement with North Korea, known as the "Sunshine Policy," had prompted Korean abductee families to mobilize. The rapidity of political elites' reactions partly reflects the issue's links to core national security concerns, a connection that complicates any explanation of the form and efficacy of these movements. Most analyses focus on the fact that Japanese abductee families obtained much more societal support after gaining such elite allies. Indeed, Japanese public sympathy for the families ballooned, and they gained nearly unassailable moral authority after the late North Korean leader Kim Jong-il admitted in September 2002 that DPRK agents had kidnapped thirteen Japanese citizens in the 1970s and 1980s. As a result, Japanese abductee families and their political allies compelled significant foreign policy changes, including unilateral sanctions and the prioritization of the abductions issue at the Six-Party Talks, held intermittently among the Koreas, the United States, Russia, China, and Japan from 2003 to 2009 to address North Korea's nuclear weapons program. Korean abductee families campaigned in comparative obscurity. Although ROK abductees outnumber Japanese abductees by twenty-five-fold and refugees from the North (including nine escaped abductees) have confirmed the abductions, third parties' reactions to the families' activism are contingent on and often overshadowed by broader dynamics in inter-Korean relations.

These clear differences between the two movements, however, obscure a surprising parallel that comparison with other victim redress movements reveals: both abductees' movements have elicited partial redress. In response to families' pressure and new evidence, the Japanese and ROK governments began investigating alleged abductions and requesting information from Pyongyang in the late 1990s. Both governments also enacted reforms to thwart future abductions and prevent the kinds of hardship that abductee families had endured. Yet neither the ROK nor Japan has apologized for its treatment of suspected abductees and their families, preferring to focus more on North Korean wrongdoing. Tokyo provided financial assistance only to abductees who returned to Japan, but families of abductees who have either died or still remain in the North are not eligible for such support. The ROK government gave no-fault stipends to families of still-missing abductees and returnees while denying compensation to all but one applicant. Tokyo also has less transparent procedures than the ROK for applying to have a person recognized as an abductee.

I trace these similar levels of redress to the fact that both movements gained elite allies early on. Subsequent differences in the extent of grassroots mobilizing help account for the distinctive content of redress in each country and their government's other actions.[1] These cases, therefore, present an opportunity to explore how the costs of early access to elite allies may vary depending on dynamic interactions among redress claimants and other third-party supporters. Many observers consider the abductions issue an idiosyncratic problem without parallels in other policy domains.[2] A few scholars have started systematically comparing Japanese and South Korean abductee families' activism.[3] I aim to bring these interrelated movements into comparison with other victim redress movements. Although another state (the DPRK) is the primary villain involved, these cases still illustrate the downsides to gaining elite allies early in a conflict and the importance of analyzing social movements and their efforts to mobilize third-party supporters in dynamic and relational terms.

Naming and Blaming: The Human Toll of North Korea's Abductions

Most foreign nationals allegedly abducted or detained by North Korea after 1953 were from the ROK and Japan, although the number of people abducted and the duration of their detention in North Korea varies (see table 5.1). The ROK government lists 3,835 citizens as having been captured since 1953, primarily during

---

1. On these differences, see Celeste L. Arrington, "The Abductions Issue in Japan and South Korea," *International Journal of Korean Studies* 17, no. 2 (Spring–Summer 2013): 108–39.

2. For an exception, see Jeon Yeong-pyeong, ed., *Hanguk ui Sosuja Jeongchaek [Korea's Policies toward Minorities]* (Seoul: Seoul National University Press, 2010), chap. 10.

3. Celeste Arrington, "Interest Group Influence in Policy-Making Processes" (paper presented at the Annual Meeting of the American Political Science Association, Chicago, 2007); Richard J. Samuels, "Kidnapping Politics in East Asia," *Journal of East Asian Studies* 10, no. 3 (December 2010): 363–95; Brad Williams and Erik Mobrand, "Explaining Divergent Responses to the North Korean Abductions Issue in Japan and South Korea," *Journal of Asian Studies* 69, no. 2 (May 2010): 507–36.

TABLE 5.1 The DPRK's abductions of Japanese and South Koreans

CATEGORY	JAPANESE	SOUTH KOREANS (SINCE 1953)
Officially recognized* as abductions victims	17	425
Still detained or missing (dead?)	12	516
Returned (before 2000)	—	3,310
Returned since 2000 (after three years or more in the DPRK)	5	9
Officially suspected abductees	~ 40 (hundreds?)	3,835

* Recognized by the Japanese or ROK government.
Source: ROK Ministry of Unification, Japanese Government Headquarters for the Abductions Issue.

the 1970s and 1980s. Nearly 90 percent of these "postwar abductees" (*jeonhu nap-bukja*) were fishermen, some of whom were captured after entering DPRK waters unwittingly. North Korea welcomed some as defectors for propaganda and released others after informal negotiations. Others were used to train spies, forced to broadcast propaganda to the South, or imprisoned in work camps. In total, 86 percent of these abductees were released within a year. Nine of the remainder have escaped and returned to the South since 2000 after having been stuck in the North for decades, but 516 are still missing and may have died. Among those still detained are 458 fishermen, the 11 crew members from a KAL flight hijacked in 1970, 30 soldiers and policemen, 6 students kidnapped from South Korean soil, and 12 ROK nationals kidnapped abroad.[4]

South Korean abductees and their families endured not only separation and abuse in North Korea but also persecution in the South. Before the 1990s, the ROK's anticommunist rulers suspected anyone who had been detained in the North or whose relatives (whether abducted or not) were in North Korea of being a potential threat to national security and labeled those missing defectors (*wol-bukja*). ROK nationals did occasionally defect, lured by economic opportunity and ideology or driven away by the South's brutal dictators. But most abductees and their families were unjustly branded as communist sympathizers. Under the principle of "guilty by association" (*yeonjwaje*), ROK authorities systematically barred these individuals from civil and military service or foreign travel and deprived them of educational opportunities.[5] Many also endured questioning, surveillance, or torture by ROK police and intelligence officials. The ROK's policy of denying seamen's licenses to abductees or their families caused particular economic hardship since most abductees had been fishermen. Although South

4. Ministry of Unification, *2015 Tongil Baekseo [Unification White Paper]* (Seoul: MOU, 2015), 113.
5. Interview with Lee Geum-sun, Korean Institute for National Unification, Seoul (July 29, 2009).

Koreans knew about the DPRK's detaining fishermen because most were repatriated, Seoul did not publish a list of still-missing abductees until 1999.

The Japanese government, meanwhile, contends that North Korea abducted seventeen people from Japan in the 1970s and 1980s. Most were young adults, although Yokota Megumi—the most famous abductee—was just thirteen when she disappeared in Niigata in 1977. DPRK agents apparently sought Japanese nationals to supply Japanese language instruction and Japanese identities to North Korean agents. Unlike many Korean abductee families, the families of most Japanese abductees heard nothing for years. In January 1980, the conservative newspaper *Sankei Shimbun* published an unprecedented story suggesting "foreign agents' involvement" in three couples' disappearances from Japan's western coasts in 1978. But the media did not pursue the story because officials would not confirm it.[6] "High thresholds for evidence" and "jurisdictional divisions" also hampered information sharing and coordination among government agencies investigating these cases.[7] As a result, the police quietly closed many suspected abductions cases because of insufficient evidence.

Circumstances changed in November 1987, however, when two DPRK agents traveling with fake Japanese passports planted a bomb on KAL flight 858, killing all 115 passengers. The surviving female agent told ROK interrogators that an abductee had taught her Japanese in Pyongyang.[8] A lawmaker from the Japan Communist Party (JCP) submitted questions about this revelation to the Diet in early 1988. In response, Japan's national public safety commissioner stated publicly for the first time that he had enough evidence to show that DPRK agents had kidnapped Japanese citizens. Later that year, the family of a suspected abductee also received a letter from their missing son, who mentioned another suspected abductee. The family showed the letter to the other abductee's parents and Foreign Ministry officials, but these officials persuaded the families to keep quiet so as not to endanger their offspring in the DPRK. Ultimately, neither the Diet testimony nor the letter sparked any action by the Japanese government.[9] Yet evidence linking North Korea to Japanese nationals' disappearances mounted until Kim Jong-il confirmed suspicions in 2002. The five surviving abductees and their children returned to Japan in 2002 and 2004, respectively. Since then, Tokyo has tried to confirm the alleged deaths of the eight other abductees and ascertain the

---

6. ReACH, *The Families* (Washington, DC: Rescuing Abductees Center for Hope, 2007), 12.

7. Interview with a government official, Tokyo (December 17, 2008).

8. The bomber, Kim Hyeon-hui, confessed in ROK custody. She was sentenced to death in 1990 but later pardoned.

9. Eric Johnston, "The North Korea Abduction Issue and Its Effect on Japanese Domestic Politics" (JPRI Working Paper No. 101, Japan Policy Research Institute, 2004), http://www.jpri.org/publications/workingpapers/wp101.html.

whereabouts of four additional people it claims were also kidnapped. Pyongyang maintains that these twelve either died or never entered the DPRK.[10] For the North, Kim Jong-il's admission and the surviving abductees' return resolved the abductions issue, but Tokyo continues to demand a complete resolution. Under pressure from activists and their elite allies, the Japanese National Police Agency revealed in late 2012 that it was investigating nearly nine hundred other disappearances in which DPRK involvement could not be ruled out.[11]

Aside from the people who were literally kidnapped by North Korean agents or detained after involuntarily venturing into DPRK territory since 1953, there are others unable to leave North Korea. They include tens of thousands of Korean families separated by the division of the peninsula (*isan gajok*); an estimated five hundred surviving South Korean prisoners of war (POWs) and captured intelligence agents; more than ninety-six thousand civilians kidnapped by the DPRK at the start of the Korean War to obtain intellectuals and professionals for the new communist country;[12] approximately ninety-three thousand ethnic Korean former residents of Japan who were encouraged by the North Korean Red Cross and some Japanese to relocate to North Korea during the "repatriation movement" (*kikoku jigyō*) of the 1960s and 1970s;[13] several thousand Japanese wives (*nihonjinzuma*) who went with these "returnees"; and members of the Japanese Red Army Faction that hijacked a Japanese plane (nicknamed *Yodogō*) to the DPRK in 1970. The plight of these others allegedly detained against their will in North Korea provides important context for Japanese and Korean abductee families' activism.

Abductees' Families Organize to Hold Their Governments Accountable

The emergence of new information about the abductions in the late 1990s first led suspected abductees' family members in Japan and South Korea to mobilize to claim redress. Previously these families had faced significant obstacles to collective action. Japanese abductee families suffered alone without information about their relatives. The ROK, meanwhile, branded most abductees defectors,

---

10. The Japanese government deemed suspect the death certificates North Korea produced in September 2002 and the alleged remains (ashes) of the deceased abductees. Headquarters for the Abductions Issue, "Points of Contention with the North Korean Position," Government of Japan, n.d., www.rachi.go.jp/en/mondaiten/index.html.

11. "Zenkoku 868nin [868 People Nationwide]," *Yomiuri Shimbun*, December 29, 2012.

12. See the Korean War Abductees Family Union (KWAFU) website, http://www.625.in.

13. Tessa Morris-Suzuki, *Exodus to North Korea* (Lanham, MD: Rowman & Littlefield, 2007).

which discouraged their families from speaking openly about their disappearances. The DPRK refused to answer humanitarian inquiries made through Red Cross channels, as doing so would have been tantamount to acknowledging the abductions. Additionally, until the late 1990s, decision makers who formulated North Korea policy in Seoul and Tokyo considered the abductions a minor issue that interfered with broader national interests, and they rebuffed families' requests for information and the return of their relatives.

Until the late 1990s Japanese policymakers downplayed the abductions issue within the country's unofficial "two Koreas policy" of cultivating equidistance in relations with the ROK and the DPRK. A series of Japanese politicians, including some from the ruling LDP, served as "pipes" (*paipu*) to the DPRK in lieu of diplomatic relations. Hopes of diplomatic or economic opportunities led them to either not mention the suspected abductions to their interlocutors or accept assurances that the abductions were a myth. The multipartisan Diet Members' League for the Promotion of Japan-North Korea Friendship (*Nitchō Giren*) also advocated exchange and business ventures with the DPRK from 1971 until its dissolution in 2002.

Yet the domestic political risks of promoting normalized relations with the DPRK grew with the North Korean nuclear crisis in 1994 and the Taepodong missile launch over Japanese airspace in 1998.[14] The demise of the Soviet bloc, the rise of China, the Japanese left's decline, Japan's economic stagnation, and international criticism of Japan's inability to share international peacekeeping burdens also emboldened hawks in Japan. They revived debates on issues such as Japan's defense posture, the constitution's pacifist Article 9, and contingency plans for regional crises.[15] Still, proponents of dialogue with North Korea persevered. As late as 1999, a Ministry of Foreign Affairs (MOFA) official warned the LDP's Foreign Affairs Committee not to derail Japan-DPRK normalization talks because of unproven suspicions that a few Japanese had been abducted years ago.[16] Indeed, when Tokyo had inquired about "missing persons" (not "abductees") in normalization talks in 1992, North Korean officials had walked out of the talks. But as hardline views toward the DPRK gained traction in Japanese politics during the 1990s, the number of potential elite allies for Japan's abductee families increased.

By comparison, Korean abductee families faced more substantial obstacles to collective action. Until the late 1980s, the South's conservative anticommu-

---

14. Christopher W. Hughes, *Japan's Economic Power and Security* (London: Routledge, 1999), 154–56.
15. Richard J. Samuels, *Securing Japan* (Ithaca: Cornell University Press, 2007), 65–68, 171–76.
16. Johnston, "North Korea Abduction Issue."

nist regime treated abductees and their families as potential security threats and prevented them from organizing. South Korea's democratization in 1987 began to enable public discussions about authoritarian governments' past wrongdoing and enhanced citizens' rights, including those of abductees and their families. Yet the abductions issue remained a tough sell for both the political left and right. Progressive activists and politicians avoided the issue so as not to antagonize the DPRK, even though they fought to rehabilitate other individuals whom past regimes had branded as communist sympathizers. Efforts at North-South rapprochement gained momentum with the 1997 election of Kim Dae-jung, South Korea's first progressive president. For South Korean conservatives, the abductions had the potential to highlight the North's misdeeds and the costs of rapprochement. But abductee families' hardship also revealed the excesses of conservatives' authoritarian predecessors. As a result, the families had comparatively fewer potential elite allies.

In the late 1990s, however, new information about the abductions encouraged victims' families in both Japan and Korea to organize. Abductions-related activism in Japan was catalyzed in late 1996 by compelling new evidence about the country's youngest abductee, Yokota Megumi, from a former North Korean spy. The Korea expert Satō Katsumi publicized the information and determined to help abductee families organize in order to "indirectly make amends" for having encouraged ethnic Koreans' "repatriation" to the DPRK as a leftist in the 1960s.[17] In January 1997, therefore, Satō and several colleagues contacted the Yokotas and other abductees' families and persuaded their fellow former Democratic Socialist Party (DSP) member-turned-hawkish-legislator, Nishimura Shingo, to submit questions about this new evidence to the Diet.[18] Japanese news outlets competed to cover the shocking revelation that a girl who had disappeared from Niigata had been seen in Pyongyang. Nishimura's questions and the publicity also prompted the government to reopen police investigations. Brought together by Satō and several other issue entrepreneurs, the Yokotas and six other families formed the Association of Families of Victims Kidnapped by North Korea (AFVKN, or Kazokukai) in March 1997. Families of suspected abductees, whom the Japanese government did not officially recognize as abductees, subsequently organized with help from one of these issue entrepreneurs in early 2003. The AFVKN, however, initially sought support from anyone who would listen, targeting both political elites and ordinary citizens. The group held a tearful press conference in Tokyo with photos of missing relatives and distributed flyers on street corners in Niigata. The

---

17. Interview with Araki Kazuhiro, COMJAN, Tokyo (March 24, 2009).
18. Araki Kazuhiro, ed., *Rachi Kyūshutsu Undō no 2000nichi [The First 2,000 Days of the Movement to Rescue Abductees]* (Tokyo: Sōshisha, 2000), 49.

families also met with lawmakers, the police, and foreign ministry officials. As the next section details, the AFVKN would gain third-party support from local and national politicians, vast networks of ordinary citizens, lawyers, journalists, and foreign groups.

In contrast, Korean abductee families initially mobilized on their own accord after the ROK government published a list of suspected abductees for the first time in 1999. The list included almost four thousand individuals, of whom 454 were noted as still missing. After hearing nothing about her father for years, Choi U-yeong—the daughter of a kidnapped fisherman—discovered his name on this list by reading it in a newspaper rather than hearing directly from the ROK government.[19] Angered, she began mobilizing other abductee families. After Choi was invited to speak at a rally for Japan's AFVKN in Tokyo in 1999, she convinced seven other Korean abductee families to form a similar group in Korea. In conjunction with launching the Abductee Families' Union (Napbukja Kajok Moim, AFU) in February 2000, Choi put ads in newspapers, contacted friends, and spoke at churches around Korea to find similarly afflicted families and raise awareness of the issue. Yet many abductee families had little time for activism, as they struggled with poverty. Others worried that revealing their family's history would expose them to renewed prejudice. But just before legislative elections in April 2000, President Kim Dae-jung announced that he would hold an unprecedented summit meeting with Kim Jong-il in Pyongyang in June. The AFU nearly tripled in size amid families' hopes that the summit might yield information about whether their relatives were still alive.

Thus, much as victims of harsh leprosy-control policies and hepatitis C-tainted blood products had, abductees and/or their families mobilized in Japan and Korea to hold their governments accountable. Rather than comparing the level of redress they achieved, most prior analyses of these movements have focused on how much more prominent the abductions issue subsequently became in Japan. Explaining variations in the extent to which the movements "captured" policymaking processes (but not variations in redress), for example, Samuels traces how skilled political entrepreneurs hyped "captivity narratives" in Japan but downplayed them in Korea to promote particular foreign policy agendas.[20] Yet he overlooks how each country's distinctive mediating institutions affected the movement's efforts to disseminate such narratives. In another comparison, Williams and Mobrand contend that differences in these movements stem from the fact that the abductions have distinctive connotations in each

---

19. Based on an interview with Choi U-yeong, FADN, Seoul (July 11, 2007).
20. Samuels, "Kidnapping Politics in East Asia."

country's nationalist ideology.[21] Like Samuels, though, they assume the diffusion of particular interpretations of the abductions issue without unpacking how mediating institutions filter discursive flows in the public sphere. By contrast, Lynn attributes the Japanese public's narrowed views on North Korea policy to the Japanese media's unrelenting and uncritical coverage of abductee families after 2002. Yet he neither compares Japan with Korea nor examines how Japan's activist sector amplified the impact of such "saturation coverage."[22]

In the analysis below, I do not deny that skilled political entrepreneurs, the position of the abductions in each country's nationalist ideology, and saturation coverage contributed to differences in the two movements. Indeed, partly because of the abductions issue's embeddedness in broader foreign policy concerns, interactions between abductee families and their supporters in the processes of conflict expansion differed from the dynamics observed in the previous chapters. Yet differences in the public profile that each country's abductee families acquired over time, in spite of their similarly early access to elite allies, stem at least in part from the conditions created in each country's public sphere by mediating institutions. In Japan, the mainstream media's relatively high barriers to entry and a tradition of victim-centered local activism facilitated the families' grassroots mobilizing to supplement the leverage that their elite allies had afforded before Kim Jong-il's admission regarding the abductees in 2002. Subsequently, competitive matching of content across news outlets, as well as relatively low levels of audience segmentation, helped keep the abductions issue salient. By contrast, the Korean movement was often overshadowed by bigger concerns in inter-Korean affairs. And Korea's more diverse and segmented media environment and politicized activist sector created fewer incentives and opportunities for grassroots mobilizing. Although these features of each country's public sphere explain the divergent levels of public attention the abductions issue received, the early access of both movements to political elites is crucial to an account of why both sets of families have achieved only partial (but not identical) redress.

Claiming Redress and Seeking the Abductees' Return

The Japanese and South Korean associations of abductees' families sought support from political elites, civil society groups, the media, and ordinary citizens from their inception in 1997 and 2000, respectively. Within months of forming

---

21. Williams and Mobrand, "Explaining Divergent Responses."

22. Hyung Gu Lynn, "Vicarious Traumas," *Pacific Affairs* 79, no. 3 (Fall 2006): 483–508.

associations, abductee families in Japan and Korea gained support from lawmakers, in the form of a cross-partisan lawmakers' union in Japan and a policy task force in the conservative opposition party in Korea. As this section will show, the mediocre redress outcomes ultimately obtained by both countries' abductee families stem at least in part from the movements' early access to elite allies. Yet, since the Japanese families and their political allies subsequently mobilized more public sympathy than their Korean counterparts, they have been able to overcome some of the liabilities of early elite access and wring other concessions from their government. By analyzing the families' activism, the constellation of civil society groups that supported them, media coverage, public opinion polls, and politicians' actions on their behalf, this section traces how these patterns of conflict expansion played out in each country.

Japan: Elite Allies and Grassroots Sympathy

Japan's abductions movement did not face the dearth of political opportunities that the Japanese Hansen's disease and HCV movements initially encountered. In April 1997, a multipartisan group of lawmakers founded the Diet Members' League to Help Japanese Allegedly Abducted by North Korea (abbreviated Rachi Giren).[23] The group's first meeting included more than 120 legislators, who came for a variety of reasons. Some—including the league's leader, Nakayama Masaaki of the LDP—had a history of engagement on North Korea issues and were also members of the Diet's older and conciliatory Nitchō Giren. Others, such as Nishimura Shingo, Hirasawa Katsuei, Koike Yuriko, Abe Shinzō, and Hiranuma Takeo, were conservatives with the opposite perspective, since they hoped to use the abductions issue to derail normalization talks with the DPRK and bolster Japan's foreign policy and defense posture. Multipartisan legislator leagues are common in Japan, but the Rachi Giren (especially after its 2002 reconstitution) had an unusually large number of members. Abductions-related groups also formed in most prefectural assemblies from 1997 onward.

While helping arrange meetings between abductee families and government officials, these early elite allies gave the families leverage by raising the issue's visibility and pressing for state action. Indeed, within ten days of the Rachi Giren's founding, Prime Minister Hashimoto Ryūtarō publicly mentioned the abductions issue for the first time while meeting with U.S. president Bill Clinton. The families' elite allies also arranged for the families to meet officials in the Ministry of Foreign Affairs and National Police Agency (NPA). Throughout spring and

---

23. This group's full Japanese name was Kitachōsen Rachi Giwaku Nihonjin Kyūen Giin Renmei.

summer 1997, the *Asahi* and *Yomiuri* newspapers each ran about twenty articles per month mentioning the abductions, often referring to Rachi Giren members who provided credentialed sources for reporters.[24] Although such early access to elite allies could have deterred the families from mobilizing grassroots support, characteristics of Japan's mediating institutions and choices by the movement helped overcome these disincentives.

GRASSROOTS MOBILIZING: LOCAL "RESCUE ASSOCIATIONS"

As one family member put it, "gaining ordinary citizens' support would help the movement sustain pressure on the Japanese government."[25] Hence the families encouraged grassroots mobilizing, which began in Megumi's hometown of Niigata when the activist Kojima Harunori—who had long campaigned for home visits for the Japanese wives of ethnic Koreans he had helped "repatriate" to the DPRK in the 1960s—began seeking local citizens' support for the Yokotas in March 1997. With twenty friends and neighbors, he founded Japan's first "[abductee] rescue association" (*sukūkai*), originally called the Group of Promoters of an Inquiry into Yokota Megumi's Abduction (Yokota Megumi-san Rachi Kyūmei Hakkinin Kai). Alongside the Yokotas, they "produced and distributed pamphlets and collected signatures to petition the Japanese government to address the families' demands."[26]

Such grassroots mobilization began in abductees' hometowns and drew on a distinctive Japanese organizational form: the local, issue-specific, and volunteer-run "supporter group" of citizens who mobilize around an individual or small number of aggrieved. Yokota Megumi's parents gained sympathy by portraying themselves as ordinary people who had become victims of North Korea's nefarious actions and the Japanese government's negligence. By June 1997, a rally in Niigata attracted more than a hundred people, and the movement had collected nearly $40,000 in small donations.[27] With the help of such concerned citizens, the Yokotas also collected 505,000 citizens' signatures by August to petition the state to take more assertive actions to rescue suspected abductees.[28] In Fukui, a similar supporter group for two other abductees' families gathered 70,000 signatures.[29] Rescue associations soon formed in other localities, including the Kansai region in July 1997 and Tokyo in August, but the movement remained

---

24. Author's calculations based on the national morning editions of each paper.

25. Interview with Hasuike Toru, brother of an abductee, Tokyo (June 25, 2009).

26. Interview with Yamazaki Haruya, a former member of Kojima's rescue association, Tokyo (March 26, 2009).

27. Araki, *Rachi Kyūshutsu Undō*, 77.

28. Ibid., 76–80, 97–100.

29. Interview with Shimada Yoichi, NARKN, Tokyo (November 20, 2008).

locally rooted. By late 1997, an AFVKN event in Niigata attracted a thousand people, while one in Tokyo attracted just 250 people. Yet Rachi Giren members often attended such rallies and criticized the government's "weak foreign policy that does not aim to protect its own citizens' lives."[30]

To coordinate such local activism more effectively with the AFVKN and the Rachi Giren, the activist Satō Katsumi and his fellow issue entrepreneurs started preparing for a national federation of local rescue associations. In April 1998, therefore, thirty-nine local supporter groups formally affiliated to form the National Association for the Rescue of Japanese Kidnapped by North Korea (NARKN, or Sukūkai) and named Satō their leader.[31] Alongside NARKN, local rescue associations continued to organize and staff local events for the families, collect signatures for petitions, receive donations, and produce pamphlets to raise citizens' awareness. By NARKN's official launch, more than one million citizens had signed petitions. Such societal support helped the movement "capture" foreign policymaking and public debate after Kim Jong-il's admission in 2002.

ELITE ALLIES' ASSISTANCE AND AGENDAS

Although the Japanese abductions movement would be constrained by the close ties it had developed early on with political elites, it also benefited from these elite allies' efforts to bolster the families' domestic and international activism. During Diet questioning in 1998, for instance, the lawmaker Nishimura Shingo compelled Prime Minister Hashimoto Ryūtarō to promise more forceful policies and a meeting with abductee families (neither was fulfilled). After the DPRK lobbed a missile over the Japanese archipelago in August, lawmakers arranged meetings for the families at MOFA and the Ministry of Justice's Human Rights Protection Bureau. In addition, the Rachi Giren reportedly subsidized movement leaders' visits to Washington, DC for meetings with the U.S. Department of State, Amnesty International, and experts.[32]

Abductee families also had their elite allies to thank for meetings with Japanese prime ministers in 1999 and 2000, which elevated the abductions issue to a national concern. Prime Minister Obuchi Keizō cited both Rachi Giren pressure and the multitude of signatures the movement had collected when he agreed to meet briefly with abductee families, their supporters, and several sympathetic lawmakers in March 1999. But the emerging "pressure faction" within the LDP—in which the future prime minister Abe Shinzō played a leading role—probably

---

30. Araki, *Rachi* Kyūshutsu *Undō*, 124.

31. Full name of the group: Kitachōsen ni Rachi Sareta Nihonjin wo Kyūshutsu Suru tame no Zenkoku Kyōgikai.

32. Araki, *Rachi Kyūshutsu Undō*, 129.

catalyzed this meeting by rendering the government vulnerable with criticisms about its inability to prevent a suspicious vessel (*fushinsen*) from the DPRK, that was intercepted within Japanese waters, from escaping, despite being fired upon.[33] Obuchi pledged to work with the UN, South Korea, and countries with diplomatic ties to the DPRK to seek suspected abductees' return.[34] Yet his chief cabinet secretary, Nonaka Hiromu; the more than 150 members of the conciliatory Nitchō Giren; and the LDP's coalition partner Kōmeitō still supported dialogue with the DPRK.[35] Abductee families, NARKN, and prefectural legislators subsequently staged a sit-in outside MOFA and LDP headquarters to denounce the Obuchi government's secret talks with Pyongyang and its provision of rice aid in early 2000, to little avail.[36] After Obuchi's sudden death in April 2000, however, Mori Yoshirō became prime minister. Sympathetic to abductee families and an opponent of Nonaka's faction, Mori met with the families in September 2000. He pledged not to pursue normalization with the DPRK without resolving the abductions issue but then announced a large shipment of food aid just three days later. The families' meetings with the prime ministers indicated both their elite allies' influence and the extent to which the movement was subject to broader political maneuvering by these allies.

Indeed, lawmakers' disagreements, especially within the Rachi Giren, over dialogue versus pressure as the best policy for Japan vis-à-vis the DPRK contributed to a lull in the abductions movement in 2001. On the one hand, Kim Dae-jung's summit with Kim Jong-il and U.S. secretary of state Madeleine Albright's trip to the DPRK in 2000 made some Japanese officials and lawmakers fear that Japan would get left behind or once again be excluded from regional security discussions.[37] On the other hand, hawks such as Nishimura Shingo argued that food aid and bilateral talks had not achieved any progress on the abductions issue and called for Japan to develop the capabilities to defend itself from the increasingly menacing North Korean threat. Indicative of the threat, another suspicious ship from the DPRK entered Japanese waters in December 2001, but this time was fired upon and sunk by the Marine Self-Defense Forces.[38]

Such disagreements among elites contributed to the collapse and reconstitution of the Rachi Giren in early 2002, leading to a closer association of the movement with hawkish foreign policy views. The collapse was catalyzed by new

---

33. David R. Leheny, *Think Global, Fear Local* (Ithaca: Cornell University Press, 2006), 158.
34. Araki, *Rachi Kyūshutsu Undō*, 188–94.
35. Johnston, "North Korea Abduction Issue."
36. Araki, *Rachi Kyūshutsu Undō*, 289–94.
37. Victor D. Cha, "Japan's Engagement Dilemmas with North Korea," *Asian Survey* 41, no. 4 (August 2001): 556.
38. Leheny, *Think Global, Fear Local*, 157–64.

evidence of North Korean involvement in the abductions, which emerged in March 2002, when the wife of a *Yodogō* plane hijacker confessed during the trial of another hijacker's wife in Tokyo that she had met Arimoto Keiko (a suspected abductee) in Europe in 1983 and lured her to the DPRK. The woman's confession and subsequent apology to Arimoto's parents were well publicized: the *Asahi* and *Yomiuri* newspapers ran about sixty and eighty articles, respectively, on the abductions in March 2002, as compared with a dozen articles each in the previous month. Since the confession provided the first firm evidence of North Korean involvement in the abductions, public sympathy toward the families grew, especially in Arimoto's hometown, and the police formally recognized her as an abductee for the first time. But Nakayama Masaaki, who had led the Rachi Giren since its inception and had also been elected to lead the conciliatory Nitchō Giren in 2000, apparently called the Arimotos to tell them that the publicity about their daughter was endangering Japan-DPRK dialogue.[39] Angered, the Arimotos publicized Nakayama's "treachery," and hardliners from the Rachi Giren resigned en masse to form a new group. They called it the Diet Members' League for the Speedy Rescue of Japanese Kidnapped by North Korea, also abbreviated Rachi Giren.[40] Abe Shinzō, Nishimura Shingo, Hirasawa Katsuei, and Koike Yuriko were among the new group's initial twelve members, who gave 2.72 million yen (about $26,000) to the AFVKN.[41] Their platform included not compromising on the abductions, cutting off cash transfers to the DPRK from ethnic Koreans in Japan, and prohibiting ethnic Korean residents of Japan (*zainichi*) from visiting the DPRK. Bureaucratic resistance to such hawkish recommendations had decreased because scandals within the MOFA in 2001 had cost several proponents of dialogue with the DPRK their jobs. By summer 2002, therefore, the movement had the backing of a new and less moderate Rachi Giren.

KIM JONG-IL'S BOMBSHELL AND REDRESS

On September 17, 2002, the late DPRK leader Kim Jong-il stunned the world by admitting that his government had abducted thirteen Japanese nationals in the 1970s and 1980s. A national movement organization, elite political support, and a network of concerned citizens enabled the families and their supporters to seize this opportunity and dominate Japanese foreign policymaking. Expectations of some information about the abductions had enticed Prime Minister Koizumi to travel to Pyongyang for a summit with Kim. Yet Kim Jong-il's frank admission

---

39. Johnston, "North Korea Abduction Issue."

40. In Japanese, Kitachōsen ni Rachi Sareta Nihonjin wo Sōki Kyūshutsu Suru tameni Kōdō Suru Giin Renmei.

41. Araki, *Rachi Kyūshutsu Undō*, 460.

caught most Japanese political elites and the media by surprise. Few people, least of all Kim Jong-il, had predicted the upwelling of public outrage that would follow this bombshell.[42] The Japanese public was particularly outraged by the DPRK's claim that eight of the thirteen abductees had died and by the fact that one of the thirteen had not been on the Japanese government's list of suspected abductees. Public ire over the abductions overshadowed even Pyongyang's disclosure to U.S. assistant secretary of state James Kelly several weeks later that the DPRK had a highly enriched uranium program. A full year after the summit, 90 percent of Japanese citizens still considered the abductions a concern vis-à-vis North Korea, whereas just 66 percent listed the DPRK's nuclear development as worrisome.[43] The Koizumi-Kim summit marked a notable step forward in Japan's quest to develop a more proactive foreign policy, as both sides signed the Pyongyang Declaration, which outlined a positive path forward for the two countries and included, among other things, statements of Japanese remorse for its colonial-era abuses and a DPRK pledge to maintain a moratorium on missile tests.[44] Koizumi may have bargained on a political victory; indeed, his approval ratings rose 10 percent between August and September 2002.[45]

But the summit also gave abductee families incontrovertible moral legitimacy. The families' combination of elite and grassroots support interacted in powerful ways with the structure and norms of Japan's media to magnify the public's outrage and hamstring Japanese leaders. Epitomizing "competitive matching," every news outlet covered Koizumi's return from Pyongyang and abductee families' reaction to the news. One observer noted that "the Japanese government seemed unprepared for the media furor, even though it had known some news about the abductions would emerge from the summit."[46] In this political vacuum, the better-prepared leaders of NARKN established the AFVKN as the sole authority on the abductions. Consequently, all news media covered the families' criticisms that the Japanese government had conveyed as indisputable fact the DPRK's claims that eight of the thirteen abductees had died in North Korea. Thereafter, Japanese news outlets competed to be the most sympathetic toward the families, and this resulted in emotionalized, uncritical coverage that saturated

---

42. Yoichi Funabashi, *The Peninsula Question* (Washington, DC: Brookings Institution Press, 2007), 36–37.

43. Cabinet Public Information Office, "Gaikou ni Kansuru Yoron Chōsa [Public Opinion Survey about Diplomacy]," October 2003, survey.gov-online.go.jp/h15/h15-gaikou/index.html.

44. Ministry of Foreign Affairs, Japan, "Pyongyang Declaration," September 17, 2002, http://www.mofa.go.jp/region/asia-paci/n_korea/pmv0209/pyongyang.html.

45. "Seifu Hyōka ni Anshin-Kan [Government Relief over Public Approval]," *Asahi Shimbun*, September 19, 2002.

46. Interview with Eric Johnston, *Japan Times* editor, Osaka (December 3, 2008).

the public sphere. The number of abductions-related articles in the *Asahi* and *Yomiuri* newspapers jumped from about 40 each in August 2002 to more than 250 per paper in September and about 300 in October. Between 2002 and 2003, donations to the AFVKN more than doubled, to about $725,000. And the entire Japanese delegation to the Japan-DPRK talks held in late October 2002 wore the AFVKN's signature blue ribbon pins.[47]

The families' elite allies in the Rachi Giren both contributed to and benefited from this media furor. Most famously, Abe Shinzō, who did not become a particularly outspoken supporter of the families until early 2002, gained popularity and influence within the LDP because of his firm stance on the abductions issue.[48] He had apparently been personally interested in the abductions for years, though. As Koizumi's deputy chief cabinet secretary and more of a hard-liner than the prime minister, Abe pushed for the five surviving abductees to remain in Japan, even though their return visit in October 2002 was supposed to be temporary. At a time when television and politicians' images were gaining importance in Japanese politics, news and talk shows' uncritical and unending coverage of the abductions provided opportunities for Rachi Giren members such as Abe to gain visibility and claim credit.[49]

AFVKN-NARKN grassroots activism prior to 2002 had also primed ordinary citizens to be eager consumers of such coverage, which gave news outlets economic reasons to continue it. Koizumi's second trip to Pyongyang in 2004 to escort surviving abductees' children back to Japan received more than three times as many hours of Japanese TV coverage as had the September 11, 2001, terrorist attacks on the United States.[50] The abductions combined the scandal of Japanese government negligence, the human-interest dimension of the families' separation and quest for justice, and the entertainment value of the DPRK's bizarre behavior to make ideal television content. The media granted abductee families' supporters—even if they were right-wing—unprecedented coverage because of their affiliation with the families. Leveraging constant and uncritical media coverage, NARKN and local rescue associations rendered questions about the movement's motives and activities virtually taboo.

In this milieu, consensus among Japanese lawmakers, rather than abductee families' pressure per se, underpinned the enactment of the first redress policies

---

47. The light blue color of the ribbons symbolizes the color of the Sea of Japan, which divides the abductees from their families, and of the sky, which is the only thing that unites the victims with their families.

48. Williams and Mobrand, "Explaining Divergent Responses," 10–13.

49. Masaki Taniguchi, "Changing Media, Changing Politics in Japan," *Japanese Journal of Political Science* 8, no. 1 (2007): 147–66.

50. Lynn, "Vicarious Traumas," 491.

in late 2002. Rachi Giren member and chief cabinet secretary Abe spearheaded an initiative to create a division within the Cabinet Office—instead of in MOFA—to coordinate abductions-related policy and assist abductees and their families. This move signaled the government's political commitment to resolve the issue and transform the way relevant policies were decided, albeit without apologizing for ignoring families' pleas for decades. The government also introduced the Law Regarding Support for Abductees and Others Affected by the Abductions by North Korean Authorities (hereafter the Support Law), which the Diet passed within a week of its introduction in December 2002.[51] The law provided monthly allowances, resettlement stipends, employment assistance, and full pensions for abductees who returned to Japan. Compared with legislation related to Hansen's disease and hepatitis C victims, discussions about these redress measures involved less input from the movement. Instead, Rachi Giren members—especially from the ruling coalition—led legislative efforts. Indeed, the AFVKN and NARKN did not consider the Support Law a "big success . . . because it passed with ease after the Pyongyang Summit and applied only to returnees."[52]

As might be expected, the abductions became a key issue in the general elections in November 2003. Both the ruling LDP and the DPJ backed the families. As the elections approached, more than one hundred additional politicians formally joined the Rachi Giren, though not all were equally active.[53] These might be considered late-arriving elite allies, given their reasons for taking up the issue. NARKN had established itself as a "combination support group and political action committee" that exposed candidates' positions on the abductions issue.[54] AFVKN-NARKN's ability to mobilize ordinary citizens appealed to many candidates wanting to get out the vote. Indicative of the movement's political influence, Social Democrat powerhouse Doi Takako was defeated by a staunch supporter of the Arimotos, who lived in her district and publicized the fact that Doi had denied their daughter's abduction years previously. The movement's early elite allies also benefited from association with the movement. For instance, Nishimura Shingo won overwhelmingly as a new member of the DPJ because of his support of the families, even though he had only narrowly won the previous election. Yet the movement's elite allies subsumed redress objectives into broader

---

51. Kitachōsen Tōkyoku ni yotte Rachi Sareta Higaisha nado no Shien ni kansuru Hōritsu (law no. 143, December 11, 2002) pledges monthly allowances of 170,000 yen (about $1,600) per repatriated abductee, or 240,000 yen ($2,300) per two-person household with 30,000 yen ($290) per additional family member.

52. Interview with Nishioka Tsutomu, NARKN, Tokyo (November 25, 2008).

53. Lynn, "Vicarious Traumas," 501.

54. Johnston, "North Korea Abduction Issue."

foreign policy goals; about two-thirds of those elected to the Diet in November 2003 favored tougher measures toward North Korea.[55]

SANCTIONS AND ABDUCTIONS-RELATED LEGISLATION

Although not related to redress, Japan's debate over sanctions against North Korea exemplified how much influence the families' elite allies had acquired since Kim Jong-il's admission about the abductions in 2002. Despite resistance from Prime Minister Koizumi, the ruling LDP started studying how to revise Japan's Foreign Exchange and Trade Control Law (FETCL) as early as December 2002 to shut off remittances to the DPRK unilaterally. Koizumi opposed such sanctions because he felt that they would constitute an abrogation of the Pyongyang Declaration, which he had signed with Kim Jong-il.[56] A NARKN survey of Diet members in late 2004, however, revealed that 85 percent of LDP legislators and 78 percent of DPJ legislators favored sanctions to pressure the DPRK into releasing the remaining abductees.[57] Only the socialists, communists, and ex-socialists within the DPJ opposed sanctions outright. Thus, Rachi Giren members submitted revisions to the FECTL, banning remittances to the North, which passed in January 2004. Later that year, they also passed the Law for Special Measures concerning Interdiction of Port Entry by Specific Ships, which curbed ship traffic and trade from the DPRK. Humanitarian aid to North Korea was then frozen in December 2004, once Koizumi secured the release of surviving abductees' children.

The movement supported such sanctions, in part because its elite allies and other supporters had promoted such nonredress objectives and also because sanctions put pressure on the DPRK. The AFVKN and NARKN launched a petition drive urging the government to cut off "people, money, materials, and information" to North Korea because differences of opinion between the Diet and the cabinet hindered the enforcement of sanctions until the summer of 2006. The movement submitted an unprecedented five million signatures to the Japanese government in February 2005. It also instigated a nationwide boycott of North Korean clams, the highest-value item in bilateral trade. As a result of the boycott and stricter insurance requirements for ships importing the clams, the clam trade fell by half from 2004 to 2005.[58] Lawmakers met with abductee families

---

55. Samuels, *Securing Japan*, 150.

56. Miyamoto Satoru, "Economic Sanctions by Japan against North Korea: Consideration of the Legislation Process for FEFTCL (February 2004) and LSMCIPESS (June 2004)," *International Journal of Korean Unification Studies* 15, no. 2 (2006): 36.

57. NARKN Survey of Upper and Lower House Diet Members, December 2004, http://www.sukuukai.jp/H16enquete.

58. James L. Schoff, *Political Fences & Bad Neighbors* (Institute for Foreign Policy Analysis Project Report, June 2006), 7, http://www.ifpa.org/pdf/fences.pdf.

multiple times per month in 2006 to coordinate their advocacy for enhanced sanctions, which enabled a rapid response to the DPRK's testing of seven missiles in July 2006. The Japanese government immediately and unilaterally enacted unprecedented nine-part sanctions. The UN Security Council took eleven days to implement sanctions. Then in October 2006, North Korea tested a nuclear device underground, leading the Security Council to unanimously impose sanctions on all transfers of military, technological, and luxury goods to the DPRK. The Japanese government expanded its sanctions to prohibit port calls by North Korean ships, all imports from North Korea, exports of luxury goods to the North, and entry of any DPRK nationals. With the LDP's Abe Shinzō's becoming prime minister in September 2006, U.S. support for sanctions, and the DPRK's undeniable abrogation of the Pyongyang Declaration, these measures passed with relative ease in the Diet.[59]

Despite being assisted by this confluence of forces, NARKN claimed the sanctions regime as one of its "biggest successes."[60] It is unclear, however, how much of a success the families thought the sanctions were. Although they avoided publicly criticizing their loyal supporters in NARKN, some subsequently questioned the efficacy of sanctions and their ramifications for abductees still in the North.[61] Moreover, the sanctions did not provide redress.

The Japanese Abductions and North Korean Human Rights Act—passed in June 2006 and amended in July 2007—provided more direct benefit to abductee families.[62] It required national and local officials to raise public awareness about the abductions and North Korea's other human rights violations, especially during a week in December every year. This provided the AFVKN and NARKN with ready audiences. The law also stipulated the government's obligation to promote international efforts to resolve the abductions issue and oppose initiatives by international financial institutions to aid the DPRK. One activist called the law "Japan's version of the U.S. North Korean Human Rights Act [H.R.4011] of 2004," which had inspired the AFVKN and NARKN to form an advocacy coalition with Mamorukai and Life Funds for North Korean Refugees (LFNKR)—two civic groups that assist refugees from North Korea.[63] In early 2005, these groups had submitted a list of demands to the DPJ's Nakagawa Shōichi, who had publicized North Korean human rights previously and was vice chairman of the Rachi

---

59. Miyamoto, "Economic Sanctions by Japan against North Korea," 46.
60. Interview with Shimada Yoichi, NARKN.
61. Interview with Hasuike Toru, brother of an abductee.
62. Rachi Mondai sonota Kitachōsen Tōkyoku ni yoru Jinken Shingai Mondai e no Taisho ni kansuru Hōritsu (law no. 96, June 23, 2006).
63. Interview with Kim Cheol-sam, North Korean Escapee Assistance Center at Mindan, Tokyo (March 30, 2009).

Giren.[64] After the DPJ submitted a bill on North Korean human rights to the Diet in 2005, the ruling LDP hurriedly drafted its own version in early 2006. The LDP's version became law later that year. Thus although the movement's early access to elite allies facilitated the drafting of these bills, its grassroots mobilizing and lawmakers' perceptions about the public's contempt toward the DPRK ensured their passage.

Abe's first premiership in 2006 and 2007 marked the peak of state responsiveness to abductee families' demands. Days after becoming prime minister, he turned the Cabinet Office division he had established several years earlier into a powerful headquarters that would manage abductions-related policy and consult with abductee families. Abe increased the headquarters' staff to thirty-five persons and expanded its budget tenfold in 2007.[65] Institutionally, this headquarters tackled the interagency coordination problems that had at least partly caused Japanese authorities to discount the families' pleas for decades. It also gave the families and their allies a direct line to the chief cabinet secretary, reducing the need to navigate complex bureaucratic channels when articulating demands. To raise awareness, the headquarters produced brochures, a multilingual documentary, and an animated film about the abductions and started transmitting radio broadcasts to North Korea. It also subsidized abductee families' travel to and lodging in Tokyo for briefings. As one official in the headquarters explained, "The state owed abductee families a debt [*oime*] for having failed to address the abductions issue earlier."[66] As we shall discuss below, however, families of recognized abductees (AFVKN members) had greater access to the headquarters than did those of suspected abductees.

ELUSIVE REDRESS AND LITIGATION

The situation of the families of potential abductees who do not appear on Tokyo's official list reveals that the level of redress remains partial in Japan, despite the overwhelming influence of the AFVKN and its supporters. The state sets the criteria to grant recognition of missing persons as North Korean abductees. Yet the administrative process of applying to have a case considered remains opaque in Japan. For the Japanese government, limiting the number of officially recognized abductions may make resolving the issue more feasible. Since 2002, Tokyo has recognized only four additional cases, but the DPRK may have abducted other Japanese nationals not on the government's list. Indeed, one of the thirteen Kim Jong-il admitted to having kidnapped was unknown to the Japanese government.

---

64. Interview with Kato Hiroshi, LFNKR, Tokyo (March 27, 2009).
65. Interview with a Japanese government official, Tokyo (July 19, 2007).
66. Interview with a Japanese government official, Tokyo (December 17, 2008).

Araki Kazuhiro, a central figure in NARKN, formed the Investigation Commission on Missing Japanese Probably Related to North Korea (COMJAN) in early 2003 to help families of suspected abductees lobby the Japanese government for recognition. Although independent, COMJAN received grants from AFVKN-NARKN. The commission also has support from a lawyers' group headed by the Tokyo cause lawyer Kawahito Hiroshi. Kawahito had first learned of the abductions issue while defending Japanese citizens accused of aiding DPRK agents in the early 1980s, but most of his pro bono work involved cases of *karōshi* (death by overwork). At first, few lawyers joined his *bengodan* "due to the issue's conservative associations," but the group grew to include about thirty attorneys by 2008.[67]

COMJAN and the lawyers' group have filed lawsuits to press the Japanese government into investigating suspected abductions, which COMJAN estimates may number more than a thousand. In April 2005, COMJAN and the lawyers helped Furukawa Noriko's family file an administrative lawsuit against the Japanese government to have their daughter, who disappeared in July 1973, recognized as an abductee. The family contended that the state had not provided clear procedures for such recognition and charged the government with negligence for failing to investigate cases of suspected abductions. Matsumoto Kyoko's family also contemplated filing a lawsuit until the government recognized her as the seventeenth abductee in 2006, partway through the Furukawa lawsuit. After the government promised to change its behavior toward unrecognized abductees' families, the Furukawa lawsuit went into settlement talks without a ruling. In contrast to the lawsuits discussed in chapters 3 and 4, the Furukawa suit garnered virtually no publicity and did little to advance the broader redress movement. In part, this was because the recognized abductees' families who constitute the AFVKN—the core of the movement—were not involved. Despite the lawsuit's failure, COMJAN continued to investigate potential abductions, lobby the state for more investigations, and broadcast abductee families' voices by radio to the DPRK. The families of about forty unrecognized abductees are actively involved in COMJAN, but they still have less ready access to the media or to government officials than do AFVKN members.[68]

THE MOVEMENT'S LONGEVITY AMID PARTIAL REDRESS

The continuing influence of the abductee families' movement is impressive considering that they have elicited only partial redress. In part, the structure of Japan's public sphere helped the families retain public interest. Established as an important source of news among Japan's relatively homogeneous mainstream

---

    67. Interview with Kawahito Hiroshi, lawyer, Tokyo (June 8, 2009). Home page: http://web01.cpi-media.co.jp/kawahito/tokutei/tokutei.htm.
    68. Interview with Araki Kazuhiro, COMJAN.

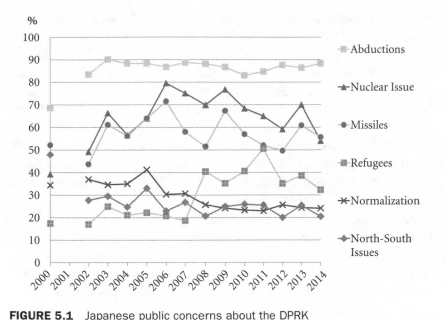

FIGURE 5.1 Japanese public concerns about the DPRK

Source: Cabinet Office, Public Opinion Survey about Foreign Policy, survey.gov-online.go.jp/index-gai.html. "If there are things that concern you about North Korea, which of the following would they be?" (not asked before 2000 or in 2001).

media, the AFVKN continues to attract coverage. For instance, when Barack Obama won the U.S. presidency in 2008, the NHK's extended prime-time news coverage included reactions from only one citizen group—the AFVKN.[69] Additionally, the families still receive support from local rescue associations, most of which remain nonpartisan and volunteer, like most Japanese civil society organizations. Asagao-no-kai, for example, is a group based in the Yokotas' apartment complex and helps them manage their mail.[70] The families of unrecognized abductees have particularly strong incentives to sustain such grassroots activism as they pressure the government to recognize their relatives. Ultimately, abductee families' and their political allies' activism and the favorable structure of Japan's public sphere have sustained public concern about the abductions: the abductions issue still outstrips all other issues related to the DPRK (see figure 5.1).

Yet members of the movement worry about whether they can sustain pressure for redress and their relatives' rescue. Abe's successors from the LDP, Prime Ministers Fukuda and Aso, "let the activity of the cabinet's abductee headquarters decline," much to the dismay of the AFVKN and its supporters.[71] Moreover, none

---

69. NHK's News 7, extended to one hour, November 5, 2008.
70. The group's English website is http://www.asagaonokai.jp/eg/index.html.
71. Interview with Nishioka Tsutomu, NARKN.

of the five candidates for the LDP party presidency in 2008 raised the abductions issue. While the DPJ controlled the government from 2009 to 2012, successive prime ministers still met with AFVKN members upon taking office. But DPJ governments also reassigned many of the abductions headquarters' tasks to other parts of the Cabinet Office and focused more on broader Asian diplomacy and multilateral efforts to curb the North Korean nuclear program than on the abductions issue per se.[72] Kim Jong-il's death and the subsequent leadership change in late 2011 presented an opportunity for Japan to reopen talks with the DPRK in 2012 about repatriating the remains of Japanese who had died in the North after World War II and the abductees. But the DPRK's provocative behavior in late 2012 and 2013 scuttled these talks.

As time passes and redress remains elusive, divisions have emerged within the Japanese abductee movement. The Yokotas started questioning the motives of politicians who seem to use them for photo ops instead of advancing their quest for redress.[73] Some abductee families also question the efficacy of sanctions and their political allies' hard-line approach, which has yet to rescue their missing relatives. Bill Clinton's trip to Pyongyang in 2009 to orchestrate the release of two U.S. journalists detained in the DPRK contrasted sharply with the lack of progress on the still-missing Japanese abductees. One jaded brother of a repatriated abductee suggested that NARKN leaders may have an interest in keeping the movement going to retain their political influence.[74] Yet amid the rightward shift in Japanese politics, some of the families and their political allies continue to use the issue to press for harsher policies toward the North and more assertive defense policies.

In fact, some of the movement's early elite allies continue to benefit from association with the issue. For example, Abe Shinzō, who had long supported the families, helped lead a defeat of the DPJ in 2012 and the LDP-Kōmeitō coalition's victory in the July 2013 upper-house elections. Since his return to the premiership in late 2012, he has faithfully worn the AFVKN's blue ribbon pin and allocated substantial resources to the abductions issue. Public sympathy for the families also remained high. As of May 2013, an unprecedented ten million citizens had signed a petition urging the Japanese government to rescue all abductees, spurred in part by the DPRK's December 2012 missile (or satellite, as North Korea claimed) launch and its third nuclear test in February 2013.[75] And Japanese journalists still worry that "attempts to foster debate

---

72. *Asahi Shimbun*, October 13, 2009, cited in Samuels, "Kidnapping Politics in East Asia."
73. Kitano Ryūichi, "Kōshō Chansu [Chance for Negotiations]," *Asahi Shimbun*, April 20, 2012.
74. Interview with Hasuike Toru, brother of abductee.
75. NARKN website, http://www.sukuukai.jp.

about broader humanitarian and human rights concerns in North Korea might spark right-wing protests."[76] Nevertheless, the NPA started investigating hundreds of cases of suspected abductions in 2012. Marking a major advance at the international level, the UN Commission of Inquiry on Human Rights in the DPRK agreed to hear testimony from abductees' relatives in Tokyo and Seoul in 2013 and condemned the North Korean abductions forcibly in its final report.[77] Furthermore, thanks to Abe's government, the Yokotas were able to meet Megumi's North Korean daughter in Mongolia in early 2014, and Pyongyang temporarily reopened investigations into the whereabouts of still-missing Japanese abductees. Such international advocacy and several rounds of secret talks between Japan and the DPRK have yielded few concrete results, though. Ultimately, it may cost the Japanese government little to keep the abductions issue alive while DPRK provocations persist, even if full redress for abductee families remains elusive.

South Korea: Early Elite Allies and Low Public Interest

The expansion of South Korean abductee families' conflict with the state similarly began from the top down, when the Grand National Party formed the Special Committee on Abductions and POW Policy in summer 2000, amid the historic transformation that the first North-South summit had engendered in South Korean attitudes toward the DPRK. Unlike the multipartisan Rachi Giren in Japan, this committee included only GNP legislators, who were emboldened by the fact that President Kim Dae-jung's party had ended up winning fewer seats than the GNP in the April 2000 election. The committee signaled conservative political elites' opposition to Kim Dae-jung's Sunshine Policy. For the opposition GNP, the government's dismissive attitude toward abductee families' plight highlighted the hypocrisy of President Kim Dae-jung's calls for humanitarian aid for the DPRK and reunions of separated families. The families also supplied GNP legislators with vivid personal stories to illustrate the brutality of the North Korean regime.

After the historic summit awakened previously unimaginable hopes, the abductee families and their elite allies in the GNP pressed the administration to include the abductions and POWs on the summit agenda, albeit unsuccessfully. Although Korean abductees are more numerous than Japanese, they were outnumbered by a different population that was discussed at the summit: the nearly

---

76. Conversation with an NHK producer (September 27, 2012).

77. UN General Assembly, *Report of the Detailed Findings of the Commission of Inquiry on Human Rights in the Democratic People's Republic of Korea* (February 7, 2014), 270–318, http://www.ohchr.org/EN/HRBodies/HRC/CoIDPRK/Pages/ReportoftheCommissionofInquiryDPRK.aspx.

one hundred thousand families separated since the Korean War. As the summit was the capstone of the Sunshine Policy, the administration was loath to risk the "big losses [of upsetting the talks] for a small potential gain [for abductees' families]."[78] The ROK agreed instead to send humanitarian aid to North Korea and even to release sixty-three unconverted North Korean prisoners (*bijeon-hyang janggisu*) after the summit. Outraged, abductee families wrote letters to the president, threatened to sue the state for failing to protect ROK citizens, held demonstrations, spoke to civic and religious leaders, and lobbied lawmakers.[79] The movement may have gained elite allies quickly and had its claims bolstered by the first escape of a long-term South Korean abductee in 2000 (discussed below), but the North-South summit and associated shifts in discourses related to the DPRK rendered South Korean society and many mediating institutions less receptive to abductee families' demands than was the case in Japan.

REDRESS LEGISLATION AS A CRITIQUE OF THE SUNSHINE POLICY

More than in Japan, the abductee movement's earliest elite allies took up the families' cause for partisan reasons, which had strong overtones in the context of inter-Korean relations. Conservative GNP legislators wanted a concrete way to criticize the Sunshine Policy and the release of sixty-three DPRK prisoners. In 2000, the GNP chairman, Lee Hoi-chang, and other lawmakers met with about forty relatives of abductees, who recounted the hardships they had endured in South Korea. Members of the GNP's Special Committee on the Abductions and POW Policy also began drafting the country's first bill related to postwar abductees, and Choi U-yeong and other abductee family members testified before the committee in public hearings. The bill GNP legislators proposed in November 2000 acknowledged the material and psychological suffering of abductee families and called for welfare assistance (but not reparations) for them.[80] By supporting the bill, more than 130 GNP legislators signaled their criticism of the government's policy of subsuming the abductions within the broader category of "separated families" in North-South negotiations. They also introduced into the

---

78. Kim Young-dai and Jeong Young-pyoung, "Sosujaroseo Napbukja Kajok ui Jeongchaek Hoikdeuk Gwajeong Yeongu [A Study of the Process by Which the Families of Those Kidnapped by North Korea Attained Certain Policies]," *Jeongbuhak Yeongu [Government Studies Research]* 13, no. 1 (2007): 134.

79. Gwon Jae-hyeon, "Eumji ui Isan Gajokdeul: (2) Napbukja [Neglected Separated Families: (2) Abductees]," *Kyunghyang Shinmun*, September 8, 2000.

80. Napbukja Gajok Senghwal Anjeong Jiwon Beop An [Draft Bill for Abductee Families' Social Security Assistance], proposed by the GNP's Gang Sam-jae and eight other legislators, November 29, 2000.

political agenda the question of rescuing abductees still detained by the DPRK.[81] Yet the bill received little media coverage and was never put to a vote because its main author's term ended. Infighting within the abductee families' association also constrained the group's influence over this effort to legislate redress.

The abductee families and their elite allies also tried to use events beyond their control to raise the profile of their cause and shame the state. For example, the ROK's release of North Korean prisoners contrasted especially sharply with Lee Jae-geun's escape from the DPRK in 1998 and eventual return to the ROK. Lee was the first known abductee to have escaped North Korea after having been detained for more than three years. He sought asylum from the ROK just two weeks before the 2000 summit, after having escaped from North Korea to China with his wife and son two years earlier. Choi Seong-yong, an abducted fisherman's son and active member of the AFU, had brought a reporter with him to China to witness and cover Lee's request for asylum. When Lee phoned an ROK consulate in China to request asylum, the diplomat who answered demanded to know why the ROK should help when Lee had not paid taxes in the ROK for decades.[82] In a classic example of shaming, Choi and the reporter publicized the diplomat's unhelpfulness, which spawned public discussions about the ROK's negligence toward abductees. Lee further embarrassed ROK officials by telling them about the more than thirty South Korean abductees he had met in reeducation camps in the North—including seven who were not on the ROK's official list. The AFU's allies in the GNP also questioned what Kim Dae-jung had conceded to achieve the historic summit and called on the state to do more for the abductees.

KOREAN ABDUCTEE FAMILIES' DIVERGENT ACTIVISM

Because of the greater number of Korean abductees and the variety of circumstances among them, Korea's abductee families became more divided than those in Japan. Disagreements over who should lead the AFU and what tactics the families should adopt caused the group to split in October 2000. A subset of families gave leader Choi U-yeong a vote of no confidence and selected Choi Seong-yong (no relation) to be the new leader of the revamped Abductee Families' Union. With her disgruntled supporters, Choi U-yeong formed the Families of the Abducted and Detained in North Korea (Napbukja Gajok Hyeopuihoe, FADN). Apparently, disagreements among families and their leaders had worsened after Choi U-yeong and a handful of other family members visited the unconverted

---

81. Park Jeong-won, "Jeonhu Napbuk Pihaeja Jiwon Ipbeop ui Gwaje wa Jeonmang [Legal Issues and Prospects for Legislation to Support Postwar Abductees]," *Beophak Noncheong* 22, no. 1 (2009): 78–79.

82. Interview with Choi Seong-yong, AFU, Seoul (February 3, 2009).

North Korean prisoners in August 2000 to request that they convey the families' appeals to the DPRK government after the ROK released them.[83] Indicative of the emotions involved in questions of inter-Korean affairs, Choi Seong-yong's faction denounced this act as capitulation to the progressive Kim administration's plan to release the prisoners.

Despite this split, the AFU and FADN continued to work—sometimes even in tandem—to raise public awareness about the abductions and pressure the ROK government. One observer noted that "the few *active* relatives of abductees frequently participated in both AFU and FADN initiatives."[84] The AFU and FADN also periodically partnered with the Korean War Abductee Family Union (KWAFU), which in 2000 became the first organization since the 1950s to represent families of the ninety-three thousand people kidnapped by the North during the war. Since most abductees were fishermen and because Choi Seong-yong used to work for South Korea's fishermen's union, the AFU acquired a small office in the union's building. FADN had a separate office, but neither group had paid staff or a supporter network like NARKN and the local rescue associations in Japan.

From their split until fall 2002, the AFU and FADN adopted distinctive approaches to activism. As leader of FADN, Choi U-yeong devoted herself to giving domestic and foreign media interviews, writing public letters to Kim Jong-il, and cooperating with the Japanese abductees. She joined members of the Japanese AFVKN in asking Amnesty International and UN agencies to investigate the abductions. To increase domestic awareness of the abductions, FADN festooned trees near the DMZ with thousands of yellow ribbons. Twenty-six FADN members, represented by one lawyer, also sued the ROK government in January 2002 for shirking its constitutional duty to protect its citizens and for returning DPRK prisoners without making serious efforts to rescue the abductees. When the court ruled against the plaintiffs in 2004, they decided not to appeal. As Choi U-yeong recounted, it "seemed hopeless; the court did not want a small issue [the abductions] to trump the bigger goal of reunification."[85]

The AFU leader Choi Seong-yong used more confrontational tactics to pressure the ROK government and attract media attention. He and AFU members marched on the President's Blue House, protested until officials at the Ministry of Unification (MOU) or Ministry of Public Administration and Security (MOPAS) met with them, launched balloons filled with leaflets and North Korean currency

83. Yun Jihui, "Buksori: Napbukja Gajok Moim Jajung Jiran [Northern Sounds: The Abductee Family Association's Internal Fighting]," *Segye Ilbo*, October 30, 2000.

84. Interview with An Jun-ho, *Chosun Ilbo* journalist, Seoul (February 11, 2009).

85. Interview with Choi U-yeong, former leader of FADN, Seoul (July 28, 2009).

into the DPRK, and called for regime change in the North. Choi Seong-yong also claims he "helped broker seven abductees' and twelve POWs' escapes from the DPRK."[86] Since he and AFU members protested in advance of all North-South meetings to publicize the ROK's failure to take steps to rescue abductees, some South Koreans criticized him for hampering North-South reconciliation. But he prides himself on being "a headache for the South Korean government."[87] Although Choi Seong-yong was wary of cooperating with other activist groups for fear of diluting abductee families' demands, the AFU worked closely with the Citizens Coalition for the Human Rights of Abductees and North Korean Refugees (CHNK). CHNK was founded in 2001 by the right-leaning activist Do Hee-yun to coordinate among North Korean refugees, abductees, POWs, and human rights advocates. Do took up this cause because he "regretted having listened to North Korean radio broadcasts while a leftist student activist in the authoritarian era in South Korea."[88] Like many of the Japanese abductee families' supporters, Do saw supporting Korean abductee families as a way to "atone for his past misperceptions about the DPRK." In addition to peopling AFU protests, CHNK helped Choi Seong-yong identify and aid abductees trying to escape the North. In late 2001, for example, Jin Jeong-pal—the second abductee to have escaped after more than three years' captivity—returned to the South with Choi's assistance.

Even though the AFU and FADN adopted such different approaches to activism, they struggled to sustain salience in South Korea. Korea's diverse traditional and online news outlets provided many venues through which abductee families could try to broadcast their demands, but one observer commented that "most outlets focused more on the greater numbers of North Korean refugees in South Korea and northeastern China."[89] Coverage of the abductions issue briefly surged in December 2000, when an abductee and his elderly mother were included—but not singled out as abductions victims by the ROK government—for the first time in the family reunions made possible by the North-South summit.[90] Between March 2001 and Kim Jong-il's bombshell about Japanese abductees in September 2002, however, the abductees were rarely mentioned in the Korean news.

---

86. Interview with Choi Seong-yong, AFU, Washington, DC (September 11, 2012).

87. Martin Fackler, "Serving a Father by Bringing Long-Lost Koreans Home," *New York Times*, January 2, 2010.

88. Interview with Do Hee-yun, CHNK, Seoul (July 31, 2009).

89. Interview with Horiyama Akiko, *Mainichi Shimbun* journalist, Seoul (June 7, 2008).

90. Since 2000, nearly 4,500 families (about 22,500 people) have briefly met their relatives in seventeen rounds of face-to-face reunions in North Korea or video reunions. These reunions included 18 abductee families (about 80 people). Family reunions were suspended in November 2010 after North Korea shelled Yeonpyeong Island. Ministry of Unification, *2015 Tongil Baekseo [Unification White Paper]* (Seoul: MOU, 2015), 110.

The abductions' relation to progressive and conservative agendas also made it difficult for the AFU and FADN to gain salience. Progressives avoided the issue because it had the potential to derail inter-Korean dialogue and cooperation.[91] On the other side of the political spectrum, abductee families provided conservatives a way to criticize the Sunshine Policy, and GNP legislators became helpful political allies. But one abductee's relative explained that many families were also "wary of being too closely associated with conservatives who called for regime change because it might endanger their relatives still detained in North Korea."[92] Thus, the AFU and FADN struggled to connect with progressive and conservative groups in Korea's vibrant activist sphere and mobilize the kind of broad support that their Japanese counterparts had through local rescue associations. Instead, both family associations pursued ad hoc coalitions with different organizations such as CHNK or KWAFU, as is common in Korea's public sphere.

Still, Kim Jong-il's surprise admission spurred a period cooperation and visibility for South Korea's abductee family organizations. Amid widespread South Korean media coverage of Prime Minister Koizumi's diplomatic overture to Pyongyang and the five surviving Japanese abductees' return to Japan in October, the AFU and FADN publicly set aside their differences to jointly pressure their own government. With the help of sympathetic lawmakers, they met with officials from the MOU and MOPAS to demand information about whether their relatives were still alive in North Korea, an official acknowledgment of their past suffering in the ROK, financial aid, and institutional reforms to prevent future abductions and discrimination against abductee families. Overwhelming political and public support for Japanese abductee families after the admission also served as an example that the AFU and FADN used to try to shame the ROK government and public into caring more about Korea's abductee families. The families' plight did resonate with some Korean citizens: one survey found that more than 53 percent of South Korean respondents wanted their government to address North Korean terrorism and abductions, as Japan had done.[93] In this milieu, *Yonhap News* published a series of articles based on interviews with abductee families in January 2003. The series concluded with an analysis of the ROK government's responsibility for abductee families' suffering and called for redress legislation.[94] But media interest subsided. Only the third escaped abductee (Kim

91. Jeong Jae-yong, "Napbukja Gajok Keuleoangi Bunuigi Tattda [Following the Atmosphere of Embracing the Abductees' Families]," *Jugan Kyunghyang*, February 21, 2006.

92. Interview with Hwang In-cheol, KAL Abductee Family Union, Seoul (August 4, 2009).

93. Mun Gwan-hyeon, "Seongin 53% 'Napbuk Munje Il Sujun Jegiheya' [53% of Respondents 'Raise the Abductions Issue to the Japanese Level']," *Yonhap News*, September 25, 2002.

94. Reprinted in FADN, *Napbukja Ingwon Bogoseo II [Abductees' Human Rights Report II]* (Seoul: Families of the Abducted and Detained in North Korea, 2008), 101–26.

Byeong-do), who returned to ROK soil in June 2003, spawned a brief burst of media coverage. And the AFU and FADN, still suffering from disagreements among their leaders, drifted apart again in 2003.

AFFIRMATION FROM THE NATIONAL HUMAN RIGHTS COMMISSION OF KOREA

As redress legislation seemed elusive, the abductee families had pursued claims in several other venues, much as the Korean hepatitis C movement had. For example, the AFU had filed a complaint with the National Human Rights Commission of Korea in November 2002 regarding the ROK government's past mistreatment of abductees and their families. Since the NHRCK had not ruled on the AFU's complaint by December 2003, Choi Seong-yong led twelve wives of still-missing fishermen on a four-day hunger strike and sit-in at the NHRCK offices. The bitter cold, the women's advanced age, and the disruption they caused attracted sympathetic coverage from the conservative *Cho-Joong-Dong* newspapers but not from the more progressive *Hankyoreh* and *Kyunghyang* newspapers, despite their long-standing support of and frequent coverage of other issues before the NHRCK. As a result of the sit-in, Roh Moo-hyun's presidential secretary came to hear the victims' demands, and the NHRCK held a public hearing on the abductions. The GNP lawmaker Lee Ju-yeong also proposed another bill to provide financial aid to abductees and their families, but it expired without being put to a vote.[95] The bill's failure confirms the liabilities of elite access without societal backing. After the sit-in and the bill, though, AFU members "met often with NHRCK staff" in early 2004.[96]

In April 2004, the NHRCK issued a formal recommendation (*gweongo*) calling for an abductions special law (*teukbyeolbeop*). The commission proposed measures to restore the honor of abductions victims, compensate them for past wrongs, and aid escaped abductees. It also argued that the state should investigate the whereabouts of missing abductees and, more important, the discrimination, surveillance, interrogation, imprisonment, or torture that abductee families had endured under past ROK regimes.[97] Although the recommendation was not

---

95. Guihwan Napbukja ui Boho mit Jeongchak Jiwon e Gwanhan Beopryul An [Law concerning the Social Security and Resettlement Assistance for Repatriated Abductees (draft)], proposed December 12, 2003.

96. Interview with Kim Min-tae, NHRCK, Seoul (February 10, 2009).

97. The NHRCK subsequently issued weaker opinions (*uigyeon*) calling for the ROK government to provide aid and state compensation for pre-1953 abductees (June 12, 2006); for the government to include an affected person on the Postwar Abductees Compensation and Assistance Review Committee (July 27, 2006); for the government to provide compensation and medical care to bereaved families of victims of abductions-related violence in the ROK (June 5, 2008); for a special law assisting and compensating pre-1953 abductees (July 18, 2008).

legally binding and received virtually no media attention, a government official said it "put pressure on the government and lawmakers to do something about the abductions."[98]

LEGISLATING ASSISTANCE FOR ABDUCTIONS VICTIMS

Disagreement about which ministry should be responsible for implementing abductee family assistance programs initially stymied the government's response to the NHRCK recommendation. As an NHRCK staffer explained, "While the NHRCK believed the issue lay within the MOU's jurisdiction, MOU officials argued in 2004 and 2005 that MOPAS actually bore responsibility because compensation and financial assistance were domestic programs and because ROK intelligence and law enforcement officials had mistreated abductees and their families in the past."[99] MOPAS officials countered that rescuing and confirming whether abductees were alive in the DPRK was the MOU's domain.

In an effort to end this buck-passing and rekindle public awareness of the abductions in early 2005, AFU leader Choi Seong-yong released a photo of thirty missing ROK fishermen together in North Korea. The unprecedented photo, which Choi Seong-yong had obtained from an anonymous source in North Korea, received substantial media coverage. Since both AFU and FADN members' relatives appeared in the photo, both groups publicized this evidence. They also continued to lobby lawmakers, the MOU, and MOPAS. This new publicity and the U.S. Congress's passage of the North Korean Human Rights Act in late 2004 aided efforts by the AFU and FADN to shame the ROK government into passing abductions-related legislation.

As a result of the new evidence and AFU and FADN lobbying at the National Assembly, a handful of politicians—early elite allies who had proven more attentive than the general public to the families' activism—again drafted legislation to aid abductees and their families in 2005. The GNP lawmaker Kim Mun-su worked particularly closely with AFU leaders, although his bill was neither the first nor the last abductee-related bill proposed. Kim apparently sympathized with the persecution that abductees' families had endured under the ROK's authoritarian regimes because he had endured similar hardship as a labor activist in the 1980s. As a member of the National Assembly's Foreign Affairs, Trade, and Unification Committee, Kim was also well positioned to introduce a bill. He did so in June 2005, just before the fourth escaped abductee (Ko Myeong-seop) returned to South Korean soil. The bill proposed financial assistance to abductees and their families and highlighted how the ROK government had failed in its

---

98. Interview with Koo Byeong-sam, MOU, Seoul (February 10, 2009).
99. Interview with Kim Min-tae, NHRKC.

basic duties to protect citizens.[100] At the public hearing on the bill in September 2005, Choi Seong-yong tearfully testified about his father. The recently escaped abductee Ko Myeong-seop also shared his story.[101] The three main papers each carried about twenty articles per month on the abductions in fall 2005. The GNP chairwoman and future ROK president Park Geun-hye also attended the hearing and later joined FADN leader Choi U-yeong in tying yellow ribbons to a tree at GNP headquarters. Meanwhile, in August 2005 the GNP lawmaker Choi Byeong-guk proposed a separate bill focused on providing financial aid to escaped abductees.[102] Indicative of the ongoing dispute over which ministry should be responsible for abductee policy, both bills were submitted to the Foreign Affairs, Trade, and Unification Committee in the National Assembly but were then sent to the Public Administration and Security Committee months later.[103] With such delays, neither bill was put to a vote in the full assembly.

Only in 2006 did efforts to legislate redress for South Korean abductees and their families progress, as a result of the appointment of a minister of unification who was willing to take on the abductions issue amid sustained pressure from abductee families and their allies and more evidence about still-missing abductees. The first development occurred in early 2006, when President Roh Moo-hyun appointed Lee Jong-seok, a specialist on the North Korean Workers' Party and Kim Il-sung, as minister of unification. Lee had been part of the ROK delegation to the North in June 2000 and considered relations with the DPRK special among all the ROK's international relationships. Although he was considered a left-leaning scholar before his political appointments, he saw "redressing the ROK government's past mistreatment of abductees and their families as connected with the administration's broader commitment to resolving authoritarian-era issues [*gwageosa hegyeol*]."[104] After two years as deputy secretary of the Korean National Security Council, Lee also felt "confident that [he] could manage the inter-ministerial coordination needed to draft a special law for abductees."[105]

Thus, an MOU-led task force, in coordination with MOPAS, began preparing a government bill in early 2006. The task force's teams—one of which included several activists and scholars from outside government—apparently "consulted Kim

---

100. Napbuk Pihaeja Jiwon deung e Gwanhan Beopryul An [Law concerning Abductions Victims' Assistance (draft)], June 24, 2005.

101. Yang Jung A., "Much Effort to Put on the '4+1 Acts,'" *Daily NK*, September 12, 2005.

102. Guihwan Napbukja ui Boho mit Jeongchak Jiwon e Gwanhan Beopryul An [Law concerning Social Security and Resettlement Assistance for Returning Abductees (draft)], August 2005.

103. Park, "Jeonhu Napbuk Pihaeja Jiwon Ipbeop eui Gwaje wa Jeonmang," 79–80.

104. Interview with Kim Jong-gwan, AFU, Seoul (August10, 2009).

105. Interview with Lee Jong-seok, former Minister of Unification, Seoul (August 13, 2009).

Mun-su's defunct bill from 2005 closely."[106] One team's investigations, a member explained, "unearthed and consolidated extant ROK government documents related to the abductions for the first time," facilitating the subsequent work of determining victims' eligibility for financial support or compensation.[107] A second team composed of lawyers studied legal precedents, and a third team negotiated with relevant ministries. Throughout 2006, AFU and FADN members also met with Minister Lee and lobbied lawmakers for backing in conjunction with the country's May 2006 local and regional elections, which the opposition GNP won handily amid public dissatisfaction with the Roh administration and its seemingly indulgent attitude toward North Korea. But Choi Seong-yong contends that "the MOU did not listen to the families' demands and that Minister Lee seemed most interested in hammering out legislation for which he could claim credit."[108]

As the ROK government prepared this law, the Japanese government revealed that the abductee Yokota Megumi had married a South Korean abductee named Kim Yeong-nam in the DPRK. This announcement received widespread media coverage in Korea, with the three main newspapers each running about fifty articles on the abductions in April 2006. Kim Yeong-nam's mother and sister visited Japan to participate in rallies alongside the Yokotas, who likewise traveled to Korea to participate in public rallies in 2006. The DPRK permitted Kim Yeong-nam to meet his mother at the separated-family reunions held in June 2006, just weeks before North Korea's missile tests led the ROK to suspend the reunions. Although Kim Yeong-nam declared that Megumi had committed suicide in North Korea, his existence added evidence that the DPRK had kidnapped ROK citizens. Unlike the majority of ROK nationals abducted or detained by the DPRK, Kim Yeong-nam had been kidnapped from a beach in South Korea as a teenager. Shortly after the reunion, the AFU's Choi Seong-yong announced that another abducted fisherman had tried but failed to escape from North Korea. These new pieces of evidence added urgency to efforts to draft legislation to assist Korean abductee families since the ROK's inaction contrasted with Japan's attitude toward its abductee families.

In October 2006, therefore, the MOU submitted the Law concerning the Compensation and Assistance of Persons Kidnapped by North Korea after the Armistice Agreement (hereafter Victim Assistance Law) to the National Assembly.[109] As the Unification and Foreign Affairs Committee was considering the bill, the

106. Interview with Yun Yeo-sang, North Korea Data Base, Seoul (July 14, 2012).
107. Interview with an MOU official, Seoul (August 19, 2009).
108. Interview with Choi Seong-yong, AFU (February 3, 2009).
109. Gunsa Jeongjeon e Gwanhan Hyeopjeong Chegyeol Ihu Napbukpihaeja ui Bosang mit Jiwon e Gwanhan Beopryul (law no. 8393, October 27, 2007).

abductee Choi Uk-il escaped in January 2007. Choi Seong-yong posted an online video of ROK consular officials in China "repeatedly refusing to recognize Choi Uk-il as an abductee" and organized protests at government buildings in Seoul.[110] Korean public outrage at consular officials' callousness led MOFAT to apologize several days later and promise a speedy repatriation process for Choi Uk-il. Although all major news outlets covered his return, media and public awareness of the abductions issue again subsided relatively quickly. In spite of the victims' inability to sustain publicity, the Victim Assistance Law passed in April 2007 with backing from GNP legislators.

IMPLEMENTING THE VICTIM ASSISTANCE LAW AND ANOTHER NORTH-SOUTH SUMMIT

The Victim Assistance Law emphasized the ROK's duty to protect citizens, required that the state help repatriate abductees or discover whether they were alive, and called on the state to compensate or provide financial relief to victims and their families. In contrast to Japanese policy, the Korean law spelled out how abductees would be recognized by the state, what levels of assistance each family applying for recognition would receive, and a schema for compensating abductees and family members who were tortured or killed by ROK authorities. The law defined three categories of victims: abductees who had returned to the ROK after being in the DPRK for three or more years, abductees who had not been able to return or who died in North Korea, and abductees or family members who were injured or killed while being investigated by ROK authorities. Escaped abductees were deemed eligible for resettlement stipends, while missing abductees' families received only condolence payments unless they could prove severe abuse by ROK authorities and thereby gain compensation. Limiting the definition of abductees to those detained in the DPRK for three or more years eliminated 80 to 90 percent of South Korean abductees, and thus the law offered only partial redress.

The most difficult part of deliberations to prepare the law, one official explained, had been "over budget and financial concessions."[111] For equity reasons MOPAS advocated capping assistance to abductee families at 10 million won per family (about $9,090), which was the amount of "condolence money" (*wirogeum*) given to victims of serious crimes. The AFU demanded 200 million won (about $182,000) per family, arguing that "governmental condolence money for crime victims does not require any acknowledgment of blame and was therefore an inappropriate model for abductee families' financial assistance."[112] The MOU

---

110. Interview with An Jun-ho, *Chosun Ilbo* journalist.
111. Interview with Koo Byeong-sam, MOU, Seoul (February 10, 2009).
112. Interview with Kim Jong-gwan, AFU (August 10, 2009).

TABLE 5.2 Public Opinion Poll—Most important subjects for upcoming North-South summit (2007)

SUBJECT	PRIORITY (BY PERCENTAGE OF RESPONDENTS)
Nuclear weapons issue	29.2%
Easing military tensions	27.9%
North-South economic cooperation	16.1%
Separated families' reunions	11.0%
Agreement on reunification procedure	8.9%
POW and abductions issue	6.7%
Don't know/No answer	0.3%

proposed a compromise of 45 million won (about $40,900) per family, which was ultimately what the law stipulated. Through a clearer process than that in Japan, applications for gaining state recognition and such financial assistance would be accepted for three years from when the law went into force in October 2007.

Yet the law failed to satisfy abductee families. In particular, members of the AFU criticized it for having been hammered out behind closed doors without families' input. In fact, AFU members lashed out at MOU officials and FADN members who gathered in July 2007 for a post facto public hearing concerning the law. AFU members punched the leader of FADN, overturned tables, and threatened the experts who were called to testify at the hearing. As a result, the hearing was abruptly terminated, and the MOU charged the AFU with obstructing its work. AFU members, in turn, staged a candlelight vigil outside the unification minister's home and harassed other officials by phone. Choi Seong-yong was arrested for this behavior. Although the AFU has since campaigned to increase the compensation and assistance provided by the law, the families face stiff opposition from the state for budgetary reasons.

In addition, President Roh Moo-hyun's decision to hold a summit with Kim Jong-il in August 2007 deflected attention from the Victim Assistance Law. A poll conducted in advance of this second North-South summit revealed that Korean citizens rated resolving the POW and abductions issue lower than all other potential priorities (table 5.2).[113]

Reports differ as to whether Roh Moo-hyun actually raised the abductions and POW issue with Kim Jong-il, but it was not an agenda item, and the DPRK continued to deny any wrongdoing. In September, another abductee (Lee Han-seop) returned to South Korea, and the AFU publicized his escape as more evidence of

---

113. Gallup Korea survey, "Which of the following do you think is the most important agenda item that should be raised at the upcoming North-South summit meeting?" 814 respondents, August 8, 2007, http://panel.gallup.co.kr.

the ROK government's neglect of abductees. Partly as a result, one opinion poll indicated that South Koreans were most dissatisfied with the way the refugee and abductee issues had been handled at the summit.[114] While 24 percent of respondents thought that the expansion of economic cooperation was the best outcome of the summit, 27 percent thought that questions about refugees and abductees represented the most disappointing outcome (16 percent thought that denuclearization was least well handled). The election to the presidency of conservative candidate Lee Myung-bak in late 2007 also partly reflected public disappointment with the results of Kim Dae-jung's and Roh Moo-hyun's conciliatory policies toward the DPRK. Both he and his opponent, Lee Hoi-chang, pledged to work to repatriate abductees.

Aside from the violent public hearing and the AFU's ongoing complaints about the Victim Assistance Law, the implementation of partial redress for Korea's abductee families was relatively smooth. In late 2007, the MOU assigned an official to supervise policies related to abductees and POWs. Like Abe's cabinet headquarters, this official provides abductee families a place to contact if they have questions or problems and coordinates relevant policies. In accordance with the Victim Assistance Law, the Abductee Compensation and Assistance Review Committee (the Review Committee) received and reviewed applications for victim status from 2007 to 2011. Composed of government officials, lawyers, North Korea experts, and one member nominated by abductee families, this committee met monthly and decided how much compensation or financial aid each claimant should receive.[115] The MOU also established the Abductions Victim Support Team to collect and investigate claims for victim status. The size of this team shrank after budgetary cuts under Lee Myung-bak. As a result, an official involved acknowledged that "its investigations into families' past suffering were not particularly thorough."[116]

Nevertheless, the Review Committee and its support team uncovered forty previously unknown cases of North Korean abductions. It also granted 31 million won each (about $28,200) in victim condolence money to 416 of the 428 cases reviewed.[117] The nine escaped abductees have each received on average 191 million won (about $174,000) in resettlement funds. One of the ways in which the ROK government curtailed the scope of this redress law was by making compensation

114. "Yeoron Josa: Choidae Seonggwa neun Gyeonhyeop . . . Napbukja Munje Miheum [Opinion Poll: Best Outcome Was Economic Cooperation . . . Disappointment with Abductions Issue]," *Hankook Ilbo*, October 7, 2007.

115. Interview with Lee Geum-sun, KINU, Seoul (July 19, 2009).

116. Interview with Koo Byeong-sam, MOU, Seoul (July 5, 2012).

117. Ministry of Unification, *2015 Tongil Baekseo*, 119.

(*bosanggeum*), as opposed to condolence money, available only for abductees and family members who were injured or killed in the process of interrogation by the ROK authorities. As a result, 68 million won (roughly $61,000) in compensation, which entails a government admission of responsibility, was granted to only one of the thirteen applicants. Additionally, one recently escaped abductee sued the Review Committee because it had reduced his financial aid after discovering that he had worked for North Korean intelligence services. He claimed that the DPRK had forced him into this work. Choi Seong-yong, meanwhile, refused to take money from the committee (and encouraged other AFU members to do so, mostly in vain) because he argued the law was flawed. He also complained that "in Japan, the government comes looking for you when you're an abductee's family. We don't expect our government to come to us, but [in Korea], it's practically impossible for a victim's family to see a government official."[118]

IN PURSUIT OF MORE COMPREHENSIVE REDRESS

Dissatisfied with redress, elements of the Korean movement continue to try to overcome the liabilities of early access to elite allies and the issue's interconnectedness with North-South relations. Since 2008, the AFU has actively campaigned for more generous redress legislation, while FADN has essentially ceased its activities. In November 2008, the GNP National Assembly member Shin Sang-jin—who apparently "knew AFU leader and journalist Kim Jong-gwan from his district outside Seoul"—proposed revisions to the Victim Assistance Law to increase financial, housing, and welfare support for abductees and their families.[119] After the draft revision faced resistance in committee for budgetary reasons, the GNP legislator Yun Sang-hyeon proposed a curtailed version to the Foreign Affairs and Unification Committee in February 2010. Kim Jong-gwan and Choi Seong-yong, both key figures in the AFU, supplied the gist of both bills to the two lawmakers. As had happened during the families' early activism, GNP legislators proved most receptive to the AFU's lobbying. Under Lee Myung-bak's conservative presidency, calls for measures to encourage defections from the DPRK grew and included discussions about ways to help abductees and POWs escape. The National Assembly also passed legislation in 2010 to recognize Korean War abductees and research their whereabouts. Finally, in April 2011, Shin Sang-jin's proposed revisions to the Victim Assistance Law passed.[120] They enabled the creation of an organization to advance abductee families' rights with state subsidies and co-

---

118. Park Ju-min, "While Japan Presses North on Abductions, South Korea Victims Are Forgotten," *Japan Times*, July 3, 2014.

119. Interview with Choi Seong-yong, AFU (February 3, 2009).

120. Gunsajeongjeon e gwanhan Hyeopjeong Chegyeol ihu Napbukpihaeja ui Bosang mit Jiwon e gwanhan Beopryul ilbu Gaejeong Beopryul (law no. 10602, April 5, 2011).

operation from national and local governments. But the final version did not include expanded benefits for abductee families.

To an even greater extent than in Japan, abductee families' dissatisfaction with partial redress in Korea has spawned divisions within the movement and organizational decline. The families of the eleven still-missing victims of the 1970 hijacking of a KAL plane organized separately from the AFU and FADN in 2004, but personal difficulties led the group's leader to disband it. Choi U-yeong's successor as head of FADN also proved less active, and this resulted in the group's near-complete dormancy by 2010. Meanwhile, escaped abductees formed their own organization in about 2005 because they felt that the AFU's Choi Seong-yong was subjecting them to excessive publicity, which endangered their families still in North Korea. And in 2011, Oh Gil-nam, who had been lured to the DPRK with his family in the 1980s but escaped while in Denmark on a mission to lure other ROK nationals to the DPRK, initiated a separate movement, Daughter of Tongyeong, by walking around South Korea and lobbying internationally for the release of his wife and daughters. Although Oh cooperates with Choi Seong-yong, he frames his cause in broader terms than the AFU or FADN ever did by linking his family's fate with the issue of North Korean prison camps. Finally, Choi Seong-yong faced accusations of "authoritarian leadership" from within the AFU. As a result, Kim Jong-gwan spearheaded the formation of a new group—the Federation of Postwar Abductions Victims' Families (Jeonhu Napbuk Pihae Gajok Yeonhaphoi)—in mid-2012. Kim Jong-gwan has "regular contact with Choi Seong-yong *and* the MOU," but his group has yet to receive the subsidies stipulated in Shin Sang-jin's 2011 law.[121] Kim hopes that the new group will enable recognized abductee families, who are poor and aging, to receive more welfare benefits from the state. Despite such divisions, both wartime and postwar abductees and their families were invited to testify before the UN Commission of Inquiry in Seoul in 2013 and received extensive discussion in the Commission's final report.

In sum, the Japanese and Korean abductee families' activism elicited only partial redress, despite their differing levels of societal support. Both Tokyo and Seoul responded to families' demands by investigating some suspected abductions and providing symbolic and material concessions to some abductees' families. But neither country publicly acknowledged responsibility for failing to prevent the abductions or exacerbating the families' hardship. The Japanese government kept its process for requesting an inquiry into an abductions case opaque, either to protect itself from being held liable for more citizens' disappearances or to make it easier to resolve the abductions issue. For its part, the ROK government

---

121. Interview with Kim Jong-gwan, chair of the group's board, Seongnam (July 11, 2012).

created so many conditions for official compensation that only one applicant has received it, although nearly 450 have received other government assistance. Still, both governments increased pressure on the DPRK to return suspected abductees, and abductee families have gained greater access to decision makers as a result of institutional reforms. In Japan, the establishment of the Cabinet Headquarters for the Abductions Issue in 2006 improved intragovernmental coordination on abductions-related policy. With less fanfare, the ROK's Ministry of Unification assigned an official to manage abductions and POW issues for the first time in 2006 and started officially coordinating with abductee families. Table 5.3 summarizes redress concessions in each case, scoring them according to the scale described in chapter 1.

TABLE 5.3   Redress outcomes in the abductee movements

COMPONENTS OF REDRESS	JAPAN	KOREA
Official inquiry	1—Ad hoc, and process for requesting an inquiry is opaque	1—Yes, but limited and only for people detained more than three years
Apology	0—No	1—No, but victims' names cleared
Compensation and financial assistance	1—Financial aid and benefits limited to repatriated abductees	1—Transparent application process for financial aid, but highly restricted compensation
Institutional reforms	2—Extensive	1—More interagency coordination
TOTAL	**PARTIAL REDRESS (4)**	**PARTIAL REDRESS (4)**

Note: The scores reflect the extent to which state actions fulfill each component of redress: fully (2), partially (1), or not at all (0).

These analogous outcomes of two distinctive movements highlight how early access to elite allies can have lasting effects, even if a movement subsequently gains broader societal support. Thus the cases indicate cross-issue parallels in the dynamic relational process of conflict expansion even with a policy area so different from those discussed in the two previous chapters. As the UN Commission of Inquiry report in 2014 put it, North Korea's abductions are undeniably "exceptional" behavior for "a state that seeks to live alongside others."[122] And abductee families' activism is inextricably linked to high-stakes foreign policy debates in each country. Many details about the abductions—and hence how to resolve the issue—will remain murky until North Korea opens. But the particularities of the abductions issue should not prevent us from comparing these cases with wholly domestic movements. Indeed, although full redress may seem unattainable for abductions victims and their families, restoring the status quo ante for any of the redress claimants discussed in this book is likewise impossible.

---

122. UN General Assembly, *Report of the Commission of Inquiry*, 13.

Conclusion

THE POLITICS OF REDRESS

The preceding chapters have examined democratic political participation by focusing on the experiences of people who feel they suffered a preventable harm due to government negligence or wrongdoing and exploring the ways in which they seek redress for this harm. Stigma, numerous competing voices and issues, and budget constraints complicate this process for redress claimants, who usually begin from positions of weakness vis-à-vis the government actors they seek to hold accountable. To overcome these challenges, claimants use their victimhood to try to persuade others that they deserve special treatment beyond that afforded to ordinary citizens by articulating how the government bears responsibility for their suffering and how redress policies will alleviate that suffering. As scholars and activists alike recognize, relatively powerless groups such as these depend on support from political elites, active groups in society, the media, experts, lawyers, and the attentive public in order to gain attention and sway policymakers' decisions. Yet this book transforms our understanding of *when and how* support from such third parties gives claimants leverage over the state they hold accountable.

By scrutinizing the contested processes of mobilizing and leveraging third-party support, we have seen that interactions over time among claimants and various third parties shape redress outcomes in two ways. First, these interactions affect other third parties' decisions about when and how to take up a cause. And consequently they affect incumbents' perceptions about the extent to which a redress movement and its supporters might impinge upon their electoral prospects or approval ratings. I built off the concept of conflict expansion to describe these combinations of mechanisms and processes, drawing particular attention to the sequencing or temporal order in which third parties take up a victim group's cause.[1] Evidence from comparisons of three pairs of movements in Japan and Korea indicates that early access to elite allies can be detrimental for redress movements. If alliances with lawmakers form early in a conflict, these elite allies may raise broader awareness about the victims' cause or sponsor special legislation, but their activities also tend to deter or undermine grassroots mobilizing. By contrast, the initial unavailability of elite allies encourages movement building and grassroots mobilizing, which in turn can create a political climate in which politicians have greater incentives to back a victim group's cause in order to avoid the negative consequences that might befall them if they fail to act. Thus the initial absence of political opportunities can be a good thing, especially for small claimant groups in centralized, elite-dominated polities.

We have also seen how civil society groups and other actors in the public sphere—not just political elites and the state—can organize some issues and groups in or out of politics, whether intentionally or not. Since lawyers, journalists, and activists constitute the social infrastructure behind grievance articulation and political participation, their impact on the tactical options available to claimants and on third parties' decisions about whether to take up a victim group's cause have received special attention. Even in this era of global convergence and interchange, the way such mediating institutions structure the public sphere still varies cross-nationally and helps account for apparent cross-cultural differences in societies' abilities to sympathize with certain redress claimants. Over time, Japanese and Korean mediating institutions have also contributed to and been affected by the evolution of democracy and the connotations that claims to victimhood acquired in each country's political development. Systematically comparing these institutions has uncovered dimensions that single-country analysis has overlooked. In Japan, for instance, the mainstream media's relative homogeneity, the predominance of local citizen activism, and lawyers' decentralized networks were conducive to grassroots mobilizing, often around litigation. In contrast, Korea's politically polarized and diverse public sphere tends to focus more on national-level politics and thus encouraged redress claimants to forge alliances with political elites early, often with detrimental consequences for their activism. If such facets of each society's mediating sectors determined redress outcomes, then one would expect similar outcomes across all such movements in that country. But the fact that outcomes also vary within each country, as we

---

1. E. E. Schattschneider, *The Semisovereign People* (New York: Holt, Rinehart and Winston, 1960).

saw in this book's case studies, suggests that there is still considerable space for contingency and actors' agency. As my analysis shows, the interactive and dynamic processes of conflict expansion that occur within this space best explain variations in redress outcomes.

Building off these arguments, this chapter returns to several key themes raised in the introduction and discusses areas for future research. I begin by considering the range of cases to which my arguments about the sequencing of conflict expansion best apply through comparisons of two recent redress movements in Japan and Korea and an example from France, another country with relatively centralized and elite-dominated politics. I then revisit the dilemmas entailed in political conflicts over redress and assess the extent to which redress-related activism enhances governmental accountability. I conclude by discussing some implications of my research and directions for future inquiry. I highlight three themes: the importance of an interactive and dynamic approach to analyzing redress politics, the growing role of law and courts in political processes in Japan and Korea, and the changing nature of state-society relations in Japan and Korea.

Victim Redress Movements in Comparative Perspective

Since the period of activism analyzed in the foregoing chapters, Japan and the Republic of Korea each faced a national tragedy that spawned victim redress movements and wrenching discussions about governmental accountability. These disasters provide an opportunity to consider the broader universe of cases to which my argument about sequencing in conflict expansion might apply. First, the massive earthquake and tsunami that struck northeastern Japan in March 2011 (known as 3.11) left nearly twenty thousand people dead or missing and caused more than $230 billion in economic damage. It also triggered a meltdown at the Fukushima nuclear power plant that uprooted a hundred thousand people and harmed their livelihoods. An independent inquiry commissioned by the Japanese Diet called the nuclear disaster "profoundly man-made" and faulted Japanese decision-making culture, improper regulations, and ineffective government coordination in the aftermath of the disaster.[2] More recently, in Korea in April 2014, the Sewol ferry capsized and sank, killing 304 of the 476 passengers, most of

---

2. Kurokawa Kiyoshi, *Executive Summary of the Official Report of the Fukushima Nuclear Accident Independent Investigation Commission* (Tokyo, 2012), 9.

whom were teenagers on a school trip. President Park Geun-hye's administration has faced accusations of ill-coordinated and sluggish rescue efforts, regulatory failure, and corruption. Not only did the coast guard rescue the captain and several other crew as they abandoned the illegally renovated and top-heavy vessel before it was evacuated, but it also failed to rescue scores of other passengers, who were instead picked up by fishing vessels. Since the ship's sinking, dozens of crew members and people related to the shipping company have been charged with negligence or homicide. The captain was sentenced to life in prison for murder, and President Park Geun-hye disbanded the coast guard and pledged to curb bureaucratic corruption.

These disasters differ in terms of their scale and causes, and, unlike most of the cases in this book, they fit into the category of rare events and policy failures that have such calamitous consequences that victims have little difficulty appealing for third-party support. In both cases, politicians proposed special legislation relatively quickly, and among civil society groups and ordinary citizens, concern for those affected by the disasters was widespread. Yet the redress movements that emerged from these disasters offer us a chance to examine the extent to which this book's framework about conflict expansion patterns also illuminates societal and political responses to victims' claims in the wake of such national tragedies. Even though it may be too early for definitive conclusions about the efficacy of redress movements related to these disasters, they already illustrate the downsides of early access to elite allies.

In fact, victims of both disasters have recently redoubled their efforts to mobilize grassroots societal backing to overcome what they perceive to be the insufficient redress policies that their elite allies engineered after each disaster. Korean relatives of the ferry's victims have used marches, rallies, protests, and signature-collection campaigns to persuade the state to raise the sunken vessel and establish a truly independent fact-finding inquiry into the sinking, without government officials on the committee. The growing number of Japanese lawsuits and local activism related to 3.11 have focused on clarifying the government's responsibility, improving safety regulations regarding nuclear power, and discouraging the government from restarting nuclear plants, even as other claimants continue to pursue compensation directly from the nuclear plant operator or through alternative dispute resolution channels. In their tactics and issue framing, redress movements in both countries seem to be pursuing societal backing to make up for some of the compromises their early elite allies made and to pressure decision makers for more comprehensive redress. The brief examination of a French redress movement below reveals a similar phenomenon, indicating that it is not unique to Japan and Korea.

3.11: Compensation and Compromise

Alleviating the hardships of people affected by 3.11 was a core priority for the Japanese government and other actors involved in relief efforts in the aftermath of the triple disaster. Yet because politicians, bureaucrats, and nuclear industry officials took up the question of compensation so quickly after the disaster, redress claimants did not have the time or the impetus to build up broader societal pressure specifically for comprehensive redress. As a result, redress measures were subject to multiple compromises among politicians and between the state and the nuclear plant's operator, Tokyo Electric Power Company (TEPCO). Although Prime Minister Kan Naoto (who had championed redress for HIV- and HCV-tainted blood victims) acknowledged the government's shared responsibility for having long promoted nuclear power, the duty to compensate victims fell primarily on TEPCO.[3] Kan's government therefore faced the challenge of ensuring that TEPCO could compensate victims without going bankrupt, which would jeopardize cleanup efforts and the broader Japanese economy. Within a month of the disaster, the government created the Dispute Reconciliation Committee for Nuclear Power Damage Compensation to start drafting guidelines for the compensation process.[4] But this body was criticized as nonneutral because some of its members had ties to a research institute that TEPCO and other utilities had created in the 1980s. Fact-finding and structural reforms to improve nuclear safety were also treated with less urgency, despite public concerns.

Although TEPCO started issuing temporary payouts to some people affected by the triple disaster in April, divisions within the DPJ and resistance from the opposition LDP resulted in further compromises and delayed compensation legislation until August 2011. Ozawa Ichirō, a powerful figure within the DPJ, vocally criticized Prime Minister Kan's leadership and discussed replacing Kan, whose approval ratings were falling. The April 2011 subnational elections dealt a blow to the DPJ, which would lose badly to the LDP in the December 2012 Lower House elections. Kan also narrowly survived a vote of no confidence tabled by the LDP and some fellow DPJ members in June 2011, after reaching an undisclosed deal with his opponents in the Diet, possibly that he would resign. When Kan did step down in August 2011, the Diet enacted legislation creating a fund that injected billions of dollars of government aid into TEPCO, with contributions from Japan's other utilities, ostensibly to facilitate both the compensation and the

---

3. Richard J. Samuels, *3.11* (Ithaca: Cornell University Press, 2013), 13.
4. Eri Osaka, "Corporate Liability, Government Liability, and the Fukushima Nuclear Disaster," *Pacific Rim Law & Policy Journal* 21, no. 3 (June 2012): 439–41.

cleanup processes.[5] Also in August, the government issued guidelines about who was eligible for compensation and established an alternative channel to resolve disputed claims, which, surprisingly, did not require claimants to forfeit the right to future litigation.[6]

But the rising fortunes of the LDP did not bode well for redress claims because of the party's longtime association with Japan's influential "nuclear village," which includes government and industry proponents of nuclear energy.[7] While still in the opposition, the LDP held up the authorization of additional government bonds to underwrite TEPCO's costs in late 2011 and then forced the DPJ prime minister, Noda Yoshihiko, to renege on promises to phase out nuclear power in Japan. Such political compromises resulted in what Feldman called "an extremely unwieldy and expensive administrative structure that impedes rather than facilitates compensation, fueling the view that the needs of the government and TEPCO, not the needs of the victims, predominate."[8] Complaints from claimants, low application rates, and critical media coverage led TEPCO to reduce the length of the compensation application form from sixty to thirty pages and to expand eligibility criteria beyond the twenty-kilometer exclusion zone, but the process remains opaque and slow.

Several developments suggest that redress claimants and their supporters are trying to overcome some of these frustrations by pursuing support from societal actors rather than politicians. First, victims' difficulties in obtaining redress led Japanese attorneys to form about ten large lawyers' groups (*bengodan*), primarily in Tokyo and Fukushima. While most of these groups aim to help victims with applications for compensation directly from TEPCO or through the alternative dispute resolution (ADR) channel by holding explanatory meetings (*setsumeikai*) or offering legal counsel, others have broader social reform goals related to the future of nuclear power.[9] Many of these legal teams include lawyers with experience in earlier legal mobilization campaigns like those discussed in this book. Second, the 3.11 disaster energized Japan's antinuclear movement. Large protests, the likes of which had not been seen in decades, rocked Japan in summer 2012, demanding

---

5. Genshiryoku Songai Baishō Shien Kikō Hō [Nuclear Damage Liability Facilitation Fund Law] (law no. 94, 2011).

6. Joel Rheuben and Luke Nottage, "Resolving Claims from the Fukushima Nuclear Disaster," *Japanese Law in the Asia-Pacific Socio-Economic Context* (blog), January 26, 2015, blogs.usyd.edu.au/japaneselaw/2015/01/resolving_nuclear_claims.html.

7. Jacques Hymans, "Veto Players, Nuclear Energy, and Nonproliferation," *International Security* 36, no. 2 (Fall 2011): 154–89.

8. Eric A. Feldman, "Fukushima," *DePaul Law Review* 62 (2013): 355.

9. Interview with Maruyama Teruhisa, leader of one of the largest lawyers' groups, Tokyo (July 1, 2013).

government accountability, among other things. Avenell points out parallels between such activism and earlier "victim-centered environmental activism," which suggest that activists are particularly attuned to redress claims.[10] Third, people affected by the triple disaster and their supporters are increasingly taking legal action to pursue redress and broader reforms, albeit with limited success to date. For example, criminal charges brought by 15,000 plaintiffs against Prime Minister Kan and TEPCO CEOs for professional negligence were dismissed. But in March 2013, more than 1,500 plaintiffs filed four lawsuits holding TEPCO and—for the first time—the central government liable for relying on nuclear power and having insufficient safety measures.[11] Some 4,000 plaintiffs from several countries have also joined a 2014 lawsuit against multinational nuclear plant suppliers for symbolic 100-yen payments.[12] In addition, activists have—with help from cause lawyers—turned to litigation as a way to press for the decommissioning of other nuclear power plants, which were all temporarily shut down after the 2011 disaster. In one case, the court issued a landmark injunction against restarting two nuclear reactors at a plant in Fukui prefecture in April 2015. The group of residents who had sued for the injunction and their supporters celebrated the ruling by proclaiming that "Justice is alive after all!"[13] As people affected by the disaster continue to press for accountability and redress, however, many still endure dislocation, economic hardships, sluggish bureaucratic processes, and unresponsive officials.

After the Sewol Sinking: Politicizing Redress

Whereas political elites' early actions related to redress for 3.11 victims resulted in compromises that fell short of many victims' hopes, Korean political elites' early involvement on questions of redress for victims' families and fact-finding after the Korean ferry disaster politicized the issue to the extent that partisan bickering delayed and eventually watered down redress measures. As divers battled rapid currents and murky water to recover victims' bodies from the sunken ship, lawmakers from all parties, but especially the progressive opposition party, criticized President Park and the authorities' botched rescue efforts, decried lax regulation, and called for relief for victims' families. Yellow ribbons commemorating the dead throughout the

10. Simon Avenell, "From Fearsome Pollution to Fukushima," *Environmental History* 17, no. 2 (April 2012): 244–76.

11. "Residents, Evacuees File Lawsuit against Central Government, TEPCO," *Asahi Shimbun*, March 12, 2013.

12. "Thousands Sue Nuclear Companies over Fukushima Disaster," *Japan Times*, March 13, 2014.

13. Mari Yamaguichi, "Japanese Court Rejects Bid to Restart 2 Nuclear Reactors," *Washington Post*, April 14, 2015.

country testified to the near-universal grief and outrage the accident had sparked at the societal level. President Park apologized for the government's poor handling of rescue operations and information after the disaster and called for reforms to the safety bureaucracy, but her apology was criticized for being delivered at a cabinet meeting thirteen days after the accident. She issued a second, tearful apology two weeks later on national TV. The Sewol issue was still raw at the time of the June 2014 local elections. Candidates from the opposition party, New Politics Alliance for Democracy (NPAD), blamed the Park administration for the disaster, while the ruling Saenuri Party urged support for the president's proposed overhaul to the safety bureaucracy. But voter turnout was lower than expected. The ruling party fared surprisingly well, though commentators noted the public's deepening distrust of political institutions, especially the National Assembly.[14]

Disillusionment with the National Assembly became particularly rife among victims' families, as partisan squabbling among their elite allies stalled the legislative process. The National Assembly delayed the start of a special legislative investigation into the administration's handling of the disaster because the parties disagreed over which witnesses to call. Both main parties negotiated directly with representatives of victims' families over the details of redress and fact-finding. Initially, the NPAD and Saenuri parties also formed a bipartisan task force to design special legislation for Sewol victims' families, but these efforts broke down amid mutual accusations and disagreements over the composition and investigatory powers of the inquiry committee. When the NPAD proposed a bill stipulating compensation for victims' families and an independent inquiry into the disaster, the Saenuri Party declared it unconstitutional. The NPAD in turn leveraged the terms of the 2012 National Advancement Act—which requires the consent of three-fifths of all lawmakers before a bill can be put up for a vote during a plenary session—to grind Korea's legislative process to a halt. For 150 days from May 2014, the NPAD refused to consider any bills until the ruling party agreed to the NPAD's proposed Sewol bill. Though President Park claimed to be staying above the legislative fray, her refusal to meet with victims' relatives throughout summer 2014 angered many. By August 2014, about 24,000 Koreans had joined victims' families in hunger strikes, and more than 3.5 million people had signed petitions calling on the government to launch a fully independent inquiry into the disaster.[15] Disappointment with the NPAD among victims' relatives grew as

---

14. Karl Friedhoff, "Ferry Crisis Strikes Heavy Blow to Public Trust," *Korea RealTime* (blog), *Wall Street Journal*, May 15, 2014, http://blogs.wsj.com/korearealtime/2014/05/15/ferry-crisis-strikes-heavy-blow-to-public-trust.

15. Jeong Je-hyeok, Sim Hye-ri, and Gyeong Tae-yeong, "24,000 People Join in the Sewol Hunger Strike," *Kyunghyang Sinmun*, August 25, 2014.

the deadlock persisted, however. One family member said that "we want to support the opposition to the end, but when we look at the things they are doing we have little hope."[16] When legislators finally reached a grand compromise in late September by essentially postponing contentious decisions about the precise composition of the inquiry commission, ninety pending bills were passed in a single day. The Sewol Special Law was passed several weeks later following further compromises.[17] Yet criticism of the NPAD leadership's handling of the Sewol issue and its failure to restore public trust in political parties with "new politics" led to several leadership shuffles that decimated the opposition party and deepened disillusionment among victims' families.[18]

By the first anniversary of the disaster, an official inquiry into the accident had yet to begin, the new Ministry of Public Safety and Security had left top positions unfilled, and only 15 percent of Koreans surveyed said they felt safer since the Sewol disaster.[19] Victims' families also continued to voice frustration toward the entire political establishment. Bereaved relatives spoke of feeling "excluded" from the ruling party's "political calculations" and "used as propaganda and agitation tools" by the opposition party.[20] To mobilize societal support for a more independent inquiry and raising the ferry, victims' relatives engaged in marches and sit-ins, collected signatures on petitions, shaved their heads in protest, and organized memorial events. As outlined by the progressive lawyers' organization Minbyeon and five other groups, the families and their supporters particularly criticized the government's effort to put officials on the inquiry commission, require government approval before releasing official documents to the commission, limit the inquiry's timeline, and reduce the budget and number of commissioners.[21] Meanwhile, the state offered 420 million won (about $382,000) to each deceased student's family and 760 million won (about $691,000) each to the families of teachers who died trying to save students, with compensation (*baesang-geum*) varying for other victims according to their age and professions. Bereaved

---

16. Jeong U-sang, "Park . . . Yugajok Seoldeuk . . . [Park . . . Persuade Victim Families]," *Chosun Ilbo*, August 11, 2014.

17. 4.16 Sewol-ho Chamsa Jinsang Gyumyeong mit Anjeon Sahoe Geonseol deungeul wihan Teukbyeolbeop (law no. 12843, November 19, 2014).

18. O. Fiona Yap, "South Korea in 2014," *Asian Survey* 55, no. 1 (February 2015): 136–37.

19. Kim Bong-moon, "Sewol Keeps Casting a Shadow," *JoongAng Daily*, April 16, 2015.

20. Lee Seul-bi, "'Seulpeo Hajido, Miweohajido Mapsida' ['Let's Not Be Sad, Hate']," *Chosun Ilbo*, December 29, 2014.

21. Minbyeon et al., "4.16 Sewol-Ho Chamsa Jinsang Gyumyeong mit Anjeonsahoe Geonseol Deungeul wihan Teukbyeolbeop Sihengryeong (An) ui Munjecheom mit Cheolhoe ui Pilyoseong [Joint Opinion by Six Scholarly and Legal Organizations about the Problems with the Sewol Special Law Enforcement Ordinance Draft and Need for Retraction]," April 2, 2015, http://minbyun.or.kr/?p=28280.

families would receive additional money from insurance payouts and private donations. Compensation was available to those families who agreed to forfeit the right to future legal action. But many families denounced the compensation as a government effort to disgrace the families as money-grubbers and "insult the victims with money."[22] As a sign of societal support, rallies commemorating the first anniversary of the disaster drew tens of thousands across Seoul. Several fatal accidents in the year after the sinking revitalized public concerns about safety regulations, shoddy construction, and disaster management. Bereaved families also left an anniversary commemoration early to avoid President Park, and the prime minister was blocked from attending another ceremony. President Park agreed to start raising the ferry in autumn 2015. But an anniversary march on the Blue House by dozens of families and several thousand supporters, against which the police used force and tear gas, epitomized persistent frustration with the partial redress that political elites had provided to date.

Tainted Blood and Redress in France

One might also probe the plausibility of my account of the effects of conflict expansion dynamics by looking, albeit briefly, outside East Asia at the *affaire du sang contaminé* (the [HIV] contaminated blood affair) in France. France presents a good comparison with Japan and Korea for several reasons. France's bureaucracy had historically been similarly insulated from political and societal interference, and France's legal opportunity structure was also relatively closed.[23] Yet in the late 1980s, as in Japan, thousands of hemophiliacs and transfusion recipients started blaming their HIV infections on French policymakers' decisions to privilege domestic expertise and business interests, thereby prolonging the period during which tainted blood and blood derivatives continued to circulate.[24] They mobilized to seek redress as Japanese and Korean victims of tainted blood products did. The two phases of this movement reveal conflict expansion patterns similar to those in the Japanese and Korean cases just discussed. In the first claims-making phase, French HIV victims gained elite allies readily amid heightened electoral competition between socialists and conservatives.[25] Politicians in the conservative parliament, including those on the far right, and the socialist president promoted a variety of policies aimed at tackling the AIDS issue. They also negotiated a redress scheme with the state and insurance companies

---

22. Jung Min-ho, "We Want Truth, Not Money," *Korea Times*, April 2, 2015.
23. Eric A. Feldman, "Blood Justice," *Law & Society Review* 34, no. 3 (2000): 655–58.
24. Marie-Angele Hermitte, *Le Sang et Le Droit* (Paris: Editions du Seuil, 1996).
25. Feldman, "Blood Justice," 693.

but excluded patients from the Association Française des Hémophiles (AFH) from negotiations.[26] The resulting Évin Agreement in 1989 was more a gesture of solidarity with the victims than redress, since it disavowed state wrongdoing.[27]

Tellingly, the AFH and people infected through blood transfusions started campaigning for more comprehensive redress legislation within a year of the Évin Agreement's signing. In this second stage of activism, redress claimants sought to hold the government more accountable through grassroots mobilizing, nearly two thousand court cases, and media appeals. In 1989, several hemophiliacs who had already filed legal claims in court against French factor concentrate manufacturers and government officials had also founded the Association des Polytransfusés (AP) as a more radical alternative to the AFH. While members of the AFH's local branches wrote letters to their legislators and lobbied all levels of government for more redress in 1990, the AP courted publicity and increased pressure on the state through litigation.[28] Then in April 1991, a weekly magazine published a pathbreaking article by the journalist Anne-Marie Casteret containing evidence that French officials had decided in the mid-1980s to continue distributing factor concentrates known to be contaminated with HIV. Her article set off a spate of investigative stories and outraged the French public, which combined with victims' activism to catalyze a sweeping inquiry by the General Inspectorate for Social Affairs.

The "high scandal" that characterized this second phase of the conflict produced more comprehensive redress legislation in late 1991, official inquiries into the safety of the blood supply, a criminal inquiry in the mid-1990s, convictions of individual decision makers, no-fault indemnity payments to victims and their families, and reforms to the oversight of the blood system and doctors' training.[29] Counting people who contracted HIV from medical procedures such as transfusions or while working as medical professionals (added in 1996), compensation payments of more than $1 billion and were made to about four thousand victims plus eleven thousand family members.[30] Court hearings in cases related to tainted blood also drew capacity audiences in the early 1990s and remained headline news for months, even though many of those on trial ended up with

---

26. Monika Steffen, "The Nation's Blood," in *Blood Feuds*, ed. Eric A. Feldman and Ronald Bayer (New York: Oxford University Press, 1999), 114.

27. Feldman, "Blood Justice," 687.

28. Ibid., 688.

29. Theodore R. Marmor, Patricia A. Dillon, and Stephen Scher, "The Comparative Politics of Contaminated Blood," in Feldman and Bayer, *Blood Feuds*, 355–56.

30. Secrétariat d'Etat à la santé et l'action sociale, *Rapport annuel sur le dispositif d'indemnisation des hémophiles et transfusés contaminés par le virus de l'immunodéficience humaine*, March 1997, http://www.ladocumentationfrancaise.fr/var/storage/rapports-publics/994001230/0000.pdf.

misdemeanor charges or acquittals. Although redress in the French case fell short in terms of an admission of state liability, victims still achieved comprehensive redress. As with activism related to the 3.11 and Sewol disasters, this case indicates that some degree of closure or blockage can encourage social movements to invest in grassroots mobilization (even belatedly), which heightens officeholders' sense of political vulnerability and produces greater redress outcomes.

Patterns of Conflict Expansion in Comparative Perspective

To what extent does the argument presented here apply beyond the cases discussed in this book? Let me suggest that bottom-up patterns of conflict expansion are especially potent for small claimant groups—who are by their very nature dependent on third-party support—in centralized and elite-dominated political contexts, such as Japan, Korea, and France. Other cases from Japan and Korea reaffirm these dynamics, although few prior studies have directly examined how the sequencing of conflict expansion affects redress outcomes. For example, Kim's study of Korean activism related to the massacres on Jeju Island (the April third events) in 1948 emphasizes the importance of long-running local activism on Jeju, even during authoritarian rule, for eventually convincing national lawmakers to create a truth commission to investigate the events, forcing the state to apologize, and allowing memorial activities to flourish starting in 2000.[31] The Korean movement to redress sexual abuse at a school for disabled children also highlights how legal action alone had limited impact until a 2011 film (*Dogani*) stoked broader societal outrage by exposing the government's lax punishment of the perpetrators and thus catalyzed legislative reforms. Older studies of pollution victims' activism in Minamata and other parts of Japan similarly reveal the crucial role of localized citizens' movements in mobilizing and constraining national politicians, who then engineered sweeping environmental reforms and compensation schemes.[32] In writing about how Japanese deaf activists mobilized supporters through litigation, Nakamura also noted that "the public relations value of the courtroom drama was as important as the cases themselves."[33] Reich used a comparative study of redress movements related to chemical disasters in Japan, Italy, and the United States to highlight the importance of generating

---

31. Hun Joon Kim, *The Massacres at Mount Halla* (Ithaca: Cornell University Press, 2014).

32. E.g., Margaret A. McKean, *Environmental Protest and Citizen Politics in Japan* (Berkeley: University of California Press, 1981); Ellis S. Krauss and Bradford L. Simcock, "Citizens' Movements," in *Political Opposition in Local Politics in Japan*, ed. Scott C. Flanagan, Kurt Steiner, and Ellis S. Krauss (Princeton: Princeton University Press, 1980), 187–227.

33. Karen Nakamura, "No Voice in the Courtroom?," in *Going to Court to Change Japan*, ed. Patricia G. Steinhoff (Ann Arbor: Center for Japanese Studies, University of Michigan, 2014), 147–63.

a "crescendo of controversy that transforms the victims' struggle into society's conflict and turns a public issue into a political issue."[34] His study also exposes the pitfalls of being too closely associated with political elites (in the Japanese case, the socialists and especially the communists). Such examples indicate that gaining support from active groups in civil society and the attentive public gives redress claimants greater leverage over those politicians who take up their cause and gives politicians greater incentives to support them.

The wider array of access points in polities with more decentralized structures—such as in the United States—probably render it less critical that redress claimants pursue the difficult and sometimes risky process of mobilizing broad public outrage against the government in order to break onto the national political agenda and maximize redress outcomes. Nevertheless, even in polities with more favorable political and legal opportunity structures, moments of blockage or governmental stonewalling can energize a movement's constituents and become powerful examples of injustice that attract bystanders to the movement's cause. Japanese Americans campaigning for redress for wartime relocation and internment, for example, overcame opposition in Congress in the 1980s by mobilizing a broader coalition of support from such groups as the American Bar Association and other civil rights organizations, thereby transforming the issue of redress into "a matter of injustice, not just special interest."[35] And as the lawyer Kenneth Feinberg—administrator of U.S. compensation schemes related to such disasters as the 9/11 terrorist attacks, the 2007 Virginia Tech shooting, the 2010 Deepwater Horizon oil spill in the Gulf of Mexico, and the 2013 Boston Marathon bombing—noted, the public's sympathy with the victims and sense of moral necessity to redress their suffering motivated and enabled the creation of these funds.[36] Future researchers should continue to explore the extent to which the interactive and dynamic processes that I have called the sequencing of conflict expansion shape social movement outcomes in other democratic contexts.

The Politics of Redress and Governmental Accountability

Examining victim redress movements could lead one to contradictory conclusions about the politics of redress. On the one hand, some claimants have achieved incredible victories in holding their government accountable for the

---

34. Michael R. Reich, *Toxic Politics* (Ithaca: Cornell University Press, 1991), 214.
35. Elazar Barkan, *The Guilt of Nations* (New York: Norton, 2000), 42.
36. Kenneth M. Feinberg, *What Is Life Worth?* (New York: PublicAffairs, 2005), chap. 2.

consequences of its policies. The Japanese movements of Hansen's disease survivors and, to a lesser extent, victims of hepatitis C-tainted blood suggest that a government will sometimes go to great lengths to respond to public outrage, acknowledge responsibility, and grant restitution. On the other hand, seeking redress from the state remains a lengthy process of iterated claiming and shaming, fraught with challenges. In addition to the hurdles to collective action that victims face in the naming and blaming stages, the state and powerful interests, which seek to minimize the repercussions of each redress movement, often put pressure on claimants to reach settlements. Both impressions capture the complex reality of redress politics. It may take decades to achieve redress, and fully righting past wrongs is likely to be impossible. Redress is hardly guaranteed, but neither is it so rare that we cannot draw conclusions about the mechanisms and processes through which victim groups mobilize supporters to hold the state accountable and claim redress.

By analyzing how the dynamic processes of conflict expansion affect redress outcomes, this book advances our understanding of why governments *ever* accept responsibility for past wrongs. And the issues it raises concern important moral and legal dilemmas that democratic polities worldwide face. Still, I concede that there is much contingency involved in political participation on the basis of alleged victimhood, depending on how claims and claimants are perceived by potential third-party supporters. I acknowledge and have tried to elucidate the costs and benefits of redress politics—both for victims themselves and for the broader polity. For example, victims tend to achieve more redress if they spark a political crisis, but this also makes political compromise more difficult and can render conflicts hard to wind down. Campaigns for redress can diminish the distinctive features of each victim's experiences or exclude certain subsets of victims. And as Feinberg points out, achieving fairness is virtually impossible.[37] Additionally, decision makers, such as medical drug regulators, may become cautious and inefficient for fear of future redress claims, and citizens may come to expect the state to foresee every potential risk and fix every problem. In the short run, redress movements also increase the state's incentives to preempt and bureaucratize claims making, which generally produces unsatisfactory outcomes for claimants as happened historically in Japan.[38] Despite the financial costs, psychological burdens, and administrative inefficiencies that these movements can incur, redress-related activism is nonetheless contributing in the longer term to the development of more robust mechanisms of government accountability.

---

37. Kenneth Feinberg interviewed on NPR's *Talk of the Nation*, June 27, 2012.

38. E.g., Frank K. Upham, *Law and Social Change in Postwar Japan* (Cambridge, MA: Harvard University Press, 1987); Susan J. Pharr, *Losing Face* (Berkeley: University of California Press, 1990).

Implications and Future Directions for Research

This book has implications for redress claimants and their potential supporters, as well as for students of comparative politics and East Asia. For claimants, this study offers two insights. First, it indicates that seizing opportunities to forge alliances with political elites too early can have disadvantages. The movements I compared indicate that tactics that use claimants' victimhood and their image as "accidental activists" to mobilize societal support give redress claimants better leverage with which to recruit and manage elite allies and compel governmental concessions, even if gaining "insider" access to political elites may seem quicker and less risky. As previous studies have shown that protest mobilization increases not just with more open political opportunity structures but also sometimes in the face of threatened repression, I demonstrated how the unavailability of elite allies can encourage grassroots mobilizing and movement development.[39] Yet this book does not adjudicate the long-standing debate about the arguably artificial distinction between insider and outsider tactics. Both are important at different times in activism. More important, we learned that groups rarely control the form and efficacy of their activism. I show instead that dynamic relations between a victim group and its supporters, rather than just a victim group's tactics, determine the group's level of success. In this, I echo Banaszak's point that second-wave feminist activism occurred both inside and outside government institutions, and the connections among these venues explain the movement's success.[40] For redress claimants, the second takeaway is that they should be aware of how progress in one relationship with a third party can affect their other relationships.

I hope also to have persuaded students of comparative politics that the dynamic processes of conflict expansion and the multiplicity of relationships involved deserve more attention. I thus join a growing number of social movement scholars in calling for more interactive approaches to studying movement outcomes.[41]

---

39. E.g., David S. Meyer and Suzanne Staggenborg, "Movements, Countermovements, and the Structure of Political Opportunity," *American Journal of Sociology* 101, no. 6 (May 1996): 1634, 1645; Jack A. Goldstone and Charles Tilly, "Threat (and Opportunity)," in *Silence and Voice in the Study of Contentious Politics*, ed. Ronald R. Aminzade et al. (Cambridge: Cambridge University Press, 2001); Paul Y. Chang, "Unintended Consequences of Repression," *Social Forces* 87, no. 2 (December 2008): 651–77.

40. Lee Ann Banaszak, *The Women's Movement inside and outside the State* (New York: Cambridge University Press, 2010).

41. E.g., Paul Burstein, Rachel Einwohner, and Jocelyn Hollander, "The Success of Political Movements," in *The Politics of Social Protest*, ed. Bert Klandermans and J. Craig Jenkins (Minneapolis: University of Minnesota Press, 1995), 275–95; Marco G. Giugni, "Was It Worth the Effort?," *Annual Review of Sociology* 24, no. 1 (1998): 389; Kevin J. O'Brien and Lianjiang Li, "Popular Contention and Its Impact in Rural China," *Comparative Political Studies* 38, no. 3 (April 2005): 237–39.

The constellation of actors and alliances involved across different venues in a given conflict can overwhelm. As Ferree and colleagues note, each has its own rules and roles and is not independent from other actors.[42] Description, let alone explanation, is difficult. Yet by systematically comparing cases paired to minimize potential confounding factors, such as attributes of an issue or claimants and the technology available for reaching potential third parties, this book offers a model for future researchers. Focusing on politicians, societal groups, and the attentive public, I have sought to elucidate the complex interactions among different third parties who might become involved in political conflicts over redress. For example, in bottom-up patterns of conflict expansion, support from the attentive public and active groups in society both increases politicians' incentives to take up a redress cause and constrains the extent to which elite allies can compromise on claimants' core demands. Consequently, interactions among different types of third parties involved in a political conflict over redress affect those parties' perceptions and behavior and thus also redress outcomes. Rather than taking the media, legal profession, and civil society sector for granted, I have illuminated how the structures and norms of the institutions that mediate claims-making processes affect the form and efficacy of activism and the dynamic processes of activating third-party supporters.

In addition, this book suggests the need for more comparative studies about the evolving relationship between law and social change in East Asia. Several classic studies about the role of litigation and cause lawyers in Japanese social movements informed my analysis in the previous chapters,[43] although fewer studies of legal mobilization in Korea exist.[44] These earlier works emphasize that using litigation in these countries to achieve policy change is even more difficult than in the United States, where litigation has been characterized as a "hollow hope."[45] Yet the movements in this book suggest that the prospects for this sort of change are improving. While acknowledging the persistent challenges of legal mobilization, the cases provide ample evidence of how law serves multiple functions in

---

42. Myra Marx Ferree et al., *Shaping Abortion Discourse* (Cambridge: Cambridge University Press, 2002), chap. 1.

43. E.g., Upham, *Law and Social Change in Postwar Japan*; Robert L. Kidder and Setsuo Miyazawa, "Long-Term Strategies in Japanese Environmental Litigation," *Law and Social Inquiry* 18 (1993): 605–28; Eric A. Feldman, *The Ritual of Rights in Japan* (Cambridge: Cambridge University Press, 2000).

44. For notable recent exceptions, see Hyunah Yang, ed., *Law & Society in Korea* (Cheltenham, UK: Edward Elgar, 2013); Patricia Goedde, "From Dissidents to Institution-Builders," *East Asia Law Review* 4 (2009): 63–90; Joon Seok Hong, "From the Streets to the Courts," in *South Korean Social Movements*, ed. Gi-Wook Shin and Paul Y. Chang (London: Routledge, 2011), 96–116.

45. Gerald N. Rosenberg, *The Hollow Hope*, 2nd ed. (Chicago: University of Chicago Press, 1991).

political conflicts over redress, such as formally holding the state accountable, mobilizing victims, supplying issue frames and language, and structuring publicity events. I also traced how redress movements learn from one another and develop more direct connections (often through lawyers) over time, especially in Japan. Both Japan and Korea are belatedly experiencing a judicialization of politics, enabled by democratization in Korea in 1987 and more competitive electoral politics in Japan since 1993. New grievance articulation channels, new legal tools for citizens to challenge state decisions, and judicial reforms are reshaping the role of law and courts in both countries. Courts have also adopted looser interpretations of statutes of limitations, reduced the costs of suing, sped up some trials, and started recruiting judges with more diverse backgrounds. Yet few sociolegal scholars have compared Japan and Korea or explored the cross-national differences in how contemporaneous reforms to their judicial systems and legal professions—as well as redress movements—are increasing citizens' access to justice and governmental accountability, albeit in different ways. Future research should, therefore, continue to explore the distinctive and evolving political functions of litigation in Japan and Korea, the extent to which systems of "legalized accountability" now constrain even East Asia's famously autonomous bureaucracies,[46] and the ways in which lawyers and advocacy groups facilitate litigation as a form of political participation.

Finally, this book challenges scholars of civil society and state-society relations, especially in East Asia, to reconsider generalizations about the relative strength of society vis-à-vis the state. Most scholars and casual observers of Korean activism tend to highlight the strength and vibrancy of civil society in Korea.[47] Large protests frequently fill Seoul's streets, and past antiauthoritarian activities are respected credentials among political elites, even in some parts of the conservative establishment. As detailed in chapter 2, Korea's large, professionalized, and politicized civil society organizations have indeed achieved impressive victories in their efforts to promote democratic accountability since the early 1990s. Numerous studies have also suggested that Japanese civic groups are comparatively ill positioned to influence policy because they are small, volunteer-based, and nonpartisan.[48] Yet this book reaches the somewhat surprising conclusion that

46. Charles R. Epp, *Making Rights Real* (Chicago: University of Chicago Press, 2009).

47. E.g., Hagen Koo, ed., *State and Society in Contemporary Korea* (Ithaca: Cornell University Press, 1993); Miranda Schreurs, "Democratic Transition and Environmental Civil Society," *Good Society* 11 (2002): 57–64; but see also Jennifer S. Oh, "Strong State and Strong Civil Society in Contemporary South Korea," *Asian Survey* 52, no. 3 (June 2012): 528–49.

48. Robert Pekkanen, *Japan's Dual Civil Society* (Stanford: Stanford University Press, 2006); But see also Simon Avenell, "Civil Society and the New Civic Movements in Contemporary Japan," *Journal of Japanese Studies* 35, no. 2 (2009): 247–83.

the staid character of Japanese civil society organizations and homogeneity of its mainstream news may actually be beneficial in the context of redress politics. Synergies between the court process and local, issue-specific models of activism help movements build a grassroots base off which issues that get picked up by political elites and the national media can explode into political scandals that catalyze policy change. By contrast, Korea's civil society favors more top-down patterns of conflict expansion that tend to result in less redress for victim groups. I do not advocate the homogenization of public spheres, though. In fact, the distinctive structures of the Japanese and Korean public spheres have interesting implications for democracy in both countries. On the one hand, Korea's vibrant and diverse public sphere is more accessible and provides more space for rights-based claims. On the other hand, the closed and relatively more homogeneous Japanese public sphere helps victim groups obtain higher levels of redress—but only if they can break into it.

Ultimately, though, my analysis of redress politics indicates that governmental accountability is improving in both Japan and Korea. Victim groups benefited from and contributed to reforms that have enhanced citizen oversight and provided opportunities for them to participate in policymaking. As illustrated in the cases examined in this book, Japan and Korea fit into a global trend that is witnessing the expansion of courts and court-like bodies into policymaking and political conflicts. Reforms have also granted more policymaking initiative to elected politicians, improved the responsiveness of local governments, and increased the range of channels through which citizens can hold government officials accountable. The active cross-border learning and the parallels among the redress movements discussed in this book lead one to more optimistic prognoses for Northeast Asia, a region still trying to hold the Japanese government accountable for past wrongs. This book provides a counterpoint to interstate disputes over historical memory by focusing on how East Asians, harmed by their own governments, are leveraging similar democratic processes to seek redress. Greater public scrutiny over policymaking processes has created new opportunities for victim groups to name their suffering, blame the government, claim redress, and, if that does not work, then shame the government into granting redress. Indeed, the growing influence of victim organizations arguably indicates the decline of the strong state and the rise of a more responsive state in both Japan and Korea. The balance of power is shifting in favor of the citizens, toward more accountable politics.

AIDS Prevention Foundation. "Ketsueki Gyōko Ijōbyō Zenkoku Chōsa [National Coagulation Disorders Survey]." 2012. http://api-net.jfap.or.jp/library/alliedEnt/02/images/h24_research/h24_research.pdf.

Aldrich, Daniel P. *Site Fights: Divisive Facilities and Civil Society in Japan and the West.* Ithaca: Cornell University Press, 2008.

Allen, J. G. "Letter: The High Cost of Cheap Blood." *New England Journal of Medicine* 294, no. 12 (March 18, 1976): 675.

Almeida, Paul D. "The Sequencing of Success: Organizing Templates and Neoliberal Policy Outcomes." *Mobilization* 13, no. 2 (2008): 165–87.

Amato, Joseph A. *Victims and Values: A History and a Theory of Suffering.* New York: Greenwood Press, 1990.

Amenta, Edwin, Neal Caren, Elizabeth Chiarello, and Yang Su. "The Political Consequences of Social Movements." *Annual Review of Sociology* 36 (April 2010): 287–307.

Amenta, Edwin, Bruce G. Carruthers, and Yvonne Zylan. "A Hero for the Aged? The Townsend Movement, the Political Mediation Model, and U.S. Old-Age Policy, 1934–1950." *American Journal of Sociology* 98, no. 2 (1992): 308–39.

Amsden, Alice H. *Asia's Next Giant: South Korea and Late Industrialization.* New York: Oxford University Press, 1989.

Andersen, Ellen Ann. *Out of the Closets and into the Courts: Legal Opportunity Structure and Gay Rights Litigation.* Ann Arbor: University of Michigan Press, 2006.

Andrews, Kenneth T. "Social Movements and Policy Implementation: The Mississippi Civil Rights Movement and the War on Poverty, 1965 to 1971." *American Sociological Review* 66, no. 1 (2001): 71–95.

Araki Kazuhiro, ed. *Rachi Kyūshutsu Undō no 2000nichi [The First 2,000 Days of the Movement to Rescue Abductees].* Tokyo: Sōshisha, 2000.

Armstrong, Charles K., ed. *Korean Society: Civil Society, Democracy and the State.* London: Routledge, 2007.

Arnold, R. Douglas. *The Logic of Congressional Action.* New Haven: Yale University Press, 1992.

Arrington, Celeste. "The Abductions Issue in Japan and South Korea: Ten Years after Pyongyang's Admission." *International Journal of Korean Studies* 17, no. 2 (Spring–Summer 2013): 108–39.

——. "Interest Group Influence in Policy-Making Processes: Comparing the Abductions Issue and North Korea Policy in Japan and South Korea." Paper presented at the Annual Meeting of the American Political Science Association, Chicago, 2007.

——. "Leprosy, Legal Mobilization, and the Public Sphere in Japan and South Korea." *Law & Society Review* 48, no. 3 (September 2014): 563–93.

——. "Media Environment Diversity and Activism: Insights from South Korea and Japan." Unpublished manuscript.

Asahi Shimbun. "'Ningen Toshite Ikirareru,' Nagasugita Kurayami ni Hikari, Hansenbyō Kōso Dannen ['I Will Be Able to Live as a Human Being,' A Light in the Darkness, Declining to Appeal the Hansen's Disease Lawsuit]." May 24, 2001.

——. "Residents, Evacuees File Lawsuit against Central Government, TEPCO." March 12, 2013.

——. "Seifu Hyōka ni Anshin-Kan [Government Relief over Public Approval]."September 19, 2002.

ASHDL (Association to Support the Hansen's Disease Lawsuits), ed. *Hansen Byō Mondai Koremade to Korekara [The Hansen's Disease Problem: Up to Now and from Now On]*. Tokyo: Nihon Hyōronsha, 2002.

Avenell, Simon. "Civil Society and the New Civic Movements in Contemporary Japan: Convergence, Collaboration, and Transformation." *Journal of Japanese Studies* 35, no. 2 (2009): 247–83.

——. "From Fearsome Pollution to Fukushima: Environmental Activism and the Nuclear Blind Spot in Contemporary Japan." *Environmental History* 17, no. 2 (April 2012): 244–76.

Awaji Takehisa. "HIV Litigation and Its Settlement (in Japan)." Translated by Keisuke Mark Abe. *Pacific Rim Law & Policy Journal* 6 (1997): 581.

BAI (Board of Audit and Investigations). "Hyeolaek Anjeon Gwalli mit Hyeolaek Keomsa Sisutem Unyong Bujeokjeong [Improprieties in the Operations of the Blood Safety Management and Blood Inspections Systems]." February 2004.

Banaszak, Lee Ann. *The Women's Movement inside and outside the State*. New York: Cambridge University Press, 2010.

Barkan, Elazar. *The Guilt of Nations: Restitution and Negotiating Historical Injustices*. New York: Norton, 2000.

Baum, Jeeyang Rhee. *Responsive Democracy: Increasing State Accountability in East Asia*. Ann Arbor: University of Michigan Press, 2011.

Baumgartner, Frank R., and Bryan D. Jones. *Agendas and Instability in American Politics*. Chicago: University of Chicago Press, 1993.

Benford, Robert D., and David A. Snow. "Framing Processes and Social Movements: An Overview and Assessment." *Annual Review of Sociology* 26, no. 1 (2000): 611–39.

Bengodan (Hansen's Disease Lawyers' Association [Hansenbyō Iken Kokubai Soshō Bengodan]). *Hirakareta Tobira: Hansenbyō Saiban wo Tatakatta Hitobito [The Opened Door: The People Who Fought the Hansen's Disease Lawsuit]*. Tokyo: Kodansha, 2003.

Berger, Thomas U. *War, Guilt, and World Politics after World War II*. Cambridge: Cambridge University Press, 2012.

Bob, Clifford. *The Marketing of Rebellion: Insurgents, Media, and International Activism*. Cambridge: Cambridge University Press, 2005.

Bogdanich, Walt, and Eric Koli. "2 Paths of Bayer Drug in 80's: Riskier One Steered Overseas." *New York Times*, May 22, 2003.

Bourdieu, Pierre. "The Force of Law: Toward a Sociology of the Juridical Field." *Hastings Law Journal* 38 (1986–87): 805–54.

Brooks, Roy L., ed. *When Sorry Isn't Enough: The Controversy over Apologies and Reparations for Human Injustice*. New York: New York University Press, 1999.

Brown, Wendy. *States of Injury: Power and Freedom in Late Modernity*. Princeton: Princeton University Press, 1995.

Bumiller, Kristin. *The Civil Rights Society: The Social Construction of Victims*. Baltimore: Johns Hopkins University Press, 1988.

Burns, Susan L. "Making Illness Identity: Writing 'Leprosy Literature' in Modern Japan." *Japan Review* 16 (2004): 191–211.

Burstein, Paul. "Social Movements and Public Policy." In *How Social Movements Matter*, edited by Marco G. Giugni, Doug McAdam, and Charles Tilly, 3–21. Minneapolis: University of Minnesota Press, 1999.

Burstein, Paul, Rachel Einwohner, and Jocelyn Hollander. "The Success of Political Movements: A Bargaining Perspective." In *The Politics of Social Protest: Comparative Perspectives on States and Social Movements*, edited by Bert Klandermans and J. Craig Jenkins, 275–95. Minneapolis: University of Minnesota Press, 1995.

Burstein, Paul, and April Linton. "The Impact of Political Parties, Interest Groups, and Social Movement Organizations on Public Policy: Some Recent Evidence and Theoretical Concerns." *Social Forces* 81, no. 2 (December 2002): 381–408.

Calder, Kent E. *Crisis and Compensation: Public Policy and Political Stability in Japan, 1949–1986*. Princeton: Princeton University Press, 1988.

Carpenter, R. Charli. *"Lost" Causes: Agenda Vetting in Global Issue Networks and the Shaping of Human Security*. Ithaca: Cornell University Press, 2014.

Cha, Victor D. "Japan's Engagement Dilemmas with North Korea." *Asian Survey* 41, no. 4 (August 2001): 549–63.

Chang, Paul Y. "Unintended Consequences of Repression: Alliance Formation in South Korea's Democracy Movement (1970–1979)." *Social Forces* 87, no. 2 (December 2008): 651–77.

Cho, Kuk. "Transitional Justice in Korea: Legally Coping with Past Wrongs after Democratization." *Pacific Rim Law & Policy Journal* 16 (2007): 579–612.

Cho, Young K., Brian T. Foley, Heungsup Sung, Young-Bong Kim, and Ji-hyun Kim. "Molecular Epidemiologic Study of a Human Immunodeficiency Virus 1 Outbreak in Hemophiliacs B Infected through Clotting Factor 9 after 1990." *Vox Sanguinis* 92, no. 2 (2006): 113–20.

Chosun Ilbo. "Jeongbu, Hansenin Pihae Kkalkkeumhage Ilgwal Bosang eul [The Government Should Give Hansen's Disease Survivors Neat Onetime Compensation]." May 1, 2014.

Chung, Erin Aeran. "Korea and Japan's Multicultural Models for Immigrant Incorporation." *Korea Observer* 41, no. 4 (Winter 2010): 649–76.

Clemens, Elisabeth S. "Organizational Repertoires and Institutional Change: Women's Groups and the Transformation of U.S. Politics, 1890–1920." *American Journal of Sociology* 98, no. 4 (January 1993): 755–98.

Cullinane, Joanne. "Tainted Blood and Vengeful Spirits: The Legacy of Japan's Yakugai Eizu (AIDS) Trial." *Culture, Medicine and Psychiatry* 29, no. 1 (2005): 5–31.

Cumings, Bruce. *The Origins of the Korean War: The Roaring of the Cataract, 1947–1950*. Vol. 2. Princeton: Princeton University Press, 1990.

Das, Veena, Arthur Kleinman, Mamphela Ramphele, and Pamela Reynolds, eds. *Violence and Subjectivity*. Berkeley: University of California Press, 2000.

Dower, John W. *Embracing Defeat: Japan in the Wake of World War II*. New York: Norton, 1999.

Edkins, Jenny. *Missing: Persons and Politics*. Ithaca: Cornell University Press, 2011.

Elster, Jon. *Closing the Books: Transitional Justice in Historical Perspective*. Cambridge: Cambridge University Press, 2004.

Epp, Charles R. *Making Rights Real: Activists, Bureaucrats, and the Creation of the Legalistic State*. Chicago: University of Chicago Press, 2009.

——. *The Rights Revolution: Lawyers, Activists, and Supreme Courts in Comparative Perspective*. Chicago: University of Chicago Press, 1998.

Fackler, Martin. "Serving a Father by Bringing Long-Lost Koreans Home." *New York Times*, January 2, 2010.

FADN (Families of the Abducted and Detained in North Korea). *Napbukja Ingwon Bogoseo II [Abductees' Human Rights Report II]*. Seoul: FADN, 2008.

Farley, Maggie. "Japan's Press and the Politics of Scandal." In *Media and Politics in Japan*, edited by Susan J. Pharr and Ellis S. Krauss. Honolulu: University of Hawai'i Press, 1996.

Fassin, Didier, and Richard Rechtman. *The Empire of Trauma: An Inquiry into the Condition of Victimhood.* Princeton: Princeton University Press, 2009.

Feinberg, Kenneth M. *What Is Life Worth? The Unprecedented Effort to Compensate the Victims of 9/11.* New York: PublicAffairs, 2005.

Feldman, Eric A. "Blood Justice: Courts, Conflict, and Compensation in Japan, France, and the United States." *Law & Society Review* 34, no. 3 (2000): 651–701.

——. "Fukushima: Catastrophe, Compensation, and Justice in Japan." *DePaul Law Review* 62 (2013): 335–56.

——. *The Ritual of Rights in Japan: Law, Society, and Health Policy.* Cambridge: Cambridge University Press, 2000.

Feldman, Eric A., and Ronald Bayer, eds. *Blood Feuds: AIDS, Blood, and the Politics of Medical Disaster.* Oxford: Oxford University Press, 1999.

Feldman, Ofer. *Talking Politics in Japan Today.* Brighton, UK: Sussex Academic Press, 2005.

Felman, Shoshana, and Dori Laub. *Testimony: Crises of Witnessing in Literature, Psychoanalysis, and History.* London: Routledge, 1992.

Felstiner, William L. F., Richard L. Abel, and Abel Sarat. "The Emergence and Transformation of Disputes: Naming, Blaming, Claiming." *Law & Society Review* 15, no. 3–4 (1981): 631–54.

Ferree, Myra Marx. "Resonance and Radicalism: Feminist Framing in the Abortion Debates of the United States and Germany." *American Journal of Sociology* 109 (2003): 304–44.

Ferree, Myra Marx, William A. Gamson, Jürgen Gerhards, and Dieter Rucht. *Shaping Abortion Discourse: Democracy and the Public Sphere in Germany and the United States.* Cambridge: Cambridge University Press, 2002.

Fligstein, Neil, and Doug McAdam. "Toward a General Theory of Strategic Action Fields." *Sociological Theory* 29, no. 1 (March 2011): 1–26.

Foege, William. "The National Pattern of AIDS." In *The AIDS Epidemic*, edited by Kevin M. Cahill, 7–17. New York: St. Martin's, 1983.

Foreman, Christopher H. "Grassroots Victim Organizations." In *Interest Group Politics*, 4th ed., edited by Allan J. Cigler and Burdett A. Loomis, 33–53. Washington, DC: CQ Press, 1995.

Fourcade, Marion. *Economists and Societies: Discipline and Profession in the United States, Britain, and France, 1890s to 1990s.* Princeton: Princeton University Press, 2009.

Freeman, Laurie. "Mobilizing and Demobilizing the Japanese Public Sphere: Mass Media and the Internet in Japan." In *The State of Civil Society in Japan*, edited by Frank J. Schwartz and Susan J. Pharr, 236. Cambridge: Cambridge University Press, 2003.

Friedhoff, Karl. "Ferry Crisis Strikes Heavy Blow to Public Trust." *Korea Real-Time* (blog), *Wall Street Journal*, May 15, 2014. http://blogs.wsj.com/korearealtime/2014/05/15/ferry-crisis-strikes-heavy-blow-to-public-trust.

Funabashi, Yoichi. *The Peninsula Question: A Chronicle of the Second Korean Nuclear Crisis.* Washington, DC: Brookings Institution Press, 2007.

Galanter, Marc. "The Radiating Effects of Courts." In *Empirical Theories about Courts*, edited by Keith O. Boyum and Lynn Mather, 117–42. New York: Longman, 1983.

Gallup Korea. *Mirae Hanguk Report Josa Gyeolgwa [Survey Results from the Future Korea Report].* Gallup Korea, October 2010. http://panel.gallup.co.kr.

Gamson, William A. "Hiroshima, the Holocaust, and the Politics of Exclusion: 1994 Presidential Address." *American Sociological Review* 60, no. 1 (February 1995): 1–20.

———. *The Strategy of Social Protest.* 2nd ed. Belmont, CA: Wadsworth, 1990.

Gamson, William A., and Gadi Wolfsfeld. "Movements and Media as Interacting Systems." *Annals of the American Academy of Political and Social Science* 528 (July 1993): 114–25.

Gang Geon-il. *Hanguk Jeyak ui Jipyeong Noksipja wa Hyeoluhwanja Ribyu [The Prospects for Korean Pharmaceuticals: A Review of the Green Cross Corporations and Hemophilia Patients].* Seoul: Cham Gwahak, 2011.

Gil Yun-hyeong. "Gongheohada, Hansenin Teukbyeolbeop [The Hansen's Disease Special Law Is Empty]." *Hankyoreh 21*, May 25, 2007.

———. "Hansenbyeonghwanja . . . Sawoichabyeol eun Bulchiinga [Hansen's Disease Patients . . . Is Social Prejudice Incurable?]." *Hankyoreh Sinmun*, January 31, 2005.

———. "Hansenin Teukbyeolbeop Jejeong Non ui Hwalbal [Lively Debate about the Proposed Hansen's Special Law]." *Hankyoreh Sinmun*, February 20, 2005.

———. "Hyeolubyeong Hwanjadeul Jipdan Sonbaeso Jegi [Hemophilia Patients Collectively File Damages Lawsuit]." *Hankyoreh Sinmun*, July 31, 2004.

Ginsburg, Tom. "Dismantling the Developmental State—Administrative Procedure Reform in Japan and Korea." *American Journal of Comparative Law* 49 (2001): 585–626.

———. "Law and the Liberal Transformation of the Northeast Asian Legal Complex." In *Fighting for Freedom*, edited by Terrence Halliday, Lucien Karpik, and Malcolm Feeley, 43–63. Oxford: Hart, 2007.

Gitlin, Todd. "Public Sphere or Public Spheticules?" In *Media, Ritual, and Identity*, edited by Tamar Liebes, James Curran, and Elihu Katz, 168–74. London: Routledge, 1998.

———. *The Whole World Is Watching: Mass Media in the Making and Unmaking of the New Left.* Berkeley: University of California Press, 1980.

Giugni, Marco G. *Social Protest and Policy Change: Ecology, Antinuclear, and Peace Movements in Comparative Perspective.* Lanham, MD: Rowman & Littlefield, 2004.

———. "Was It Worth the Effort? The Outcomes and Consequences of Social Movements." *Annual Review of Sociology* 24, no. 1 (1998): 371–93.

Goedde, Patricia. "From Dissidents to Institution-Builders: The Transformation of Public Interest Lawyers in South Korea." *East Asia Law Review* 4 (2009): 63–90.

———. "How Activist Lawyers Mobilized the Law for Social and Political Change in South Korea, 1988–2007." PhD diss., University of Washington, 2008.

———. "Lawyers for a Democratic Society (Minbyun): The Evolution of Its Legal Mobilization Process since 1988." In *South Korean Social Movements: From Democracy to Civil Society*, edited by Gi-Wook Shin and Paul Y. Chang, 224–44. London: Routledge, 2011.

———. "The Making of Public Interest Law in South Korea via the Institutional Discourses of Minbyeon, PSPD, and Gonggam." In *Law and Society in Korea*, edited by Hyunah Yang, 131–49. Cheltenham, UK: Edward Elgar, 2013.

Goldstone, Jack A., and Charles Tilly. "Threat (and Opportunity): Popular Action and State Response in the Dynamics of Contentious Action." In *Silence and Voice in the Study of Contentious Politics*, edited by Ronald R. Aminzade, Jack A.

Goldstone, Doug McAdam, Elizabeth J. Perry, William H. Sewell, Sidney Tarrow, and Charles Tilly. Cambridge: Cambridge University Press, 2001.

Goodwin, Jeff, and James M. Jasper. "Caught in a Winding, Snarling Vine: The Structural Bias of Political Process Theory." *Sociological Forum* 14, no. 1 (1999): 27–53.

Gwon Jae-hyeon. "Eumji ui Isan Gajokdeul: (2) Napbukja [Neglected Separated Families: (2) Abductees]." *Kyunghyang Sinmun*, September 8, 2000.

Habermas, Jürgen. *Between Facts and Norms: Contributions to a Discourse Theory of Law and Democracy*. Cambridge, MA: MIT Press, 1996.

———. "Political Communication in Media Society: Does Democracy Still Enjoy an Epistemic Dimension? The Impact of Normative Theory on Empirical Research." *Communication Theory* 16, no. 4 (2006): 411–26.

———. *The Structural Transformation of the Public Sphere: An Inquiry into a Category of Bourgeois Society*. Translated by Thomas Burger and Frederick Lawrence. Cambridge, MA: MIT Press, 1989.

Haddad, Mary Alice. "Transformation of Japan's Civil Society Landscape." *Journal of East Asian Studies* 7, no. 3 (2007): 413–37.

Hadfield, Gillian K. "Framing the Choice between Cash and the Courthouse: Experiences with the 9/11 Victim Compensation Fund." *Law & Society Review* 42, no. 3 (September 2008): 645–82.

Hadfield, James. "Takashi Uesugi: The Interview." *TimeOut Tokyo*, April 1, 2011. http://www.timeout.jp/en/tokyo/feature/2776/Takashi-Uesugi-The-Interview.

Haggard, Stephan, and Jong-Sung You. "Freedom of Expression in South Korea." *Journal of Contemporary Asia* 45, no. 1 (January 2015): 167–79.

Hallin, Daniel C. *We Keep America on Top of the World: Television Journalism and the Public Sphere*. New York: Routledge, 1994.

Hallin, Daniel C., and Paolo Mancini. *Comparing Media Systems: Three Models of Media and Politics*. Cambridge: Cambridge University Press, 2004.

Handler, Joel F. *Social Movements and the Legal System: Theory of Law Reform and Social Change*. New York: Academic Press, 1978.

Hankook Ilbo. "Yeoron Josa: Choedae Seonggwa neun Gyeonhyeop . . . Napbukja Munje Miheum [Opinion Poll: Best Outcome Was Economic Cooperation . . . Disappointment with Abductions Issue]." October 7, 2007.

Hankyoreh Sinmun. "Hansenin Tanjong Naktae Haksal, Gukka Seuseuro Chaekim Jeoya [The State Should Take Responsibility for Hansen's Disease Survivors' Vasectomy and Abortion Massacres]." October 18, 2011.

Hanvit. "Hansenin Gangje Danjong, Naktae Gukka Baesang Sosong Cheot Jaepan [First Court Date in the State Compensation Lawsuit for Hansen's Victims of Forced Vasectomies and Abortions]." *News*, February 1, 2012. www.ehanvit.org/board.php?db=news&mode=view&idx=290&page=2.

———. "Hansenin Pihae Sageon Pihaeja Myeongye Hoebok mit Bosang deung e Gwanhan Beopryul Ipbeop Gongjeonghoe Gechoe [Hosting a Public Hearing for the New Law concerning the Honor Restoration and Compensation of Hansen's Disease Victims of Incidents]." *Hanvit Magazine*, February 2009.

———. *Hansenin Pihaesgeon Pihaeja Myeongyehoebok mit Bosang deung e Gwanhan Beopryul Ipbeop Gongcheonghoe [Public Hearing for the Revised Hansen's Disease Victim Assistance Law]*. National Assembly, 2009.

Harrington, Christine B. "Outlining a Theory of Legal Practice." In *Lawyers in a Postmodern World*, edited by Maureen Cain and Christine B. Harrington, 49–69. New York: New York University Press, 1995.

Hayner, Priscilla B. *Unspeakable Truths: Confronting State Terror and Atrocity*. New York: Routledge, 2001.

HCA (Hanseong Cooperative Association). *Hansenbyeongryeokja Gwonikbohoreul wihan Gwanryeon Jeongchaek Semina [Seminar on Policies Related to the Protection of Hansen's Disease Patients' Interests]*. Seoul: HCA, March 15, 2002.

Headquarters for the Abductions Issue. "Points of Contention with the North Korean Position." Government of Japan, n.d. www.rachi.go.jp/en/mondaiten/index. html.

Hermitte, Marie-Angele. *Le Sang et Le Droit. Essai Sur La Transfusion Sanguine*. Paris: Editions du Seuil, 1996.

Heso Magazine. "Interview with Human Rights Lawyer Yasuhara Yukihiko." October 2008.

Hilbink, Thomas M. "You Know the Type: Categories of Cause Lawyering." *Law & Social Inquiry* 29, no. 3 (Summer 2004): 657–98.

Hirschman, Albert O. *The Rhetoric of Reaction: Perversity, Futility, Jeopardy*. Cambridge, MA: Belknap Press, 1991.

Hong, Joon Seok. "From the Streets to the Courts: PSPD's Legal Strategy and the Institutionalization of Social Movements." In *South Korean Social Movements: From Democracy to Civil Society*, edited by Gi-Wook Shin and Paul Y. Chang, 96–116. London: Routledge, 2011.

Howard, Marc Morjé. *The Weakness of Civil Society in Post-Communist Europe*. Cambridge: Cambridge University Press, 2003.

Hughes, Christopher W. *Japan's Economic Power and Security: Japan and North Korea*. London: Routledge, 1999.

Hymans, Jacques. "Veto Players, Nuclear Energy, and Nonproliferation." *International Security* 36, no. 2 (Fall 2011): 154–89.

IDEA. "Our Struggle and Efforts." *IDEA Newsletter*, December 2004. http://www. idealeprosydignity.org/newsletter/vol9–3/9V3.pdf.

Institutes of Medicine, Lauren B. Leveton, Harold C. Sox, and Michael A. Stoto, eds. *HIV and the Blood Supply: An Analysis of Crisis Decisionmaking*. Washington, DC: National Academies Press, 1995.

Iwasawa Michihiko. *Yakugai C Gata Kanen Onnatachi no Tatakai [The Battle of the Women Victims of Drug-Related Hepatitis C]*. Tokyo: Shogakukan, 2008.

Jager, Sheila Miyoshi, and Jiyul Kim. "The Korean War after the Cold War: Commemorating the Armistice Agreement in South Korea." In *Ruptured Histories: War, Memory, and the Post-Cold War in Asia*, edited by Sheila Miyoshi Jager and Rana Mitter, 233–65. Cambridge, MA: Harvard University Press, 2007.

Japanese Audit Bureau of Circulations. *Shimbun Hakkōsha Repōto Hanki Fukyūritsu [Newspaper Publishers' Half-Year Report on Diffusion Rates]*. December 2014. http://adv.yomiuri.co.jp/yomiuri/busu/busu01.html.

Japanese Newspaper Federation (NSK). *Beesu Media to Seikatsusha [Main Media and Ordinary People]*. Annual Report, Tokyo, 2009.

Japan Times. "Hepatitis C Bill Offering Aid, Apology Clears Diet." January 12, 2008.

———. "Thousands Sue Nuclear Companies over Fukushima Disaster." March 13, 2014.

Javeline, Debra. "The Role of Blame in Collective Action: Evidence from Russia." *American Political Science Review* 97, no. 1 (February 2003): 107–21.

Jeon Yeong-pyeong, ed. *Hanguk ui Sosuja Jeongchaek: Damnon gwa Sarye [Korea's Policies toward Minorities: Discourses and Cases]*. Seoul: Seoul National University Press, 2010.

Jeong Jae-yong. "Napbukja Gajok Keuleoangi Bunuigi Tattda [Following the Atmosphere of Embracing the Abductees' Families]." *Jugan Kyunghyang*, February 21, 2006.

Jeong Je-hyeok, Sim Hye-ri, and Gyeong Tae-yeong. "24,000 People Join in the Sewol Hunger Strike: Citizens Putting the Pressure on Politicians." *Kyunghyang Sinmun*, August 25, 2014.

Jeong Jonggwon. "Simin Undong e daehan Bipanjeok Pyongga [Critical Assessment of the Citizens' Movement]." *Gyeongje wa Sahoe [Economy and Society]*, no. 45 (2000): 132–48.

Jeong U-sang. "Park . . . Yugajok Seoldeuk . . . [Park . . . Persuade Victim Families]." *Chosun Ilbo*, August 11, 2014.

Johnson, Chalmers A. *MITI and the Japanese Miracle: The Growth of Industrial Policy, 1925–1975*. Stanford: Stanford University Press, 1982.

Johnston, Eric. "The North Korea Abduction Issue and Its Effect on Japanese Domestic Politics." JPRI Working Paper No. 101, Japan Policy Research Institute, 2004. http://www.jpri.org/publications/workingpapers/wp101.html.

Joo, Jaehyun. "Dynamics of Social Policy Change: A Korean Case Study from a Comparative Perspective." *Governance* 12, no. 1 (January 1999): 57–80.

JoongAng Ilbo. "Gamgeum, Haksal, Gangje Noyeok Hansenin Pihaeja 6,462myeong: Samang 1,754myeong . . . Gicho Chasangui 4,000myeong Wol 15 Man Won Jigeup [6,462 Hansen's Disease Patients Victims of Imprisonment, Massacre, Forced Labor: 1,754 of Them Deceased . . . 4,000 Low-Income Patients to Receive 150,000 Won Per Month]." July 18, 2013.

Jung Min-ho. "We Want Truth, Not Money." *Korea Times*, April 2, 2015.

Kabashima, Ikuo, and Gill Steel. "The Koizumi Revolution." *PS: Political Science & Politics* 40, no. 1 (2007): 79–84.

Kagan, Robert A. *Adversarial Legalism: The American Way of Law*. Cambridge, MA: Harvard University Press, 2003.

Kage, Rieko. "Making Reconstruction Work: Civil Society and Information after War's End." *Comparative Political Studies* 43, no. 10 (2010): 163–87.

Kang Hun. "Hyeolubyeong Hwanja 23myeong 'Hyeolaek Gwanli Chal Mot' 10eok Sonbaeso [23 Hemophilia Patients File a Billion Won Lawsuit for 'Faulty Blood Management']." *Chosun Ilbo*, July 30, 2004.

Kang Yang-gu. "Hyeolubyeong Hwanja 23myeong, Jeoksipjasae 10eok Gyumo Sonhaebaesang Cheonggu [23 Hemophilia Patients File a Damages Lawsuit against the KNRC for 1 Billion Won]." *Pressian*, July 30, 2004. http://www.pressian.com/news/article.html?no=27452.

Kapur, Ratna. "The Tragedy of Victimization Rhetoric: Resurrecting the 'Native' Subject in International/Post-Colonial Feminist Legal Politics." *Harvard Human Rights Journal* 15 (2002): 1–37.

Keck, Margaret E., and Kathryn Sikkink. *Activists beyond Borders: Advocacy Networks in International Politics*. Ithaca: Cornell University Press, 1998.

Keio University. "Research Survey of Political Society in a Multi-Cultural and Pluri-Generational World." July 2007. http://www.coe-ccc.keio.ac.jp/data_archive_en/data_archive_en_csw_download.html.

Kenshōkaigi [Verification Committee]. *Hansenbyō Mondai ni Kansuru Kenshōkaigi Saishū Hōkokusho [Final Report of the Verification Committee on the Hansen's Disease Problem]*. Japan Law Foundation, Tokyo, March 2005. http://www.jlf.or.jp/work/hansen_report.shtml#higai.

Kern, Thomas, and Sang-hui Nam. "Citizen Journalism: The Transformation of the Democratic Media Movement." In *South Korean Social Movements: From*

Democracy to Civil Society, edited by Gi-Wook Shin and Paul Y. Chang, 173–89. London: Routledge, 2011.

Keshavjee, Salmaan, Sheri Weiser, and Arthur Kleinman. "Medicine Betrayed: Hemophilia Patients and HIV in the US." *Social Science & Medicine* 53, no. 8 (October 2001): 1081–94.

Kidder, Robert L., and Setsuo Miyazawa. "Long-Term Strategies in Japanese Environmental Litigation." *Law & Social Inquiry* 18 (1993): 605–28.

Kim Bong-moon. "Sewol Keeps Casting a Shadow." *JoongAng Daily*, April 16, 2015.

Kim Deok-mo. "Ilbon Hyeonji Hwaldong Gyeolgwa reul Bogo Hamnida [Reporting on Local Japanese Activism]." *Sorokdoreul Sarang Haneun Saramdeul ui Moim*, January 9, 2003. http://cafe.daum.net/ilovesosamo/5QHF/19?docid=1yqf5 QHF1920030109153906.

Kim, Eunjung. "Cultural Rehabilitation: Hansen's Disease, Gender, and Disability in Korea." *Wagadu* 4 (Summer 2007): 108–24.

Kim, Hun Joon. *The Massacres at Mount Halla: Sixty Years of Truth Seeking in South Korea*. Ithaca: Cornell University Press, 2014.

Kim Jae-hyeong. "Hanguk Hansenindanche ui Haeoe Wonjo Saeop Model ui Hyeongseong e Gwanhan Sahoehakjeok Yeongu [A Sociological Study of the Formation of Models for Foreign Aid Projects among Korea's Organizations of People with Hansen's Disease]." Master's thesis, Seoul National University, 2007.

Kim Se-jeong. "PM Apologizes to Hansen's Disease Patients for Discrimination." *Korea Times*, May 17, 2009.

Kim Su Jung. "Emerging Patterns of News Media Use Across Multiple Platforms and Their Political Implications in South Korea." PhD diss., Northwestern University, 2011.

Kim, Sunhyuk. "Civil Society in South Korea: From Grand Democracy Movements to Petty Interest Groups." *Journal of Northeast Asian Studies* 15, no. 2 (Summer 1996): 81–97.

——. "South Korea: Confrontational Legacy and Democratic Contributions." In *Civil Society and Political Change in Asia: Expanding and Contracting Democratic Spaces*, edited by Muthiah Alagappa, 138–63. Stanford: Stanford University Press, 2004.

Kim Tae-il. "HCV Sosong Gijahoegyeon Hyeonjang Seukkechi [A Sketch of the Press Conference for the HCV Lawsuit]." *Uri KOHEM [Our KOHEM]*, July 2004.

Kim Yeong-ro. "Hyeolaek Yurae Baireoseu (HIV, HCV) Sosong e Gwanhan Bogoseo (1) [Report on the Blood-Borne HIV and HCV Lawsuits (1)]." *Uri KOHEM [Our KOHEM]*, November 2009.

——. "Hyeolaek Yurae Baireoseu (HIV, HCV) Sosong e Gwanhan Bogoseo (2) [Report on the Blood-Borne HIV and HCV Lawsuits (2)]." *Uri KOHEM [Our KOHEM]*, December 2009.

——. "Hyeolaek Yurae Baireoseu (HIV, HCV) Sosong e Gwanhan Bogoseo (3) [Report on the Blood-Borne HIV and HCV Lawsuits (3)]." *Uri KOHEM [Our KOHEM]*, January 2010.

Kim Young-dai, and Jeong Young-pyoung. "Sosujaroseo Napbukja Kajok ui Jeongchaek Hoekdeuk Gwajeong Yeongu [A Study of the Process by Which the Families of Those Kidnapped by North Korea Attained Certain Policies]." *Jeongbuhak Yeongu [Government Studies Research]* 13, no. 1 (2007): 117–54.

Kingdon, John W. *Agendas, Alternatives, and Public Policies*. Boston: Little, Brown, 1984.

Kingston, Jeff. *Japan's Quiet Transformation*. London: Routledge, 2004.

Kitano Ryūichi. "Kōshō Chansu [Chance for Negotiations]." *Asahi Shimbun*, April 20, 2012.

Kitschelt, Herbert. "Linkages between Citizens and Politicians in Democratic Polities." *Comparative Political Studies* 33, no. 6–7 (2000): 845–79.

Koga Katsuhige, *Shūdan Soshō, Jitsumu Manual [A Practical Manual for Collective Litigation]* (Tokyo: Nihon Hyōronsha, 2009).

KOHEM (Korea Hemophilia Association). "C-hyeong Ganyeom (HCV) Sosong Indan Annaemun [Announcement About the HCV Lawsuit Group]." No. 122. *KOHEM Announcements*, June 30, 2004. http://www.kohem.net.

———. "Hyeolaek Oyeomsago Jaebalbangjireul wihan Gukmingyutan Daehoe [Citizens' Rally to Call for the Prevention of a Reoccurrence of Tainted Blood Disasters]." September 13, 2005.

———. "Hyeoluhwanu Wonwecheobang Hoetsu e daehan Seolmunjosa [Survey about the Prescription Benefits of Hemophilia Patients]." *Uri KOHEM [Our KOHEM]*, June 2006.

Koizumi Jun'ichirō. "Hansenbyō Mondai no Sōkikatsu Zenmenteki Kaiketsu ni Mukete no Naikaku Sōridaijin Danwa [Prime Ministerial Statement Concerning the Swift and Comprehensive Solution of the Hansen's Disease Issue]." May 25, 2001. http://www.kantei.go.jp/jp/koizumispeech/2001/0525danwa.html.

Koo, Hagen. "Civil Society and Democracy in South Korea." *Good Society* 11, no. 2 (2002): 40–45.

———, ed. *State and Society in Contemporary Korea*. Ithaca: Cornell University Press, 1993.

Korea Hemophilia Foundation. *Hyeolubyeong Baekseo [Hemophilia White Paper]*. 2012. http://www.kohem.org/_data/board_list_file/8/2013/1305040914501.pdf.

Korea Press Foundation. *The Korea Press*. Seoul: Korea Press Foundation, 2012.

———. "Suyongja Uisik Josa [Survey of Media Users]." Media Statistics Information System, 2013. http://mediasis.kpf.or.kr/surveyStatistics/KPF_mediaSurvey.aspx?MASTER_CODE=99928&menu_Index=0.

Krauss, Ellis S. *Broadcasting Politics in Japan: NHK and Television News*. Ithaca: Cornell University Press, 2000.

Krauss, Ellis S., and Bradford L. Simcock. "Citizens' Movements: The Growth and Impact of Environmental Protest in Japan." In *Political Opposition in Local Politics in Japan*, edited by Scott C. Flanagan, Kurt Steiner, and Ellis S. Krauss, 187–227. Princeton: Princeton University Press, 1981.

Kriesi, Hanspeter, Ruud Koopmans, Jan Willem Duyvendak, and Marco G. Giugni. *New Social Movements in Western Europe: A Comparative Analysis*. Minneapolis: University of Minnesota Press, 1995.

Kunimoto Mamoru. *Ikite Futatabi [Alive Again]*. Tokyo: Mainichi Shimbunsha, 2001.

Kunimune Naoko. "Signature Petition Report." http://www15.ocn.ne.jp/~srkt/syomei.htm.

Kurokawa Kiyoshi. *Executive Summary of the Official Report of the Fukushima Nuclear Accident Independent Investigation Commission*. Tokyo, 2012.

Kwak, Jun-Hyeok, and Melissa Nobles, eds. *Inherited Responsibility and Historical Reconciliation in East Asia*. New York: Routledge, 2013.

Kwak Ki-Sung. *Media and Democratic Transition in South Korea*. London: Routledge, 2012.

Kyunghyang Sinmun. "Hansenin Pihae Bosang eun Ingweon Munje Ida [Compensation for Hansen's Disease Victims is a Human Rights Issue]." November 7, 2005.

Lee Kyung-mi, and Jung Hwang-bong. "Media Workers' Union Protests Launch of ChoJoongDong Networks." *Hankyoreh Sinmun*, December 2, 2011.

Lee, Namhee. *The Making of Minjung: Democracy and the Politics of Representation in South Korea*. Ithaca: Cornell University Press, 2009.

Lee Sang-il. "Sorokdo Sarang Haneun Areumdaun Saramdeul [Beautiful People Who Love Sorokdo]." *Kookmin Ilbo*, March 31, 2001.

Lee Seul-bi. "'Seulpeo Hajido, Miweohajido Mapsida' ['Let's Not Be Sad, Hate']." *Chosun Ilbo*, December 29, 2014.

Lee, Seung-Ook, Sook-Jin Kim, and Joel Wainwright. "Mad Cow Militancy: Neoliberal Hegemony and Social Resistance in South Korea." *Political Geography* 29 (2010): 359–69.

Lee, Sook-Jong. "Democratization and Polarization in Korean Society." *Asian Perspective* 29, no. 3 (2005): 99–125.

Lee, Sook Jong, and Celeste Arrington. "The Politics of NGOs and Democratic Governance in South Korea and Japan." *Pacific Focus* 23, no. 1 (2008): 75–96.

Leheny, David R. *Think Global, Fear Local*. Ithaca: Cornell University Press, 2006.

Lew, Joon. "Leprosy in Korea, Past and Present: A Model for the Healing of Leprosy in Korea." *Korea Observer* 23, no. 2 (Summer 1992): 197–213.

Lewis, Linda S. "Commemorating Kwangju: The 5.18 Movement and Civil Society at the Millennium." In *Korean Society: Civil Society, Democracy, and the State*, edited by Charles K. Armstrong, 165–86. New York: Routledge, 2002.

Lewis, Linda S., and Ju-na Byun. "From Heroic Victims to Disabled Survivors: The 5–18 Injured after Twenty Years." In *Contentious Kwangju: The May 18 Uprising in Korea's Past and Present*, edited by Gi-Wook Shin and Kyung Moon Hwang, 53–66. Lanham, MD: Rowman & Littlefield, 2003.

Lind, Jennifer. *Sorry States: Apologies in International Politics*. Ithaca: Cornell University Press, 2008.

Lipsky, Michael. "Protest as a Political Resource." *American Political Science Review* 62, no. 4 (1968): 1144–58.

Lohmann, Susanne. "A Signaling Model of Informative and Manipulative Political Action." *American Political Science Review* 87, no. 2 (June 1993): 319–33.

Lynn, Hyung Gu. "Vicarious Traumas: Television and Public Opinion in Japan's North Korea Policy." *Pacific Affairs* 79, no. 3 (Fall 2006): 483–508.

Mackie, Vera. "In Search of Innocence: Feminist Historians Debate the Legacy of Wartime Japan." *Australian Feminist Studies* 20, no. 47 (July 2005): 207–17.

Maclachlan, Patricia L. *Consumer Politics in Postwar Japan*. New York: Columbia University Press, 2002.

——. "Information Disclosure and the Center-Local Relationship in Japan." In *Local Voices, National Issues: The Impact of Local Initiatives in Japanese Policy-Making*, edited by Sheila A. Smith, 9–30. Ann Arbor: University of Michigan, 2000.

Mansfield Foundation, trans. "Nikkei Shimbun Opinion Polls (conducted Dec. 14–16, 2007)." December 2007. http://www.mansfieldfdn.org/polls/2007/poll-07-34. htm.

Marmor, Theodore R., Patricia A. Dillon, and Stephen Scher. "The Comparative Politics of Contaminated Blood: From Hesitancy to Scandal." In *Blood Feuds: AIDS, Blood, and the Politics of Medical Disaster*, edited by Eric A. Feldman and Ronald Bayer, 350–66. Oxford: Oxford University Press, 1999.

May, Marlynn L., and Daniel B. Stengel. "Who Sues Their Doctors? How Patients Handle Medical Grievances." *Law & Society Review* 24, no. 1 (1990): 105–20.

McAdam, Doug. *Political Process and the Development of Black Insurgency, 1930–1970*. Chicago: University of Chicago Press, 1982.

McAdam, Doug, Sidney Tarrow, and Charles Tilly, eds. *Dynamics of Contention*. New York: Cambridge University Press, 2001.

McCann, Michael W. "Law and Social Movements: Contemporary Perspectives." *Annual Review of Law and Social Science* 2 (2006): 17–38.

———. *Rights at Work: Pay Equity Reform and the Politics of Legal Mobilization.* Chicago: University of Chicago Press, 1994.

McCarthy, John D., and Meyer N. Zald. "Resource Mobilization and Social Movements: A Partial Theory." *American Journal of Sociology* 82, no. 6 (1977): 1212–41.

McCurry, Justin. "Japan Compensates Some of Its Hepatitis C Victims." *Lancet* 371, no. 9618 (2008): 1061–62.

McKean, Margaret A. *Environmental Protest and Citizen Politics in Japan.* Berkeley: University of California Press, 1981.

———. "Political Socialization through Citizens' Movements." In *Political Opposition in Local Politics in Japan,* edited by Kurt Steiner, Ellis S. Krauss, and Scott C. Flanagan, 228–75. Princeton: Princeton University Press, 1981.

McNeill, David. "Japan's Contemporary Media." In *Critical Issues in Contemporary Japan,* edited by Jeff Kingston, 64–76. New York: Routledge, 2014.

McWilliams, Monica. "Struggling for Peace and Justice: Reflections on Women's Activism in Northern Ireland." *Journal of Women's History* 6, no. 4 (1995): 13–39.

Meyer, David S., and Debra C. Minkoff. "Conceptualizing Political Opportunity." *Social Forces* 82, no. 4 (June 2004): 1457–92.

Meyer, David S., and Suzanne Staggenborg. "Movements, Countermovements, and the Structure of Political Opportunity." *American Journal of Sociology* 101, no. 6 (May 1996): 1628–60.

MHLW (Ministry of Health, Labor, and Welfare). *Fibrinogen Seizai ni yoru C Gata Kanen Virus Kansen ni Kansuru Chōsa Hōkokusho [Report on the Investigation into Hepatitis C Infections from the Product Fibrinogen].* August 29, 2002. http://www.mhlw.go.jp/houdou/2002/08/h0829–3.html.

———. "Hansenbyō Mondai wo Tadashiku Tsutaeru Tameni: Hansenbyō no Mukōgawa [Correctly Communicating the Hansen's Disease Issue: The Other Side of Hansen's Disease]." 2003. http://www.mhlw.go.jp/houdou/2003/01/h0131–5.html.

Minbyeon, Professors for Democracy, Democratic Legal Studies Association, Korean Professors' Union, Hangyojo, and Korean Progressive Academy Council. "4.16 Sewol-ho Chamsa Jinsang Gyumyeong mit Anjeonsahoe Geonseol deungeul wihan Teukbyeolbeop Sihengryeong (An) ui Munjecheom mit Cheolhoe ui Pilyoseong [Joint Opinion by Six Scholarly and Legal Organizations about the Problems with the Sewol Special Law Enforcement Ordinance Draft and Need for Retraction]." April 2, 2015. http://minbyun.or.kr/?p=28280.

Ministry of Foreign Affairs (Japan). "Pyongyang Declaration." September 17, 2002. http://www.mofa.go.jp/region/asia-paci/n_korea/pmv0209/pyongyang.html.

Ministry of Internal Affairs and Communications. *Jōhō Tsūshin Hakusho [Information and Communications White Paper].* 2011. http://www.soumu.go.jp/johotsusintokei/whitepaper/ja/h23/pdf/index.html.

Ministry of Unification. *2015 Tongil Baekseo [Unification White Paper].* Seoul: MOU, 2015.

Minow, Martha. "Surviving Victim Talk." *UCLA Law Review* 40 (1992–93): 1411–45.

Mitsubishi Tanabe Pharma Corporation. "Standard for Our Company's Payment Burdens Related to Fees Required for Benefit Payments and Other Operations, Based on the Special Relief Law Concerning the Payment of Benefits to the Patients of Hepatitis C." April 10, 2009. http://www.mt-pharma.co.jp/e/release/nr/2009/pdf/eMTPC090410.pdf.

Miyamoto, Satoru. "Economic Sanctions by Japan against North Korea: Consideration of the Legislation Process for FEFTCL (February 2004) and LSMCIPESS (June 2004)." *International Journal of Korean Unification Studies* 15, no. 2 (2006): 21–46.

Moon, Katharine H. S. "Resurrecting Prostitutes and Overturning Treaties: Gender Politics in the 'Anti-American' Movement in South Korea." *Journal of Asian Studies* 66, no. 1 (2007): 129–57.

Morris-Suzuki, Tessa. *Exodus to North Korea: Shadows from Japan's Cold War.* Lanham, MD: Rowman & Littlefield, 2007.

Mun Gwan-hyeon. "Seongin 53% 'Napbuk Munje Il Sujun Jegiheya' [53% of Respondents 'Raise the Abductions Issue to the Japanese Level']." *Yonhap News,* September 25, 2002.

Na Gwon-il. "Sorokdo reul Ingwon Jaehwal ui Ddang euro [Turning Sorokdo into a Land of Rehabilitating Human Rights]." *Sisa Jeoneol,* December 30, 2001. http://www.sisapress.com/news/articleView.html?idxno=9129.

Nakamura, Karen. "No Voice in the Courtroom? Deaf Legal Cases in Japan during the 1960s." In *Going to Court to Change Japan,* edited by Patricia G. Steinhoff, 147–63. Ann Arbor: Center for Japanese Studies, University of Michigan, 2014.

Naoi, Megumi, and Ellis S. Krauss. "Who Lobbies Whom? Special Interest Politics under Alternative Electoral Systems." *American Journal of Political Science* 53, no. 4 (2009): 874–92.

NCLR (National Council of Leprosarium Residents). *Fukken e no Nichigestu [The Years to the Restoration of Our Rights].* Tokyo: Kōyō, 2001.

———. *Zenkankyō Undōshi: Hansenshibyō Kanja no Tatakai no Kiroku [The History of Activism by the National Council of Leprosarium Patients: The Record of Hansen's Disease Patients' Battle].* Tokyo: Ikkōsha, 1977.

NHRCK (National Human Rights Committee Korea). *Hansenin Ingwon Siltae Josa [A Study of the Human Rights of Persons Affected by Hansen's Disease].* NHRCK, December 2005.

Noble, Gregory W. "Let a Hundred Channels Contend: Technological Change, Political Opening, and Bureaucratic Priorities in Japanese Television Broadcasting." *Journal of Japanese Studies* 26, no. 1 (January 2000): 79–109.

Nobles, Melissa. *The Politics of Official Apologies.* Cambridge: Cambridge University Press, 2008.

———. "The Prosecution of Human Rights Violations." *Annual Review of Political Science* 13 (2010): 165–82.

O'Brien, Kevin J., and Lianjiang Li. "Popular Contention and Its Impact in Rural China." *Comparative Political Studies* 38, no. 3 (April 2005): 235–59.

Oh, Jennifer S. "Strong State and Strong Civil Society in Contemporary South Korea: Challenges to Democratic Governance." *Asian Survey* 52, no. 3 (June 2012): 528–49.

Olson, Susan M. *Clients and Lawyers: Securing the Rights of Disabled Persons.* Westport, CT: Greenwood Press, 1984.

Open Source Center. "Japan—Media Environment Open; State Looms Large." Director of National Intelligence, August 18, 2009. http://www.fas.org/irp/dni/osc/japan-media.pdf.

Orr, James Joseph. *The Victim as Hero: Ideologies of Peace and National Identity in Postwar Japan.* Honolulu: University of Hawai'i Press, 2001.

Osaka, Eri. "Corporate Liability, Government Liability, and the Fukushima Nuclear Disaster." *Pacific Rim Law & Policy Journal* 21, no. 3 (June 2012): 433–59.

Ota, Shozo, and Kahei Rokumoto. "Issues of the Lawyer Population: Japan." *Case Western Reserve Journal of International Law* 25 (1993): 315–32.

Ōtani Fujio. *The Walls Crumble: The Emancipation of Persons Affected by Hansen's Disease in Japan* (English trans. of Japanese 1996 ed.). Tokyo: Tōfu Kyōkai, 1998.

Page, Benjamin I. "The Semi-Sovereign Public." In *Navigating Public Opinion*, edited by Jeff Manza, Fay Lomax Cook, and Benjamin I. Page, 325–44. Oxford: Oxford University Press, 2002.

Park Jeong-won. "Jeonhu Napbuk Pihaeja Jiwon Ipbeop ui Gwaje wa Jeonmang [Legal Issues and Prospects for Legislation to Support Postwar Abductees]." *Beophak Noncheong* 22, no. 1 (2009): 71–107.

Park Ju-min. "While Japan Presses North on Abductions, South Korea Victims Are Forgotten." *Japan Times*, July 3, 2014.

Pekkanen, Robert. *Japan's Dual Civil Society: Members without Advocates.* Stanford: Stanford University Press, 2006.

Pempel, T. J. *Regime Shift: Comparative Dynamics of the Japanese Political Economy.* Ithaca: Cornell University Press, 1998.

Petryna, Adriana. "Biological Citizenship: The Science and Politics of Chernobyl-Exposed Populations." *Osiris*, 2nd ser., 19 (January 1, 2004): 250–65.

Pharr, Susan J. *Losing Face.* Berkeley: University of California Press, 1990.

Picart, Caroline Joan (Kay) S. "Rhetorically Reconfiguring Victimhood and Agency." *Rhetoric & Public Affairs* 6 (2003): 97–125.

Pierson, Paul. *Politics in Time: History, Institutions, and Social Analysis.* Princeton: Princeton University Press, 2004.

Powell, Jerry S. "Recombinant Factor VIII in the Management of Hemophilia A: Current Use and Future Promise." *Therapeutics and Clinical Risk Management* 5 (May 2009): 391–402.

Prime Minister's Office. *Heisei 18nendo Shimin Katsudō Dantai Kihon Chōsa Hōkokusho [2006 Report on Citizen Activities' Associations].* April 2007.

ReACH. *The Families.* Washington, DC: Rescuing Abductees Center for Hope, 2007. http://reachdc.net/bookTableOfContents.html.

Reich, Michael R. *Toxic Politics.* Ithaca: Cornell University Press, 1991.

Repeta, Lawrence. "Limiting Fundamental Rights Protection in Japan: The Role of the Supreme Court." In *Critical Issues in Contemporary Japan*, edited by Jeff Kingston, 37–51. New York: Routledge, 2013.

Rhee June-woong. "Tendentiousness of Korean Journalism and the Problem of the 'Distinction between Facts and Opinions.'" *Korea Journalism Review* 4, no. 2 (Summer 2010): 52–70.

Rheuben, Joel, and Luke Nottage. "Resolving Claims from the Fukushima Nuclear Disaster." *Japanese Law in the Asia-Pacific Socio-Economic Context* (blog). January 26, 2015. blogs.usyd.edu.au/japaneselaw/2015/01/resolving_nuclear_claims.html.

Rosenberg, Gerald N. *The Hollow Hope: Can Courts Bring About Social Change?* 2nd ed. Chicago: University of Chicago Press, 1991.

Rucht, Dieter. "Movement Allies, Adversaries, and Third Parties." In *The Blackwell Companion to Social Movements*, edited by David A. Snow, Sarah A. Soule, and Hanspeter Kriesi, 197–216. Malden, MA: Blackwell, 2004.

Sabatier, Paul A., and Christopher M. Weible. "The Advocacy Coalition Framework: Innovations and Clarifications." In *Theories of the Policy Process*, edited by Paul A. Sabatier, 189–220. Boulder: Westview, 2007.

Samuels, Richard J. "Kidnapping Politics in East Asia." *Journal of East Asian Studies* 10, no. 3 (December 2010): 363–95.

———. *Securing Japan: Tokyo's Grand Strategy and the Future of East Asia.* Ithaca: Cornell University Press, 2007.

———. *3.11: Disaster and Change in Japan.* Ithaca: Cornell University Press, 2013.

Sano Ryūsuke. "Hemofilia Tomo no Kai Zenkoku Nettowaaku ni Tsuite [About the National Network of Hemophilia Associations] Comment No. 2998." CHPNet, September 30, 2008. http://log.chpnet.info/bbs3_pre/pslg2998.html#2998.

Sarat, Austin, and Stuart A. Scheingold, eds. *Cause Lawyering and the State in a Global Era.* Oxford: Oxford University Press, 2001.

———, eds. *Cause Lawyering: Political Commitments and Professional Responsibilities.* New York: Oxford University Press, 1998.

Sato, Hajime, and Minoru Narita. "Politics of Leprosy Segregation in Japan: The Emergence, Transformation and Abolition of the Patient Segregation Policy." *Social Science & Medicine* 56, no. 12 (2003): 2529–39.

Schattschneider, E. E. *The Semisovereign People: A Realist's View of Democracy in America.* New York: Holt, Rinehart and Winston, 1960.

Schedler, Andreas. "Conceptualizing Accountability." In *The Self-Restraining State: Power and Accountability in New Democracies,* edited by Andreas Schedler, Larry J. Diamond, and Marc F. Plattner. Boulder: Lynne Rienner, 1999.

Scheingold, Stuart A., and Austin Sarat. *Something to Believe in: Politics, Professionalism, and Cause Lawyering.* Stanford: Stanford Law and Politics, 2004.

Schoff, James L. *Political Fences & Bad Neighbors: North Korea Policy Making in Japan & Implications for the United States.* Institute for Foreign Policy Analysis Project Report, June 2006. http://www.ifpa.org/pdf/fences.pdf.

Schreurs, Miranda. "Democratic Transition and Environmental Civil Society." *Good Society* 11 (2002): 57–64.

Schumaker, Paul D. "Policy Responsiveness to Protest-Group Demands." *Journal of Politics* 37, no. 2 (1975): 488–521.

Scott, W. Richard, and John W. Meyer. "The Organization of Societal Sectors." In *Organizational Environments: Ritual and Rationality,* edited by John W. Meyer and W. Richard Scott, 129–53. Beverly Hills: Sage, 1983.

Secrétariat d'Etat à la santé et l'action sociale, *Rapport annuel sur le dispositif d'indemnisation des hémophiles et transfusés contaminés par le virus de l'immunodéficience humaine,* March 1997. http://www.ladocumentation francaise.fr/var/storage/rapports-publics/994001230/0000.pdf.

Sellers, Patrick J. "Strategy and Background in Congressional Campaigns." *American Political Science Review* 92, no. 1 (March 1998): 159–71.

Shimura Yasushi. *Watashi No Tomurai Gassen [My Avenging Battle].* Kumamoto, 1999.

Shin Dong-ho. "Hyeolubyeong 10yeomyeong Eiju Kamyeom [About 10 Hemophiliacs Infected with HIV]." *DongA Ilbo,* September 13, 2002.

Shin, Gi-Wook, Soon-Won Park, and Daqing Yang, eds. *Rethinking Historical Injustice and Reconciliation in Northeast Asia: The Korean Experience.* New York: Routledge, 2007.

Shin Gwang-yeong. "'Sum Suiryeoneun Ne Agi Reul Geudeuleun Binile Dama Beoryeotda' ['They Threw Away My Still Breathing Child in a Plastic Bag']." *DongA Ilbo,* October 19, 2011.

Shin Hye Son. "KFDA to Destroy 22 Batches of Tainted Hemophilia Drug." *Korea Herald,* January 29, 2000.

Sikkink, Kathryn, and Carrie B. Walling. "The Justice Cascade and the Impact of Human Rights Trials in Latin America." *Journal of Peace Research* 44, no. 4 (2007): 427–45.

Simon, Jonathan. *Governing through Crime: How the War on Crime Transformed American Democracy and Created a Culture of Fear*. London: Oxford University Press, 2007.

Skocpol, Theda, Morris P Fiorina, Brookings Institution, and Russell Sage Foundation, eds. *Civic Engagement in American Democracy*. Washington, DC: Brookings Institution Press, 1999.

Soh, Chunghee Sarah. *The Comfort Women: Sexual Violence and Postcolonial Memory in Korea and Japan*. Chicago: University of Chicago Press, 2008.

Soule, Sarah A., and Brayden G. King. "The Stages of the Policy Process and the Equal Rights Amendment, 1972–1982." *American Journal of Sociology* 111, no. 6 (May 2006): 1871–1909.

Soule, Sarah A., and Susan Olzak. "When Do Movements Matter? The Politics of Contingency and the Equal Rights Amendment." *American Sociological Review* 69, no. 4 (2004): 473–97.

Starr, Douglas. *Blood: An Epic History of Medicine and Commerce*. New York: Knopf, 1998.

Stearns, Linda Brewster, and Paul D. Almeida. "The Formation of State Actor–Social Movement Coalitions and Favorable Policy Outcomes." *Social Problems* 51, no. 4 (November 2004): 478–504.

Steffen, Monika. "The Nation's Blood: Medicine, Justice, and the State in France." In *Blood Feuds: AIDS, Blood, and the Politics of Medical Disaster*, edited by Eric A. Feldman and Ronald Bayer, 95–126. New York: Oxford University Press, 1999.

Steinhoff, Patricia G. "Doing the Defendant's Laundry: Support Groups as Social Movement Organizations in Contemporary Japan." *Japanstudien: Jahrbuch des Deutschen Instituts für Japanstudien* 11 (1999): 55–78.

Stern, Rachel E., and Jonathan Hassid. "Amplifying Silence: Uncertainty and Control Parables in Contemporary China." *Comparative Political Studies* 45, no. 10 (October 2012): 1230–54.

Stone, Deborah A. "Causal Stories and the Formation of Policy Agendas." *Political Science Quarterly* 104, no. 2 (1989): 281–300.

Strother, Jason. "Korean Leprosy Victims Seek Redress; Time Is Running Out for Many Who Allege Forced Abortions, Sterilizations Decades Ago." *Wall Street Journal*, June 24, 2014.

Sung, Heungsup, Brian T. Foley, In G. Bae, Hyun S. Chi, and Young K. Cho. "Phylogenetic Analysis of Reverse Transcriptase in Antiretroviral Drug-Native Korean HIV Type 1 Patients." *AIDS Research and Human Retroviruses* 17, no. 16 (2001): 1549–54.

Taniguchi, Masaki. "Changing Media, Changing Politics in Japan." *Japanese Journal of Political Science* 8, no. 1 (2007): 147–66.

Tarrow, Sidney. *Power in Movement: Social Movements and Contentious Politics*. 3rd ed. Cambridge: Cambridge University Press, 2011.

———. "The Strategy of Paired Comparison: Toward a Theory of Practice." *Comparative Political Studies* 43, no. 2 (February 1, 2010): 230–59.

Third Sector Institute. *The Explosion of CSOs and Citizen Participation: An Assessment of Civil Society in South Korea*. CIVICUS Civil Society Index Report for South Korea, Hanyang University, 2006. http://www.civicus.org/media/CSI_South_Korea_Country_Report.pdf.

Thompson, Dennis F. "Moral Responsibility of Public Officials: The Problem of Many Hands." *American Political Science Review* 74, no. 4 (December 1980): 905–16.

Tilly, Charles. "Repertoires of Contention in America and Britain, 1750–1830." In *The Dynamics of Social Movements*, edited by Meyer N. Zald and John D. McCarthy. Cambridge, MA: Winthrop, 1979.

Tokyo HCV Supporter Group. *Yakugai Kanen Soshō wo Shien Suru Kai (Tokyo) Kirokushū [Collected Documents from the Tokyo Association to Support the Iatrogenic Hepatitis Lawsuit]*. March 1, 2012. http://www.gaiki.net/yakugai/hc/lib/12318yha.pdf.

Tsujinaka, Yutaka. "From Developmentalism to Maturity: Japan's Civil Society Organizations in Comparative Perspective." In *The State of Civil Society in Japan*, edited by Frank J. Schwartz and Susan J. Pharr, 83–115. Cambridge: Cambridge University Press, 2003.

Tsutsui, Kiyoteru, and Hwa Ji Shin. "Global Norms, Local Activism, and Social Movement Outcomes: Global Human Rights and Resident Korean in Japan." *Social Problems* 55, no. 3 (2008): 391–418.

Underwood, William. "Redress Crossroads in Japan: Decisive Phase in Campaigns to Compensate Korean and Chinese Wartime Forced Laborers." *Asia-Pacific Journal* 30–31–10 (July 26, 2010).

UN General Assembly. *Report of the Detailed Findings of the Commission of Inquiry on Human Rights in the Democratic People's Republic of Korea*. February 7, 2014. http://www.ohchr.org/EN/HRBodies/HRC/CoIDPRK/Pages/ReportoftheCommissionofInquiryDPRK.aspx.

Upham, Frank K. *Law and Social Change in Postwar Japan*. Cambridge, MA: Harvard University Press, 1987.

——. "Litigation and Moral Consciousness in Japan: An Interpretive Analysis of Four Japanese Pollution Suits." *Law & Society Review* 10, no. 4 (Summer 1976): 579–619.

Uri KOHEM [Our KOHEM]. "Interview with an HCV Plaintiff." December 2009.

Vallinder, Torbjörn. "The Judicialization of Politics—A World-Wide Phenomenon: Introduction." *International Political Science Review* 15, no. 2 (April 1, 1994): 91–99.

Verification Committee. *Verification Committee Concerning the Hansen's Disease Problem, Final Report (English Summary Version)*. Tokyo: Japan Law Foundation, March 2005. http://www.mhlw.go.jp/english/policy/health/01/pdf/01.pdf.

Westney, D. Eleanor. "Mass Media as Business Organizations: A U.S.-Japanese Comparison." In *Media and Politics in Japan*, edited by Susan J. Pharr and Ellis S. Krauss, 47–88. Honolulu: University of Hawai'i Press, 1996.

Williams, Brad, and Erik Mobrand. "Explaining Divergent Responses to the North Korean Abductions Issue in Japan and South Korea." *Journal of Asian Studies* 69, no. 2 (May 2010): 507–36.

Woolford, Andrew, and Stefan Wolejszo. "Collecting on Moral Debts: Reparations for the Holocaust and Pořajmos." *Law & Society Review* 40, no. 4 (2006): 871–902.

Yamaguichi, Mari. "Japanese Court Rejects Bid to Restart 2 Nuclear Reactors." *Washington Post*, April 14, 2015.

Yang Hye-In. "10nyeonkan Muryo Byeonron Beopjeong Tujaeng . . . Hyeolaekgwanri Jaejeongbi Gihoero Samaya [After Giving Pro Bono Legal Services to a 10-Year Long Legal Battle . . . We Must Use This Opportunity to Revise Blood Management]." *Medical Today*, October 4, 2011.

Yang, Hyunah, ed. *Law and Society in Korea*. Cheltenham, UK: Edward Elgar, 2013.

Yang Jung A. "Much Effort to Put on the '4+1 Acts.'" *Daily NK*, September 12, 2005.

Yap, O. Fiona. "South Korea in 2014: A Tragedy Reveals the Country's Weaknesses." *Asian Survey* 55, no. 1 (February 2015): 132–41.

Yomiuri Shimbun. "Kyū Midori Jūji no Ketsueki Seizai, Bei de Kinshigo Mo 10nen Hanbai 'Yakugai Kanen' Meihaku ni [Drug-Induced Hepatitis Clear from Sales of Former Green Cross's Blood Product Ten Years after US Prohibition]." March 21, 2002.

——. "Zenkoku 868nin [868 People Nationwide]." December 29, 2012.

Youm, Kyu Ho. "South Korea's Experiment with a Free Press." *International Communication Gazette* 53, no. 1–2 (January 1994): 111–26.

Yumoto Hiroshi, and Nakayama Shozo. "Poll Worries Prompted Government HCV U-Turn." *Daily Yomiuri*, December 25, 2007.

Yun Jihui. "Buksori: Napbukja Gajok Moim Jajung Jiran [Northern Sounds: The Abductee Family Association's Internal Fighting]." *Segye Ilbo*, October 30, 2000.

Index

3.11 disaster (2011 earthquake, tsunami, and
nuclear power plant meltdown in
Japan): compensation payments for
victims of, 19, 190–93; damage caused
by, 189; government responsibility in
events of, 190; lawyers and, 192–93;
media coverage of, 56, 58, 192; protests
and, 192–93; preventive reform following, 190–91, 193
"418 List" (of hepatitis C-tainted blood
victims in Japan), 131–32

Abductee Compensation and Assistance
Review Committee (Korea), 183–84
Abductee Families Union (AFU; Korea):
Citizens Coalition for the Human Rights
of Abductees and North Korean Refugees
(CHNK) and, 175; compensation claims
for abduction victims and, 184; divisions
within, 173, 185; escapees from North Korea
and, 173, 177, 178–79, 181–85; Families of
the Abducted and Detained by North Korea
(FADN) and, 173–78, 182; founding of, 155;
Grand National Party and, 173; leadership
vote in, 173; lobbying by, 178, 180, 184–85;
National Human Rights Commission Korea
and, 177; obstacles faced by, 175–76; protests by, 174–75, 182; Victim Assistance Law
(2007 and 2011) and, 180–85
Abductees' Support Law (Japan, 2002), 164
abductions by North Korea: apologies for,
148–49; civil society organizations and,
156–57, 166, 169, 176; compensation for
victims of and their families, 148–49, 164,
177–84, 186; discrimination faced by victims and their families following (yeonjwaje,
guilty by association), 147–48, 150, 154–55,
177, 181, 184; durations of detentions and,
149–50, 181; elite allies and, 17, 148–49,
152–60, 163–65, 167, 170–73, 178, 184, 186;
escapees and, 19, 150, 172–73, 175, 178–79,
181–84; fact-finding inquiries and, 147,
152–54, 158, 168, 176, 185–86; of fishermen, 150–51, 174, 177–78; of Japanese
nationals, 17, 19, 147–71, 176, 180, 186;
Japanese public opinion regarding, 169;

KAL flight 858 bombing (1987) and impact
on policy regarding, 151; of Korean nationals, 17, 19, 147–50, 153–56, 171–86; Korean
public opinion regarding, 182–83; lawyers
and, 155, 168, 174, 180, 183; media coverage
of, 19, 151, 154, 156, 158, 162–63, 169, 173,
175–78, 181; motivations for, 17, 147, 150;
non-abducted detainees in North Korea
and, 152; petitions for victims of, 159, 170;
preventive reforms and, 181, 186; return
of children of abductees to Japan and, 163;
sanctions on North Korea and, 165–66,
170; Six-Party Talks (2003–2009) and, 148;
"Sunshine Policy" and, 148, 154; victims'
families and, 17, 19, 147–48, 150–54,
156–60, 162, 165–66, 169–77, 181–82,
184–86
Abduction Victim Assistance Law (Korea, 2007
and 2011), 180–85
Abe Shinzō: Cabinet Headquarters for the
Abductions Issue and, 167, 183; conservative ideology of, 157, 163; hepatitis
C-tainted blood product victims and,
130–31; North Korean abduction cases and,
157, 159–61, 163–64, 167, 170–71; as prime
minister of Japan, 166–67, 170–71
abortions: Hansen's disease litigation and,
104–7; forcible, 2, 70, 73–75, 77, 91, 97,
104–7
accidental activists. See also specific causes:
avoidance of partisanship by, 35, 37, 63;
limited leverage of, 25; moral legitimacy of,
13, 27, 30, 37, 201
accountability. See responsibility
activist sector. See civil society organizations
Agent Orange, 19
AIDS. See HIV
American Bar Association, 30, 199
apologies: to Hansen's disease victims, 2–3, 71,
76, 91, 93, 96, 103, 106, 108; to
hepatitis C-tainted blood product victims,
111, 134–35, 145; to HIV-tainted blood
product victims, 76, 116; in Jeju Island suppression case, 198; North Korean abduction
cases and, 148–49; in Sewol sinking case,
194

Comprehensive Blood Safety Policy (Korea, 2003), 138
condolence payments (*mimaikain/wirogeum*), 23, 181
conflict expansion: bottom-up forms of, 16, 20, 35–36, 54–55, 85–95, 110, 124, 135, 145, 198, 202; in comparative perspective, 198–99; definition of, 6; iterative and dynamic nature of, 37–40, 69, 186, 189, 200–202; mediating institutions and, 7–8, 16, 18, 40, 46–47; Schattschneider on, 6, 35–36, 66; sequencing of, 6, 17–18, 20, 26, 31, 35–37, 84, 148, 156–57, 189–90, 196, 199, 201; top-down forms of, 35–36, 51, 53, 95–108, 148, 204
Constitutional Court (Korea), 29, 143
Council on the Hansen's Disease Issue (Kyōgikai), 93–95

Democratic Party (Korea), 143
Democratic Party of Japan (DPJ): 3.11 disaster (2011) aftermath and, 191–92; abductions by North Korea and, 164–67, 170; Hansen Gikon and, 89; hepatitis C-tainted blood products and, 117, 129–33, 135, 137; media's relations with, 55; Democratic Socialist Party (DSP, Japan), 154
Diet (Japanese parliament): 3.11 disaster compensation policies and, 189–91; abductions by North Korea and, 148, 151, 153–54, 157, 159, 161, 164–67; Hansen Gikon and, 89–91, 94–95; Hansen's disease and, 74, 79, 86, 89–90, 93–95, 99–100; hepatitis C-tainted blood products and, 117, 125–26, 129–34, 137; Nitchō Giren and, 153, 157, 160; Rachi Giren and, 157–61, 163–65; sanctions against North Korea and, 165–66
Dokdo/Takeshima territorial dispute (Japan and Korea), 99
DongA Ilbo, 59, 117, 177

Eastern Japan Lawyers' Group (Higashinihon Bengodan), Hansen's disease lawsuits and, 86
elite allies: crises as a form of leverage over, 28; definition of, 5; in French HIV-tainted blood cases, 196; Hansen's disease victims and, 3–4, 71, 89–90, 92–97, 108, 137; hepatitis C-tainted blood product victims and, 110, 117, 124, 129–31, 133, 137–40, 144–46; incentives and motivations among, 3, 5–6, 33–34, 67–68, 89, 92–93, 129, 137,

145; insider information and, 4, 67; legislation and, 5, 26, 28, 32–35, 67–68, 84, 96–97; North Korean abduction cases and, 17, 148–49, 152–60, 163–65, 167, 170–73, 178, 184, 186; sequencing of support from, 4–6, 17, 20, 26, 31–35, 48, 69, 71, 108, 110, 140, 144, 148–49, 157, 187–88, 190, 199, 201–2; Sewol ferry sinking cases and, 193–94

factor IX (blood clotting agent), 112, 117, 121–22
factor concentrates, 111–12, 121–23, 138, 197
Families of the Abducted and Detained by North Korea (FADN; Korea): Abductee Families Union (AFU) and, 173–78, 182; decline of, 184–85; founding of, 173; lawsuit and, 174; lobbying by, 178, 180; obstacles faced by, 175–76
Federation of Postwar Abductions Victims' Families (Korea), 185
Feinberg, Kenneth, 199–200
fibrinogen, 121–22, 125, 129
fishermen. *See under* abductions by North Korea
"focusing events," 29–30
Food and Drug Administration (FDA; United States), 122, 125, 129
Foreign Exchange and Trade Control Law (FETCL, Japan), 165
France, 196–98
Fujī Hirohisa, 89
Fukuda Eriko, 134
Fukuda Yasuo, 95, 132–33, 169
Fukushima disaster. *See* 3.11 disaster
Furukawa lawsuit (Japan), 168

gijashil (Korean press clubs), 56–57
Grand National Party (GNP; Korea): abduction of Korean citizens by North Korea and, 171–73, 176–81, 184; Hansen's disease and, 101–3; hepatitis C-tainted blood products and, 137, 139, 141, 143; Special Committee on Abductions and POW Policy (Korea) and, 171–72
Green Cross Corporation (GCC; Korea): hepatitis A-tainted blood products and, 136; hepatitis C-tainted blood products and, 123, 137, 140; HIV-tainted blood products and, 114–15, 117–19, 140, 144; libel cases filed by, 118; litigation against, 115, 118–19, 123, 140, 144; plasma-derived and recombinant factor produced by, 143

Studies of the
Weatherhead East Asian Institute
Columbia University

Selected Titles

(Complete list at: http://www.columbia.edu/cu/weai/weatherhead-studies.html)

The Age of Irreverence: A New History of Laughter in China, by Christopher Rea. University of California Press, 2015

The Nature of Knowledge and the Knowledge of Nature in Early Modern Japan, by Federico Marcon. University of Chicago Press, 2015

The Fascist Effect: Japan and Italy, 1915–1952, by Reto Hoffman. Cornell University Press, 2015

The International Minimum: Creativity and Contradiction in Japan's Global Engagement, 1933–1964, by Jessamyn R. Abel. University of Hawai'i Press, 2015

Empires of Coal: Fueling China's Entry into the Modern World Order, 1860–1920, by Shellen Xiao Wu. Stanford University Press, 2015

Casualties of History: Wounded Japanese Servicemen and the Second World War, by Lee K. Pennington. Cornell University Press, 2015

City of Virtues: Nanjing in an Age of Utopian Visions, by Chuck Wooldridge. University of Washington Press, 2015

The Proletarian Wave: Literature and Leftist Culture in Colonial Korea, 1910–1945, by Sunyoung Park. Harvard University Asia Center, 2015.

Neither Donkey Nor Horse: Medicine in the Struggle Over China's Modernity, by Sean Hsiang-lin Lei. University of Chicago Press, 2014.

When the Future Disappears: The Modernist Imagination in Late Colonial Korea, by Janet Poole. Columbia University Press, 2014.

Bad Water: Nature, Pollution, & Politics in Japan, 1870–1950, by Robert Stolz. Duke University Press, 2014.

Rise of a Japanese Chinatown: Yokohama, 1894–1972, by Eric C. Han. Harvard University Asia Center, 2014.

Beyond the Metropolis: Second Cities and Modern Life in Interwar Japan, by Louise Young. University of California Press, 2013.

From Cultures of War to Cultures of Peace: War and Peace Museums in Japan, China, and South Korea, by Takashi Yoshida. MerwinAsia, 2013.

Imperial Eclipse: Japan's Strategic Thinking about Continental Asia before August 1945, by Yukiko Koshiro. Cornell University Press, 2013.

The Nature of the Beasts: Empire and Exhibition at the Tokyo Imperial Zoo, by Ian J. Miller. University of California Press, 2013.

Public Properties: Museums in Imperial Japan, by Noriko Aso. Duke University Press, 2013.

Reconstructing Bodies: Biomedicine, Health, and Nation-Building in South Korea Since 1945, by John P. DiMoia. Stanford University Press, 2013.

Taming Tibet: Landscape Transformation and the Gift of Chinese Development, by Emily T. Yeh. Cornell University Press, 2013.

Tyranny of the Weak: North Korea and the World, 1950–1992, by Charles K. Armstrong. Cornell University Press, 2013.

The Art of Censorship in Postwar Japan, by Kirsten Cather. University of Hawai'i Press, 2012.

Asia for the Asians: China in the Lives of Five Meiji Japanese, by Paula Harrell. MerwinAsia, 2012.

Lin Shu, Inc.: Translation and the Making of Modern Chinese Culture, by Michael Gibbs Hill. Oxford University Press, 2012.

Occupying Power: Sex Workers and Servicemen in Postwar Japan, by Sarah Kovner. Stanford University Press, 2012.

Redacted: The Archives of Censorship in Postwar Japan, by Jonathan E. Abel. University of California Press, 2012.

Empire of Dogs: Canines, Japan, and the Making of the Modern Imperial World, by Aaron Herald Skabelund. Cornell University Press, 2011.

Planning for Empire: Reform Bureaucrats and the Japanese Wartime State, by Janis Mimura. Cornell University Press, 2011.

Realms of Literacy: Early Japan and the History of Writing, by David Lurie. Harvard University Asia Center, 2011.

Russo-Japanese Relations, 1905–17: From Enemies to Allies, by Peter Berton. Routledge, 2011.

Behind the Gate: Inventing Students in Beijing, by Fabio Lanza. Columbia University Press, 2010.

Imperial Japan at Its Zenith: The Wartime Celebration of the Empire's 2,600th Anniversary, by Kenneth J. Ruoff. Cornell University Press, 2010.